"Sit Down, Stop Waving Your Arms About!"

"Sit Down, Stop Waving Your Arms About!"

The autobiography of British conductor

Anthony Inglis

With a foreword by Katherine Jenkins OBE

Matador
Unit E2 Airfield Business Park,
Harrison Road, Market Harborough,
Leicestershire. LE16 7UL
Tel: 0116 279 2299
Email: books@troubador.co.uk
Web: www.troubador.co.uk/matador
Twitter: @matadorbooks

ISBN 9781803136776

British Library Cataloguing in Publication Data.
A catalogue record for this book is available from the British Library.

Printed and bound in the UK by TJ Books Limited, Padstow, Cornwall
Typeset in 12pt Bembo by Troubador Publishing Ltd, Leicester, UK

Matador is an imprint of Troubador Publishing Ltd

For my family, past, present and future.

Contents

Contents

Acknowledgements

It has often been said that everyone has one book in them. You, dear reader, are about to find out whether that is true or not, as this is my one book.

I began what became this story by writing down a reminiscence, a fact or a thought, so my children would know a little about their father's life, the majority of which will most probably be lived before they were born. Then, during 2020 and 2021 when the world stopped moving, it grew into an idea.

All autobiographies are, in a way, vanity projects and this is no less true of mine. It has been an indulgence, similar to when presenting a lecture all about my life and career to the patrons of hotels, cruise ships and local societies, embarrassing to begin with, before warming to my theme and ending by surrendering and thoroughly enjoying my memories. I have jumped about in places, and you will have to forgive me for that; it really cannot be helped! A story reawakened from childhood sometimes has a relevance to adulthood and vice versa.

There are many people who require thanking: first and foremost, my wife Jan. We have been together for more than forty years and aside from coming up the with the title of this book, throughout those years she has continued to ensure there is a stable home life, full of warmth and love, allowing me a marvellous time flying all over the world, selfishly doing what

I love. Our three children: Eleanor, who spent a week with my wife and me in Corfu, making sure this book was readable and coherent – there was suddenly a window opened for publication and a hard, busy, last-minute week was spent on this beautiful island – our two sons Dominic and Alexander, who have often kept me grounded, though one does take me up into the air every now and then!

There are many others who have been important to me in my life, and three must be mentioned by name: my two oldest and best male friends Mike Reed and Vaughan Meakins, plus my best female friend and brilliant commercial agent Sue James, with whom I talk most days. They have been huge constants in my life. There are others and you know who you are!

My thanks also go to the solicitor Henri Brandman, for casting his eye over the tome, and Charles Hart for permission to quote his wonderful lyrics. Also, to all those who have employed me, giving me enormous enjoyment in pursuing my hobby. Of them, the ones who have employed me the most have been Cunard Line, Anthony Findlay, Raymond Gubbay, Katherine Jenkins, Sir Cameron Mackintosh and Lord Lloyd Webber. Now may be the time to let you know, it has been so much fun I would have done it for free!

To my late parents who gave me life, despite destiny trying desperately hard to prevent it, and my siblings for helping me survive the ordeal of early childhood and boarding schools.

Lastly, thank you for your purchase. I trust everyone finds something of interest within the pages. Of course, as when attending operas, musicals, concerts and the theatre, it is my hope you will stay and read it from overture to play-out. However, those of you who do not want to know about my RAF lineage or the trauma of six of the best at school, can skip to a subject matter that will be of more interest. The use of acts and scenes, each scene having a subheading, should make it easy to identify those subjects of interest. But please don't; if permitted to say, I think you will find my tale an interesting one.

Trust me... I'm a conductor!

Anthony Inglis
Corfu, July 2022

Foreword

As a young singer I was told by my then manager that I would be performing my first season of summer festival concerts and that I would be working with the illustrious Anthony Inglis who would be conducting the Royal Philharmonic Orchestra. Excited by all these new opportunities and feeling the need to impress Anthony (after all, he had worked for many years with Andrew Lloyd Webber who had long been a hero of mine), I put my best foot forward in the rehearsal at Marble Hill in Twickenham. Backstage, our dressing rooms were tents. I cannot remember if we had small separate tents that were just very close together or whether we all shared one which simply had dividers down the middle, but nevertheless, for someone I had never met, it was very intimate! Between his three young children having meltdowns, his poor wife Jan (who is a dear friend today) trying to keep them quiet and my endless warbling warm-ups, we definitely made a racket! It wasn't the glamorous start I had imagined, but it was the start of a beautiful friendship on and off the stage, filled most certainly with music but also with a lot of laughs. And this has been a common theme since then... in the world of classical music, where people can take themselves much too seriously, Anthony's sense of humour and desire to make the music fun brings so much to the audience as well as the performer.

From the Big Five in Africa to temples in Thailand, I have had the great fortune to see the world with Anthony. What I am most struck by is how the orchestras, whether home or abroad, fall in love with him. In a relatively short space of time, he has a way of cultivating a respect, an admiration and a great rapport with them, and a constant feedback comment is: 'that's the best we have heard them play'. And so, this big-hearted, emotional man who is fiercely patriotic, proud and has reached the top of his game (just don't ask him about pop music – he once asked me who Take That were!) continues to strive to bring classical music to a wider audience, advocates for live musicians and their well-being and, on a personal note, inspires me to be the best performer I can be.

Maestro Anthony Inglis will forever be my friend. His colourful stories have entertained me for nearly two decades on the road, and I sincerely hope you will enjoy them as much as me!

Katherine Jenkins

Overture

On 20 January 1947, at the age of forty-seven, Air Vice-Marshal Francis Frederic Inglis CB CBE DL was appointed senior air staff officer HQ Air Command Far East in Singapore. Like many, he had had a very busy and stressful war and, as head of RAF intelligence, had been reporting directly to the prime minister, Winston Churchill. In fact, after the shock of Pearl Harbour on 7 December 1941 and the thirst for revenge on Japan by the American people, Churchill had made him responsible for ensuring that Franklin D. Roosevelt, president of the United States of America, also concentrated the American war effort in Europe, rather than just the Far East. Churchill reasoned that to defeat the Axis powers, you had to cut off the head, and that meant Herr Adolph Hitler, chancellor of Germany.

Despite the opposition of Roosevelt's senior military advisors, Air Vice-Marshal Frank Inglis was successful in his task and, on 10 January 1942, shortly after the surprise attack on Pearl Harbour, American troops slowly began to cross the Atlantic and form the Allies. In February 1942, it became a torrent, with the crossing of the Cunard liners RMS *Queen Elizabeth* and RMS *Queen Mary*. Therefore, it could be said he was responsible for 'overpaid, oversexed, over here', a popular expression of the time directed by the British people at the influx of American military personnel.

No other war decision by America was more significant for Europe and the world than that one. It is to be attributed to the clear trustworthiness of Frank Inglis that his vital, single-handed mission was successful, and it is to be attributed to his modesty that his part in that happening seems never to have come to the notice of historians.

Inglis obituary, *The Times.*

For his success in the mission, he was on Adolph Hitler's list of 2,820 people singled out for execution should Germany have won the war and conquered Great Britain.

The air vice-marshal took out to Singapore with him his wife Vera, known by everyone as Midge. Apparently, the nickname Midge came about when, as the midwife delivered her, she took one look at the baby and said, "Oh what a midge!" The name stuck ever after, which was just as well as she hated the name Vera! With them to Singapore went their daughter Wendy.

However, Frank and Midge had two daughters and the younger one, Jill, had not yet attended finishing school. Finishing schools were mid-nineteenth to twentieth-century educational institutions normally sited in Switzerland, where young ladies went to be taught social graces and prepare them for married life (a different age!). It was decided that, as Wendy had left school and Jill was still of school age about to go to finishing school, Wendy would go out to Singapore and Jill would remain in the UK, spending the holidays with the family in the Far East.

At almost exactly the same time, the life of Air Commodore Ernest Howard-Williams MC, born in 1895, was no less remarkable. He had joined the Sportsmen's Battalion of the East Yorkshire Regiment as a private in 1914, transferring to the Royal Naval Air Service and Royal Flying Corps in 1915. He was one of the first into the newly formed Royal Air Force in 1918 when the RNAS and RFC merged with the Independent Brigade. At the outbreak of the Second World War, he was the acting senior air staff officer of Fighter Command, effectively 'number two' to Air Chief Marshal Sir Hugh Dowding, with whom unfortunately he would row. Rowing with senior officers was quite a feature of his life, and he maintained to the end that having witnessed the appalling horrors of the Somme and Passchendaele from the air, he never had a high opinion for those in command, always questioning decisions made by senior officers as to their effectiveness, versus the loss of life. He was subsequently sent to RAF Halton and then RAF Blackpool where he was air officer commanding.

At Blackpool, one of his tasks was ensuring there was entertainment for the thousands of RAF troops who were training there. To this end, he would put on concerts and variety shows, before finally producing a concert at the Royal Albert Hall in aid of the RAF Benevolent Fund, for whom he would claim to have raised millions. However, he argued with the commanding officer at Blackpool and retired from the RAF.

With the aid of his friend Lord Trenchard, founder of the Royal Air Force, he obtained a job for the last two years of the war as air correspondent for *The Daily Telegraph*.

After the war, Air Commodore Ernest Howard-Williams, known as Bill or Billy, moved to Africa to become an elected member of the Kenyan Government and helped form the Iraqi Air Force. As he writes in the foreword to his own unpublished autobiography of 1963:

> *I was, and still am, an air commodore in the RAF, a general in the Iraqi Army and a pasha of Iraq. I have served with many of the air chiefs who helped to win the war, and who were indeed my contemporaries, known most of the famous pioneer pilots and aircraft manufacturers, and have for long been right in the middle of the present political scene in Kenya. I have also met personally many of the stars of stage*

and screen and have served with most of our distinguished admirals and generals. I became an elected member of the Kenyan Parliament during its most difficult time and lately accepted the Ministry of Tourism at the behest of her new governor, Sir Patrick Renison. At the time of writing, I lead the opposition to the present Coalition Government of Kenya.

In 1919 he had married a lady called Norah 'Biddy' Gibson, the daughter of Dr Percy Gibson who lived and worked on the Isle of Wight and was the first man on the island to have a motorcar. He was also the founder of the famous Island Sailing Club in Cowes.

Like Air Vice-Marshal Inglis, Bill and Norah Howard-Williams also had two children, this time two boys, both born on the island.

The eldest, Peter Ian Howard-Williams, born in 1919, followed his father and went into the RAF and, during the Battle of Britain, fought in 19 Squadron out of Duxford as part of 12 Group, alongside his wing leader Douglas Bader in the 'Duxford Wing'.

He played himself in the 1942 film *The First of the Few*, which starred David Niven and Leslie Howard and told the embattled story of the design and build of the famous Spitfire aeroplane designed by Reginald J. Mitchell CBE.

The film unfolds in a series of flashbacks with David Niven playing the role of the test pilot Geoffrey Crisp, a fictional character made up of a composite between Jeffrey Quill and Joseph 'Mutt' Summers, the two original Spitfire test pilots. Niven tells the story to a group of airmen outside a dispersal hut on a typical Battle of Britain airfield. This group of seven young pilots, which included Peter Howard-Williams, were real ex-Battle of Britain pilots fighting the war, and was filmed at Ibsley, an aerodrome just outside Ringwood in the New Forest, shortly after the battle had finished. It was the only Second World War film to be sanctioned by Churchill for filming on an active RAF airfield.

While filming, the bell to scramble would go off in real life and they would run to their aeroplanes to fight the war. When they came back from the sortie, they would carry on filming as though nothing had happened. Niven was so impressed with this small group of airmen, that for the post-wrap party he sent them for the weekend to the Savoy Hotel in London. Ringing up the general manager prior to their visit, Niven told him that whatever these airmen wanted, he was to give it to them and send him the bill. Peter always went misty-eyed reminiscing about that weekend!

The other son was Jeremy Napier Howard-Williams. Having been born on 13 March 1922, he was only seventeen at the outbreak of the war and therefore too young for the Battle of Britain. Joining up shortly after, he learnt to fly Sopwith Camels and twin-engine Avro Ansons in Canada.

Like a lot of younger brothers, he was desperate to follow his older sibling, in his case into Fighter Command. Worried that his ability to fly twins meant he would go into Bomber Command, for the first and only time in his life, he appealed to his father the air commodore. When he got back, he was posted to John 'Cat's Eyes' Cunningham's 604 Squadron, based at Middle Wallop, and became a night fighter pilot flying twin-engine attackers such as Beaufighters, Blenheims and ultimately Mosquitos. In contrast, his brother was a day fighter pilot flying single-engine Spitfires.

Although he flew every type of RAF aircraft, including the Spitfire and Hurricane, many times, he always said the Mosquito was his favourite aircraft, with a cockpit ergonomically laid out so much better than anything else. On the poorly designed Blenheim interior, he would 'blob', that is put drops of glue on the top of various important switches so he could feel for them at night, as of course all cockpit lights were extinguished, a habit he would maintain for the rest of his life, particularly on his bedside radio!

Jeremy told an amusing story of how, during the war, when he was stationed at Middle Wallop and Peter stationed nearby at the satellite airfield Ibsley in the New Forest, they would often visit each other, landing at their respective airfields. One day, they spotted their old housemaster from Felsted School who was a non-commissioned officer in the Local Defence Force helping to guard the perimeter fence. This was obviously too good an opportunity for them to miss. So, the brothers, both recent school leavers and flight lieutenants, therefore senior in rank to an NCO, stood twenty feet apart and made their old housemaster march between them, ordering him to quick march, about-turn and stand to attention! When asked how their ex-housemaster had taken it, Jeremy replied, "With remarkable good humour!"

On resting from ops with John Cunningham's 604 Squadron at Middle Wallop, he volunteered for Fighter Interception Unit (FIU), who were also stationed at Middle Wallop, becoming one of the pioneers of what ultimately became Airborne Warning and Control System (AWACS): Airborne Radar. Indeed, there is an extraordinary picture of Jeremy in 1944 flying a captured German Messerschmitt 410 with its own AI (Airborne Interception) radar over the weald of Kent! Only by flying the German aeroplane could the British compare who had the more advanced system and what could be learned from the other side. In order to defend themselves from attack, the 410 was painted in RAF colours and escorted by two Mosquitos as a way of protecting the captured German aeroplane from troops on the ground or British aircraft in the air. There is a picture of this formation in his autobiographical book *Night Intruder* (and also here) published by David & Charles in 1976, reprinted 2023 by Sapere Books.

The foreword was penned by Rudolf Schoenert who, in 1943, was commanding officer of Nachtjagd Gruppe 10 at Werneuchen, the exact German equivalent of the Fighter Interception Development Squadron of which Jeremy Howard-Williams was flight commander. They were therefore opposite numbers of their respective airborne radar squadrons.

With Peter a day fighter pilot and Jeremy a night fighter pilot, their parents must have had a wretched war. Never able to relax as, for twenty-four hours a day, one of their two sons was always up in the air being shot at.

When the war finished, both sons had survived and remained in the RAF. A couple of years after hostilities ceased, Squadron Leader Jeremy Howard-Williams DFC was posted to Singapore at the same time as Air Vice-Marshal Inglis CB CBE.

The social life of the British armed services in Singapore after the war was centred around a shack on a beach to the north of the city, the home of the Changi Garrison Yacht Club or as it is known today, the Changi Sailing Club. Nowadays, the yacht club is a very smart place, with facilities to rival any in the world; from a private swimming pool to a first-class restaurant, it is home to Singaporeans of all ages. In the second half of the 1940s, it had very few facilities but was the social hub of the officers and children of serving service personnel.

Sailing, or at any rate the clubhouse, was where everyone met in the evening. Jill Inglis, daughter of the air vice-marshal and out during holidays, was surrounded by officers, loving this social life. Very soon, Jeremy Howard-Williams and Jill Inglis met and fell in love.

In 1949, the air vice-marshal was posted back to the UK and, with his family, left Singapore. He was followed shortly afterwards by Jeremy.

On 29 September 1951, Jeremy, aged twenty-nine, and Jill, aged twenty, were married to each other, for the first time…

Act 1

Scene 1: Hello; Early Years

I was born Anthony Inglis Howard-Williams at RAF Hospital Halton to Squadron Leader Jeremy and Mrs. Jill Howard-Williams on 27 June 1952, just in time for lunch on a fairly hot day. The hottest day of the year was to fall four days later, and the temperature was only falling to 18°C at night. The birth could not have come soon enough for my mother, though it was perhaps astonishing I was born at all. Before either my father and mother were born, both their fathers had fallen out of their aeroplanes while they were in the air and survived the ordeal.

It was almost de rigueur in the early years of flying to have accidents. It was merely a matter of luck, and/or skill, whether you survived them or not.

In 1916, my paternal grandfather, Bill Howard-Williams, had been an observer in a Sunbeam Short Seaplane flying at five hundred feet and the pilot, when doing a turn, forgot to put on any bank. The result was a flat spin and an accidental inversion of the aeroplane. In those days, there were no seatbelts in aircraft so my grandfather fell out, vertically, into the Suez Canal which, fortuitously, was beneath them. By doing so, he held the record of surviving the highest freefall without a parachute, only broken in the Second World War. Bill was lucky, sadly, the pilot was not.

In May 1924, my maternal grandfather, Frank Inglis, was

propelled out of a de Havilland 9A by an engine failure. His choice of a crash site was either some palm trees or the river Euphrates. He chose the latter and was observed to do a perfect swallow dive as the nose dug into the river.

Both survived their traumatic moments, which are backed up by one telling the story on tape and the other reported in the local *Mesopotamian* newspaper article. Subsequently, both went on to marry and have their children: my father and mother.

Both were also extremely brave as demonstrated by Bill being awarded the Military Cross while he was in the RFC. His citation reads:

> *For conspicuous gallantry and devotion to duty in co-operating with our artillery, often under extremely unfavourable weather conditions. On one occasion in particular, although very much hampered by mist and clouds, he ranged three of our batteries on to a hostile battery position and enabled them to demolish it. His splendid example has been of the greatest value to his squadron.*

In the early days of flying, during the First World War, there were more genteel customs observed in the midst of the horrors of war. One such custom was one side letting the other know if they had captured or killed an airman. This was done by flying over the opposition's airfield and waggling your wings so they would know your intention was communication and not attack. Then, a note weighed down with a stone would be dropped on the field which would relay the relevant information. I have on my desk in front of me one such note from a downed airman of my grandfather's squadron, addressed to him. It reads:

> *Dear Williams. Just a line to let you know that we were brought down this morning. Poor Allen was killed, and I was*

wounded in the right foot and left leg. We got five German Albatross on us and they gave us hell. The fellows who brought us down are here and are very decent to me. They are taking this across. Would you write to my brother and sister and see about sending my kit home? We were brought down on fire and hit the floor with a hell of a whang. Allen was killed when we hit. Goodbye, old thing. Give my love to everyone. Yours to a cinder, McTavish!

Not only do I have the actual note but also a photograph taken in 1976 of that very airman who had written it, Lt. Duncan McTavish, and my father, the son of the squadron commander to whom the note was addressed, both looking at it nearly sixty years after it had been dropped.

I remember very little of my early childhood, though know it was spent in a variety of places. Dad was an assistant air attaché in the embassies of Berlin, where my brother Christopher was born twenty-one months after me, and Paris, where my sister Nicola was born, twenty-two months after him. The odd fact now is that they have swapped countries, as my brother lives in France and my sister in Germany!

One of my earliest memories is of my brother Christopher falling out of a first-floor window in our Paris house into the basement below. Falling from heights seems to be a family trait! I was following my brother, tracing the walls of the room, when we came across floor-to-ceiling sliding doors which had been left open. Out he went. It was claimed that he bounced! Being about two, or whatever age he was, that may have been true. A quick check-up in hospital and no bones broken; this from a height of the first floor down to the basement!

I, on the other hand, was a sickly child. First, in Paris, it was decided that pressure needed to be relieved from my inner ear. No idea the reason, but the cure was to have my eardrums pierced with a needle. The first time it happened, I did not understand what was about to be inflicted upon me, and it only took one doctor and a couple of nurses to make sure I did not move. With the other ear, I was wiser; it took three doctors and five nurses to catch me and hold me down, while they carefully manoeuvred the needle down my ear canal until they came to the right place to give the needle a final push. Not for the last time, they could hear me the other end of the hospital! This has left me prone to ear infections ever since.

Then I contracted tonsillitis, and it was decided my tonsils needed to be removed. For some reason, in those days (or maybe I was just unlucky), they made a decision to remove them without an anaesthetic! Again, it took a number of people to hold me perfectly still. My mother and father always told me that they were waiting in a room off a corridor, listening to their eldest child screaming the place down. When it stopped and they went outside, they saw this limp, exhausted, tear-stained child in the arms of a doctor being carried down the stairs towards them, blood dribbling out of the corner of his mouth, and were told, "You can take him home now!" They refused and told the doctor to keep me in overnight.

Sadly, this wasn't the end of my various childhood medical difficulties. While in Paris, I contracted tuberculosis – my parents always thought it was from the cook in our service household. TB in the '50s could be quite a serious disease, and there were not the antibiotics to treat it effectively. Consequently, in addition to any medication that was available, I was packed off to a sanatorium. Unfortunately, we were in France, and the nearest sanatorium was a place called Jean-Lou in a town called Saint-Gervais-les-Bains, halfway up the side of a mountain. Not just any old mountain but the tallest in Europe: Mont Blanc.

It was October 1956, and I was four when my bags were packed and taken to a large building in St. Gervais, where we had spartan living conditions and freezing temperatures.

I think part of the cure for TB in those days must have been the healthy outdoor weather; we would take our meals under the house, open on three sides to the elements. That way we would get the cold biting wind and snow and eat our food quickly, otherwise it became cold, and slow eaters would have to deal with frozen food!

I became quite a good skier. At least three times a week we would all have to traipse up the snow-covered road to visit the doctor, who had his surgery higher up than we were. At the doctor's place, we would receive our injections and other treatment deemed necessary, before skiing back down. Sounds far from idyllic, and it wasn't, because eventually, they ran out of places to put the needles! Arms, legs, bottom, all covered in pinpricks! This has left me with a phobia of needles.

My experience at Jean-Lou has given me quite a collection of phobias! As the only English child in a sanitorium full of French children, I quickly forgot my mother tongue, and on leaving Jean-Lou after six months of treatment, came out speaking fluent French with absolutely no English at all. In fact, when I arrived back at Dover jabbering away in French to my grandmother who had gone to pick me up and spoke little of the language, immigration refused to let the little French boy into the country! It was only by showing my British passport and convincing them of my nationality, that entry to the UK was permitted.

My parents, quite naturally, wanted me to keep up my language skills and, in an attempt to do so, tried to have mealtimes a French-speaking-only zone. This I resolutely refused to do. Must have been similar to the road accident I may have had. I say 'may have had', as it was never admitted by the sanitorium and I remember nothing of it. However, having an X-ray a little later as part of the ongoing check-ups for TB, it was discovered that my arm had been broken and, when asked about it, I kept saying, "*Voiture, voiture!*"

It's the same with skiing. On a visit to my brother, who now lives close to Chamonix, he took us skiing. I did not want to go, but he persuaded me, and after putting the skis on and attempting to move forward, my right leg went one way, my left the other. I immediately took them off, vowing never to put them back on!

I had such an awful time as a child halfway up a mountain, unable to speak the language, needles being inserted into me at every opportunity, not seeing my family, that I never again wanted to speak French or ski as it reminded me of a very unhappy time in my life.

Actually, my parents did visit once during my time in the sanitorium, about halfway through the six-month treatment process. At the end of that day, when it was time for them to leave, they got in the car and started to drive off. As they did so, and realising what was about to happen, I ran down the drive after them, screaming for them to stop and take me with them. Of course, they couldn't. Years later, my mother confessed the visit upset her so much, particularly the end when I ran after the car, she said she couldn't face doing it again! And they didn't. I was four!

My brother, having moved to France in 1976, ended up twenty-two years later in a little town called La Roche-sur-Foron, about half an hour from Geneva and an hour from Saint-Gervais and Jean-Lou. He made it his mission to go and see if he could discover the old sanatorium. Having made enquiries at the local tourist office, he discovered it was now a private house, and when I next went and visited him, we both went to see it. The underneath of the house where we ate our meals is there (it now stores logs and tractors etc); the drive I ran down after the car is still there; and the lane going up towards the doctor's hut is, of course, also still there. We rang the doorbell, but nobody answered, so we walked around the grounds, and no one disturbed us. I wonder how many of us TB children have revisited that house?

To my great relief, when my grandmother and I arrived back at Dover from Jean-Lou, I discovered my family had left France, Paris and the embassy life for good.

Scene 2: Life in Kent; Royal Heritage

For months after coming back from Jean-Lou, a lady would come round daily to inject me; I looked like a junkie with so many needle pricks in my thighs, arms, buttocks etc. I called her 'the pricky lady'. I did not like her very much and would hide anywhere I could when the doorbell announced her visit!

Needles – the bane of my existence for so much of my life. On a recent orchestra tour to Ireland, I could hardly walk, and it turned out to be a recurrence of a Morton's neuroma, which is a sort of cyst in the toes, this time in my little toe of my left foot.

Unable to walk to the concert platform in Cork, the orchestra manager took me to a private hospital where the chief honcho said he could cure that for me! I was pleased though should have guessed what was going to happen, because when I asked whether it was going to hurt, he said it wouldn't be comfortable. What I didn't know was that he was going to slowly push a needle into the joint of my little toe so the local anaesthetic would have time to work first before the actual treatment would be injected underneath.

I had news for him: it wasn't comfortable – it was downright agony! I screamed the place down, and you are beginning to see here that screaming in hospitals is fast becoming a regular occurrence for me. Doors banged and nurses with other doctors came rushing into an already overcrowded cubicle to see who was being murdered. One of them stroked my hand and told me to calm down and breathe deeply. No doubt a sensible instruction to someone with a high tolerance to pain, but after all my medical trauma, that wasn't me. It felt as if I was having my little toe sawn off! I looked at her while taking a breath between screams and said, "Calm down? Calm down? Have you seen what this man is doing to me?" After what seemed like half an hour, but in reality was probably only two or three minutes, he withdrew the needle and it was a miracle. I got straight off the bed in the cubicle, pain-free. On sheepishly walking back to my changing room, I apologised to anyone within sight, including the cleaner.

I hurriedly dressed and, keeping my head down, went to the car waiting for me outside. This involved a journey down a few corridors, round some corners, through a couple of doors to the entrance of the hospital. Before leaving, I had to pay for the pain and trauma I had just been through and went up to the receptionist, warily asking whether she had heard screaming emanating from the depths of the hospital. To which she replied in a thick, broad Irish accent, "Oh Jeez, was that you? I thought I was back on the labour ward!"

What is it about doctors that they like injecting into joints? Every now and then, I suffer from problems with my knee joints, a hazard of standing while working for long periods of time, and they require a visit to my doctor at Ashtead Hospital. He too puts a needle into me, this time my knee. I go in with sticks and in quite a degree of pain and come out like a twenty-one-year-old!

I also have regular colonoscopies to try and prevent, what is whispered in hushed tones as, 'the family disease' from taking hold! We didn't know it at the time but now, sadly at the expense of much-loved members of the household, we do. There is a prevalence of colon/bowel cancer in the family.

For a start, my father died from a recurrence of colon cancer. He had had a permanent colostomy, and having had a large part of his colon removed, no one thought to tell him it could reappear in a part of the colon that had not been removed. It did but, when discovered, it was too late for treatment, and he died aged seventy-four. My uncle, the Battle of Britain pilot, and my aunt in 2021 also died of it. We then look back and think that my great-aunt, and maybe a great-uncle, also suffered from this vicious cancer.

After his colostomy, my father persuaded me to have a check-up in my early forties. This was done by the great Roger Leicester, surgeon to the stars. He discovered polyps, which were removed and, after analysing, found to be of the type that could turn cancerous. Dad almost wept with joy on being told. Dad, I owe you one; no, wait a minute, I owe you everything! Colonoscopies are now a regular procedure for me, just to make sure any reoccurrence is dealt with promptly. If my dad had had regular check-ups, he might have lived a lot longer.

Anyway, I digress! I fear that may be a feature! Back to my childhood.

After the embassy life of Berlin and Paris, we came back to England and moved to a house just outside Sevenoaks in Kent. It was huge! It even had a private swimming pool and a wood of its own. After the trauma of France, I loved that house. It was called, and still is to my knowledge, Longspring Wood. Our maternal grandparents lived close by in a village called Ide Hill.

During the war, the air vice-marshal had bought a house called Pigsty Barn down a little lane called Hanging Bank, as a bolthole away from the stresses and strains of high command. It was a pretty little pink cottage, and they took every opportunity to visit it, now renamed Gayshaws, in a small Kent village they had fallen in love with. If ever I am in the area, I take a nostalgic trip down Hanging Bank and look at the house. Both my grandparents are buried in the local church graveyard, where, upon retirement, the air vice-marshal had been a churchwarden.

In the grounds of the house there is a mound, which looks like a long barrow and which, legend has it, is the reason for the name of the road. During the civil war, it was reputed that one side or the other used the mound as a gallows, hanging many people there. My grandparents used to call this mound Everest, and you can see why. It is in a place where the whole of the Vale of Kent is laid out before you, with a view twenty-five miles into the distance towards East Grinstead. If there was an upside to being hanged in 1645 in Kent, the only one I can see is the fantastic view, and if you are of a religious persuasion, you get to see God's magnificent handiwork before going to meet the Maker to congratulate Him!

However, the dark history of the site sometimes makes itself known! My grandmother always hinted at mysterious secrets of the property but would never mention what they were, except to say they had a poltergeist, who was normally friendly and always very mischievous! She never told us why she believed she had one, except one day telling us this story:

The view from the top of that mound is so spectacular that when they moved in, the first thing they did was put a bench on the top, so they could sit there and enjoy the splendour of it all. The next morning, the bench was at the bottom of Everest, lying upside down. They assumed there must have been some high wind in the night to pick up that heavy bench and throw it some thirty feet down to the bottom of the mound into their garden, so they put it back up. The same thing happened again the next night. By now, perplexed, they tried it a third time and overnight it snowed. The next morning, there it was, in exactly the same position at the bottom, yet completely free of snow, proving that it had not snowed after it had moved. However, on the ground there was virgin snow between the top of Everest and where it was now resting. It was as if someone had literally picked the bench up and placed it thirty feet away. They never tried it again.

On the few occasions I have been back down the lane, there has never been anything on the top of the most obvious place to put a bench, and I can't say I blame the owners.

Whilst I am on the subject of the unexplained at that house, it was a small dwelling, and downstairs there was a living room and dining room divided by a curtain. One night the house was full of guests, and the three bedrooms upstairs were full. It was decided I would sleep on a camp bed downstairs in the dining room, which had a beautiful picture window overlooking the garden and Everest. We closed the curtain between the dining and living rooms to provide some privacy, and we all went to bed. During the night, I awoke to see an entire army dressed in civil war outfits on horseback with flags and lancers marching down the lane and through the fireplace and curtains towards me and Everest. Still to this day, at least half a century later, the memory video remains vividly imprinted in my mind. I did not go back to sleep that night and never again slept downstairs. I know what you are all thinking, nevertheless I also know what I saw!

Whilst we were living in Sevenoaks and regularly visiting my maternal grandparents down Hanging Bank, we would also meet up with my maternal great-grandparents, both of whom were still alive: Captain Cecil Willie Turner AFC, known to all and sundry as Gaffa, and his wife Emily Diana Cecilia Streatfeild, known by everyone as Gamma, and yes, that is the correct way of spelling her surname!

I'm not sure, it may have been a generational thing that everyone had nicknames. I have various relatives from that era who must have had real names but were always known as either Unky (who was married to Ola), Bunny, Dubba, Nookie, Tubby or other such endearingly odd names.

From great-grandmother Gamma's side of the family came my great-great-great-great-grandmother, the social reformer and Quaker, Elizabeth Fry. Elizabeth was part of the Gurney banking family, and she took as a husband a man by the name of Joseph Fry, named after his uncle who had founded the Fry chocolate company. Elizabeth's grandmother came from the Barclay family of

Barclays bank. Sadly, no banking or chocolate money from either the Gurney, Barclay or Fry families remains with us! Also, my first cousin twice removed is the famous author Noel Streatfeild OBE, author of children's books including the famous *Ballet Shoes*.

Although Gamma's ancestry was impressive, that of her husband's was even more so. Cecil Willie Turner AFC was born in 1874 and had served as a captain with distinction in the Duke of Cornwall's Light Infantry, gaining an MC. After the First World War, my great-grandfather was a stockbroker. However, due to being great friends with Lord Weir, who at one time had been president of the Air Council, Cecil Turner AFC had learnt to fly autogyros. When the Second World War started, being too old for active service, he was given the rank of flight lieutenant and tasked with flying autogyros around radar sites so they could calibrate their new Radio Detection And Ranging machines (RADAR)! In 1945, he was demobbed, but not before he had earned the Air Force Cross.

When my father retired for good, he used to love coming up to The National Archives in the Public Record Office in Kew and researching the family tree. No computers to aid ancestral discovery in those days!

Through the Turner line, which of course was not his own but his wife's, he was able to trace the family tree all the way back to Edward I of England and his wife Eleanor of Castile. The king and queen had at least fourteen children, and we are descended from the eighth, who was Joan of Acre, the oldest surviving child upon her father's death. This means we are also distantly related to Edward II, III and IV, plus William III. Leaving aside the fact that in the early fourteenth century, primogeniture made it theoretically impossible for females to ascend the throne, I do not believe I have any current claim to the crown of England! Nor do I expect people to leave my presence walking backwards and bowing!

Whether Gaffa knew of his illustrious ancestry or not, we young children would keep our distance and limit our time with an elderly man who tolerated the exuberance of youth for only brief periods. Both he and his wife ended their days living with their daughter and son-in-law at Gayshaws in what was affectionately known as the Gaffery. Captain/Flight Lieutenant Cecil Turner AFC died in 1965, outliving his wife by seven years.

Scene 3: Pre-Prep School; Heroics of Ancestors; Conduct for First Time

By now, us children were five, three and one, so for me, school was beckoning, and this I did locally.

First, to an independent school for girls in Sevenoaks called The Granville School, where I stayed a year, before, possibly realising the mistake, transferring to a nearby independent boys' school called Freston Lodge. My brother would join me there later.

Shortly after we left, the school never recovered from the scandal of the headmaster and his interest in the very young boys that attended. Indeed, I am extremely happy to report Mr. Claudet was discovered, went to jail and the school closed down shortly afterwards.

Bizarrely, I will always be indebted to the school, as it was there, at the age of six, that I had my first taste of what I was to do for the rest of my life.

I had shown signs of an interest and some small talent in playing the piano, and when it came to the end-of-term concert, casting around for a small child to lead the ensemble, the music teacher, a lady called Mrs. Lawford, rested her eyes on me, and I was given a baton. I would love to say that the rest, as they say, is history. But quite apart from this biography being very short, there were many obstacles before reaching whatever heights I have now done.

That end-of-term concert was memorable for two reasons. One, because I conducted for the first time and two, for an incident that made the audience laugh! The tune was a basic melody in 2/4 time, so all I had to do was go up and down in time with the music. Some people say that's what I have been doing ever since! This is another memory video where I can remember everything about the occasion: the stage, the choir in front of me, the percussion ensemble to my right and the teacher playing the piano on my left. For years, despite being able to sing the tune, I did not know the name of it. One day, giving a lecture on board the *Queen Mary 2* and recounting the story, I sang the melody! Later, and via my website, a lady emailed informing me it was an Irish traditional song called 'The Mallow Fling', solving a question I had pondered for decades.

The laughing incident was caused by me getting carried away with beating time so enthusiastically, that on one of the up beats, I lost the baton out of my hand. I only knew where it had gone from the screams of the mums in the audience who had thought bits of the ceiling were falling down as my baton fell amongst them. Looking round while the performance continued, the screams turned to laughter as the stick was solemnly handed back row by row, until eventually it ended up in the right place, and I continued with my conducting, albeit a little less frenetically!

As an aside, I very seldom lose a baton while conducting, despite being quite relaxed. On the couple of occasions it has happened, I have always been grateful it's never taken someone's eye out. There is a sharp wooden point at the end of the stick and I often think the front desks of the strings should get danger money. Conductors' hands move quite fast and when sticks are lost, they can fly anywhere.

That first concert made me realise conducting was going

to be my job for life. This is what I wanted to do, and nothing would ever deviate me from that path; I knew exactly what I was going to become from the age of six. In my teens, I became quite a good pianist and could trot out the Grieg *Piano Concerto* without notice, plus any number of difficult Liszt and Ravel piano pieces, but conducting was always going to be my career.

The days in Sevenoaks were idyllic, with long, hot summers cooled off in the swimming pool, balanced by hard, snow-filled winters cut off from civilisation. Winters in the late '50s were much harder than they are now, or maybe we are better at dealing with them; it was a happy time for us all.

My brother and I, along with cousin Richard Helmore, were able to join the Hayley Mills fan club. *Tiger Bay* and *Pollyanna* had just come out; *In Search of the Castaways* was to come shortly afterwards; and, aged six and seven, we were all in love for the first time!

I came close to meeting her in 1984 when doing a show at the Chichester Festival Theatre, and I was introduced to her parents Sir John and Lady Mills. It was not until the '90s that I actually did meet Ms. Mills, at the Regent's Park Open Air Theatre with Cameron Mackintosh. When he said, "Anthony, this is Hayley; Hayley, this is Anthony," all I could do was splutter and dribble as memories of my youth overwhelmed me. As soon as I got home, I sent a message to both Christopher and Richard and just said, *met her!* They knew instantly what I meant.

In 2015, she starred in *Cinderella* at the Richmond Theatre, and I took my family to see her, embarrassing them mightily by hollering and cheering at her every entrance as my childhood came flooding back.

There were some not-so-good times as well, like the walk we children did at this young age. For some unknown reason, Mother got it into her head to walk from our house to her mother's house in Ide Hill. This was a distance of some four miles, maybe more.

Now it would be much more difficult to do as the A225 has been built. Back then it was a walk through woods and brambles, a long walk through woods and brambles. I seem to remember my sister, only aged about three, had a pram which made it a lot easier for her, if not for mother!

About halfway, my mother realised the whole idea was a huge mistake, but it was too late, we were past the point of no return, so we carried on and on and on. I thought that walk was never going to end. Mother tried to keep our spirits up, at the same time as pushing a pram through woods and brambles. Nowadays, you'd just ring someone up on your mobile and say, come and pick us up. In the 1960s, there were no mobile phones, and we were on our own. The original idea, after reaching our destination, was to walk back. When we eventually reached Gayshaws, we all collapsed and, with the respective menfolk away in the cars, stayed the night until someone could come and pick us up the next day.

She never tried a long walk again. To this day, if anyone says, "Shall we go for an afternoon walk?" I always ask, "How far are we going?"

Still, Gayshaws was a better direction than setting off the opposite way towards my great-aunts', who lived at a house called Meadowgate in Brasted. That would have been at least double the distance. In its favour was the fact that it was an extremely interesting house!

My maternal grandfather's sisters, Nesta and Mildred Inglis, lived together just off Brasted High Street, with Mildred's husband, Air Marshal Sir Victor Goddard KB CBE DL.

The Inglis' come of good army stock. My great-great-grandfather, Colonel John Inglis, took over the siege of Lucknow in the Indian Mutiny after Sir Henry Lawrence died from the shelling at the beginning of the attack. Colonel John Inglis, now commanding, managed to repel many assaults until finally relieved by the British Army after 148 days of bombardment.

After the relief, he was promoted to major general and made KCB. His wife, my great-great-grandmother Lady Julia and the daughter of Frederic Thesiger 1st Baron of Chelmsford, who was twice the lord chancellor of Great Britain, wrote the definitive contemporary account of the siege.

Whilst I am here, a number of my relatives died in the First World War and I would like to record three who sacrificed their lives for their country. My great-great-uncle the Rev Rupert Inglis who, prior to the war, had played rugby for England before becoming a chaplain in the British Army, was killed at the age of fifty-one looking for wounded men at the Battle of the Somme. One of his sons, Vice-Admiral John Inglis KBE CB, rose to become director of naval intelligence after the Second World War.

Rupert Inglis was a fruit farmer in British Columbia prior to the war and killed in action in 1915 at Gallipoli.

My great-uncle, Lieutenant John Inglis, was a talented musician, composing his first piece of music at the age of five. He went straight from Rugby School to the Woolwich Military Academy, receiving his commission in the Royal Engineers in 1914. He died in 1915 aged twenty-two at the Battle of Loos, Vermilles, Hill 70, and the plaque given as a memorial to the relatives of those who died in service has pride of place on a wall in our house.

Nesta Inglis was John's sister, and she always said the reason she remained unmarried was that all the young single men went off to war. So many of them died in the trenches and fields of northern France and Belgium, there were not enough to go around when those who survived returned home.

Sir Victor Goddard, who was married to Mildred (maternal grandfather's sister), had an incredibly distinguished war record as senior air staff officer in France just after the outbreak of the Second World War. After returning from France, he became air commodore, chief of the air staff, Royal New Zealand Air Force and the only senior British air officer in the South Pacific in the face of attacks by the Japanese at Guadalcanal.

I cannot, though, gloss over the bit about senior air officer in France! He was senior air officer to General Lord Gort, commander of the British Expeditionary Forces at Dunkirk! When Gort could see the Germans had overwhelming superior forces, he realised he had to get his army out of there, and the only way to get them back to England was rescue across the channel.

In his book *Skies to Dunkirk*, Goddard describes how he was summoned by Lord Gort, told the situation was desperate and somehow to inform Sir Winston Churchill of the fact that unless they were rescued, the British and French Army would be defeated; not only defeated but ignominiously captured.

Goddard therefore commandeered a previously crashed Ensign aeroplane that had been partially repaired but still with no fixed seats. Taking off at night with the aid of car headlamps from a ploughed field at Dunkirk, and having to circle round the Channel until dawn as he had no password that would have allowed him through the English Air Defences, he carried on at first light, landing at Manston before continuing to London.

On arrival he met by chance an old friend Air Commodore Archie Boyle and, having just returned from the front with the most up-to-date news, persuaded the air commodore to get him into the underground headquarters of the war cabinet rooms in Whitehall, where the joint chiefs of staff were discussing the situation in France. He arrived just in time to hear Admiral Pound, the navy chief of staff, announce that all he could spare for the rescue of the BEF were six destroyers.

Victor Goddard, a group captain at the time and therefore very junior in rank compared to others in the room, interrupted to announce it was imperative that an armada of small boats from all sources should be sent to the beaches at Dunkirk – Channel

Packets, pleasure boats, fishing vessels, coasters, lifeboats, yachts, motorboats, anything that could float and cross the channel must be sent – an idea he subsequently claimed to have made up on the spur of the moment. Upon which a scandalised vice-chief of the air staff, Air Chief Marshal Sir Richard Peirce, had him escorted out of the building, telling him he was overwrought as a result of his experiences at the front.

However, as we all know, his passionate plea was subsequently accepted and orders were sent out to Admiral Ramsay in Dover, with the result that 338,226 soldiers of the British and French armies were saved in one of the most daring and ultimately inspiring rescues of the Second World War.

Of possible equal benefit was his counter-espionage coup of 1937.

A high-ranking delegation was sent by Hitler to try and broker an alliance between Germany and Britain with the intention that Germany would rule the land and Britain the waves. Victor Goddard, pretending to be pro-Nazi, was able to persuade the visiting delegation, led by the First World War fighter ace Ernst Udet, that it was not necessary to build four-engine bombers for the upcoming conflict, which Goddard agreed would unite Britain and Germany, as we already had them. Therefore, the German delegation, having accepted Goddard's assurances, never built any meaningful four-engine bombers before or during the Second World War.

On seeing the attrition the Halifax and Lancaster bombers wrought to their own cities, Udet and the Germans realised Goddard had deliberately deceived them, and in 1941, Ernst Udet shot himself in the head.

As if all that was not enough for lasting fame, after the conflict was over, it was his belief in the paranormal that was to gain him some international fame or notoriety, however you want to view it.

His psychic belief first started before the war when he claimed to have been flying a Hawker Hart biplane and to have got lost in low cloud. He recounts in his book *Flight Towards Reality* how he tried to climb above it but was unsuccessful. The weather then got worse, and he lost control of his aeroplane which spiralled down to his seeming inevitable death. Only a few feet above the land, he regained control of the aircraft, just missing a young woman pushing a pram who took no notice of him despite flying a few feet above her head. He tried to regain height, but the clouds which had unleashed their full torrent of rain were lashing at his face, and he wasn't going to enter them.

Suddenly, he saw ahead of him RAF Drem. He knew it was Drem as he had visited the site the day before and had found it in disarray. By 1935, the RAF had abandoned the airfield; the tarmac and four hangars were in disrepair; and barbed wire divided the field where cattle now grazed.

As he flew towards it, a very different scene met his eyes. He described it as flying into a different world. The aircraft was shaking violently, and the clouds had turned a strange yellowish-brown. Ahead of him, he could see a completely repaired airfield with mechanics working on three Avro 504N trainer biplanes and an unknown type of monoplane. At the time of his flight, the RAF had no monoplanes of any sort, and all four planes were bright yellow, an unknown colour in the RAF. Furthermore, the mechanics were wearing blue overalls and not the usual brown ones. He flew off, just clearing the hangars, the mechanics not appearing to see him, before once again being swallowed by the storm. He managed to return to his base safely.

He did not want to be discharged from the RAF as mentally unfit, so, apart from telling a few trusted brother officers, he kept quiet about his experience. In 1939 he watched silently as RAF trainers began to be painted yellow and mechanics switch to brown overalls. Then he heard RAF Drem had been recommissioned and was now a fully operational RAF station!

Another and equally famous event happened to him after the war. On 26 May 1951, he wrote an article for the *Saturday Evening Post*, in which he described an incident that had occurred to him four years earlier. He was in Japan, attending a cocktail party being held in his honour, when he heard from behind a naval officer by the name of Captain Gerald Gladstone, at the time commander of the cruiser HMS *Black Prince*, say to whoever he was talking to, wasn't it a tragedy to hear about the air marshal's death? At this, Sir Victor confronted a very confused captain and said he was still very much alive.

Pressing him for details, the captain replied it must have been a very vivid dream in which he knew the air marshal had flown in a Dakota aeroplane with three civilians, two men and a woman on board. The aircraft was on a flight to the north of Japan and had just flown over a mountain, when it crashed in a violent storm on a rocky shore; all had perished as a result. He was absolutely convinced it had been true, so much so that he had very nearly not come to the cocktail party as he had assumed it would be cancelled. Indeed, he had gone round the party telling everyone the air marshal was dead, until he had been overheard by Sir Victor himself.

By coincidence, Sir Victor was due to fly to the north of Japan the next day, but was fairly relaxed about his scheduled flight, as civilians were not allowed on military flights and, in any case, his aircraft was not a Dakota.

Later that evening, Sir Victor was shocked to discover that his military flight would be taking three civilians: two men and a lady stenographer. One of the civilians was the consul general and an exception had been made for him. Due to a fault, the aircraft was then exchanged for a Dakota. The air marshal became nervous and tried to prevent the civilians, especially the female stenographer, from boarding but was overruled.

The flight was fairly uneventful to begin with, until it started to unfold exactly as Captain Gladstone had described the previous evening. They flew over a mountain in a storm and the pilot had to crash land on a rocky shore. The only difference between the dream and reality was that in the real event, all the passengers survived.

Later, the two men discussed it and Captain Gladstone claimed not to remember any details of the dream, only that he knew and was convinced the air marshal was dead. He had watched it happen!

This story was made into the marvellous film *The Night My Number Came Up* and, although altering some of the plot lines (extra passengers were added to the film in order to increase the cast list and the location altered to Hong Kong), it basically gave a good account of the story. The film cast Sir Michael Redgrave as Sir Victor Goddard with Denholm Elliott, Sheila Sim, Michael Hordern, Alexander Knox and many other British names of the 1950's film industry.

As I say, an interesting house in Brasted, especially as Sir Victor had a shed at the bottom of his garden where he used to do all his paranormal writings or, as his wife, sister-in-law and others in the family called it, his woo-woo hut.

Longspring Wood was also the time I swallowed a threepenny bit. For some reason, I had in my possession one of these old dodecagonal coins and had gone to bed as our parents had guests round for dinner. I remember lying on my back on the bottom of a bunk bed and throwing it up in the air, then catching it like cricketers did with my hands cupped in front of my face, until one throw, and rather like my prowess on the sporting field, I dropped it. I must have had my mouth open, because it went straight down my throat. I ran into the supper party and caused a bit of a stir screaming that I had just swallowed a threepenny bit. Salt water was given to me in an effort to make me regurgitate it. I was very sick, but of the coin, there was no sign. It was then decided that unless it came out naturally, I was to have an operation to remove it; meanwhile, the instruction was not to flush the lavatory.

The day before the operation came and nothing had happened. As the doctors were not too sure where the coin was, it was not going to be straightforward. I went to the lavatory that morning and, horror of horrors, without thinking pulled the chain. My parents, hearing the flush, came rushing into the bathroom absolutely livid; there were dangers attached to the procedure the next day as they had been told there was a 50% chance of me not surviving. On inspecting the bowl of the lavatory, there, reclining in all its wondrousness, was the threepenny bit! Never was there such joy at the result of a defecation!

Scene 4: Move to Isle of Wight

Our time at Longspring Wood was coming to an end. Dad's father and mother had divorced, and Bill Howard-Williams had married Diana Bamber, a lady half his age and the sister of Neville Bamber. Neville, along with his wife, daughter and twin grandchildren, would ultimately be murdered at White House Farm in 1985 by his adopted son Jeremy Bamber, still in jail at the time of writing and protesting his innocence. Diana (Bill's second wife) had also died, and it was rumoured with her lover, some years previously in a car accident in Kenya.

Biddy, my grandmother, had remarried too, and in terms of my father's job-hunting prospects, rather well. She had married Chris Ratsey from the family of the famous sail-making firm Ratsey & Lapthorn in Cowes on the Isle of Wight. That firm had made some of the sails for HMS *Victory* at the Battle of Trafalgar in 1805, one of which, complete with canon ball holes, is on view in the Portsmouth Historic Dockyard. Chris Ratsey offered Dad a job. This meant selling Longspring Wood and moving to Cowes, so Dad could take up the job of sales director. Realising how cut off she would be on an island with no bridge or tunnel and limited ferry sailings, away from friends and relatives, Mother did not want to go. However, a job was a job, and move we did. To a house called The Helmain in Baring Road, which overlooked the roads of Cowes, and by the term roads, I don't mean the B3325 but the stretch of water immediately outside the harbour!

Dad, meanwhile, had his mind set on sending his two boys to the prep school he had attended. Perched on the edge of the cliffs on the road between a small village called Milford-on-Sea and Barton-on-Sea, it was an establishment called Hordle House. There was a brief hiatus as my small musical gifts were acknowledged with the thought of joining the Canterbury Cathedral Choir as a treble, which would have meant attending a local school. However, I failed the audition as a result, my mother always said, of me having a cold. I think I failed due to indifference! So, my father got his wish, and I went to his old alma mater.

To do this meant boarding, and in order to get us used to the idea of boarding throughout childhood and into adulthood, Christopher and I first boarded for a term or two at Freston Lodge in Sevenoaks; you remember, that school where the headmaster was jailed for doing unto small boys what no adult should ever do to any child?

Acknowledging the trauma of Jean-Lou, it was decided to board us both as Christopher would be company for me, and at the ages of seven and six, we spent a couple of terms coming to terms (no pun intended) without parents, in the hope that it would get us used to the concept prior to Hordle House. I wasn't so sure. I had already experienced life without parents and had not liked it.

But I never got used to the idea of being without a parent, that agonising goodbye when you wave to them as they leave and watch retreating figures until, through tears, you can see them no

THE RAF CONTINGENT 1918-Present Day

From top left clockwise: Air Vice-Marshal FF Inglis CB CBE DL (maternal grandfather). Air Commodore EL Howard-Williams MC (paternal grandfather). Group Captain Peter Helmore DFC and Bar (maternal uncle by marriage). Air Marshal Sir Victor Goddard KB CBE DL (great-uncle by marriage). I knew them all!

1

Squadron Leader Jeremy Howard-Williams DFC (father) and Diana Gillian Howard-Williams (mother)

Wing Commander Peter Howard-Williams DFC (paternal uncle)

And the next generation with some of his flying awards: Flight Lieutenant Dominic Howard-Williams (son)

Paternal grandmother Norah Gibson (Biddy) married to Air Commodore 'Bill' Howard-Williams

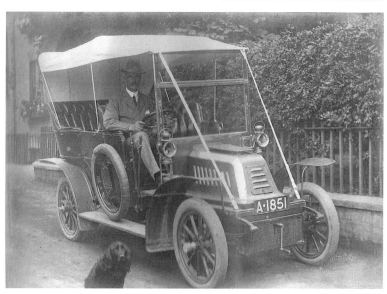

Paternal great-grandfather Dr Percy Gibson of Cowes who founded the Island Sailing Club and was the first man on the Isle of Wight to own a motorcar

Maternal great-grandmother
Emily (Gamma) Streatfeild
with two of her children
including my grandmother
Vera (in front), married to…

Maternal great-grandfather
Fl Lt Cecil Willie Turner
AFC

Maternal grandmother Vera 'Midge' Inglis on the summit of 'Everest' at Gayshaws, with her adored poodles which she successfully showed and bred

Wing Commander Peter Howard-Williams DFC in his Spitfire

Dec 1941, Plt Off J Howard-Williams with Blenheim at Church Fenton Aerodrome

Foreground: Feb 1944, Sqdn Ldr J Howard-Williams DFC (pilot) and F/O FJ MacRae (navigator) flying an ME410 in RAF colours with RAF serial number TF209. The accompanying Mosquito is an MK XVII and its crew were to be shot down and killed two weeks later

Author aged three

Four generations of the Inglises
TOP ROW: *Vera Inglis, Jeremy H-W, FF Inglis*
MIDDLE ROW: *Cecil Turner, Jill H-W, Emily Turner*
FRONT ROW: *Author, Nicola H-W, Christopher H-W*

'Everest' in 2017 with nothing on the summit

Lt Duncan McTavish with author's father looking at dropped First World War note

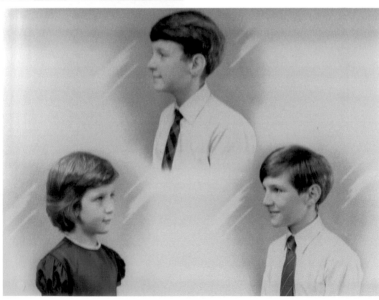

Top: Author; Left: Nicola; Right: Christopher

more. Even now, some sixty years later, I recall those moments with anxiety.

However, in those days, there was no option; you did as you were told, and off to boarding school we were packed!

Act 2

Scene 1: Prep School

Hordle House was an interesting school, all male and suffering from a lack of good teachers. This was 1960 and most potential teachers, those who should have been teaching, had had their training interrupted by a war and were now doing different occupations. Like other schools, Hordle had those who were either coming to the end of their careers or who had come out of retirement to help. I remember even at the time, none of us were overly impressed by the quality of the teaching.

There was the science teacher, a man by the name of Mr. Backhouse. A man so inept, he once asked me to take a phial of liquid outside the classroom and pour it into the ground. He did tell me to be careful, and I was, but not careful enough. Pouring it onto the concrete caused splashback over my left leg and left me with horrific burns. I was rushed to Sister (the resident nurse) who had to bathe it, put special cream with a gauze on and change the dressing for weeks after. I subsequently learnt this phial was sulphuric acid and still have four scars on my left leg from that lesson, learnt at the age of nine.

The maths teacher was a man called Captain Eriks, and he had a tin leg, though at the time we never knew how he got it, or even, we assumed, which war he had got it in. It was only later on I learnt it was as a result of a motorbike accident and nothing to do with a battle. He was the man who in a lesson would always go off at a tangent. We would try and make him do this as they were always far more interesting than the maths he was supposed to be teaching. For instance, and this is an actual example, "If the distance to a wall was ten feet and the angle to the top was twenty degrees, how tall is the wall?" He would get side-tracked and ask us if we knew how a wall was built! This was always much more interesting than the original question, and if we were clever and kept asking the right questions, we could make wall building last the entire lesson! The downside, to my detriment a few years later, we had not learnt a lot of maths.

Mr. Lewman was a teacher with a frightening temper. The rumour buzzing around the boys was that an earwig had at some time got into his ear and was still there, which would occasionally send him crazy. Being small boys, we would try and expose his temper. We used to call this perilous sport Lewman-baiting and, occasionally, it got out of hand.

Years of experience had given him an unerring accuracy with a chalk when flung at a boy, invariably hitting him on his head. One day we had Lewman-baited to excess; he picked on me and proceeded to beat me up! With no exaggeration, he had me, aged nine or ten, on the floor, kicking six bells out of me. I was only saved by the headmaster who, upon hearing the commotion created by Mr. Lewman and the screaming boys, some of whom were probably cheering him on, others genuinely concerned for my safety, came into the classroom and invited him to step outside. I shudder to think what might have happened if the headmaster had not fortuitously been passing. Nowadays, Mr. Lewman would probably be jailed for assault!

Mr. Howerd, who taught English, was the best teacher there, only he had retired and just filled in when they needed him; all too seldom in my opinion. We all cheered when we knew he was taking our lessons. He always knew his subject, was thoroughly prepared and intensely interesting to listen to.

He was, however, responsible for some small unfairness directed towards me. He read out loud to the class a passage from Arthur Conan Doyle's *Hound of the Baskervilles* and asked at the end of the passage how Sherlock Holmes had deduced something. I shot my hand up and said, "From the tobacco ash the suspect dropped outside the hut on the moor." Mr. Howerd, upset by the fact his question had been answered correctly, said it was unfair of me to answer the question if I had already read the book. I hadn't! I just realised that although the information of ash being dropped appeared insignificant, Mr. Conan Doyle never wrote anything of unimportance!

Influenced by Mr. Howerd, reading is a daily delight. It may be a book I have read before, but I get great joy out of the written word. He was a magnificent teacher.

The school was run by two brothers Peter and John Whately-Smith, the sons of the founder with whom my father and uncle had attended back in the late 1920s early 1930s. Their wives, respectively Dorothy and Diana, were in no small part the power behind the throne.

Being boys, every teacher had a nickname and, of course, they were unfair. Peter Whately-Smith was Pig and his wife Sow. I'm sorry to say their son, who was a pupil at the school, was known as Piglet. John Whately-Smith was Billy and his wife The Dragon, and they all knew their nicknames. We know this as Dorothy Whately-Smith was once taking a painting lesson and her youngest son was in the class. She made the mistake of saying that the brush demonstration would be done by Piglet. To which his memorable reply was, "Will I now, Sow?" She was furious!

Just to show there is no bias, there was a nickname at Hordle for me. It was not a very nice nickname, nor do I know how I earned it, though I can guess. Nevertheless, uttering it now in the hope it is immediately forgotten, by everyone, I was called

Bogey! Unfortunately, I saddled my brother with the name as well, for when he arrived at Hordle he was immediately called Bogey minor, and I became Bogey major! I lost it as soon as I left the school, though every now and then my cousin, who you are about to meet, perpetuates in occasionally calling me Bogey! Thank goodness he went on to Charterhouse School and not to my destination!

The matron of the school was called Miss. Trinder and even her name, uttered in hushed tones, was enough to strike terror into the hearts of us boys. Her nickname was The Trinder-Bug, and her hair brushing and toenail cutting were conducted in such harsh strokes and cuts with brush and scissors, it made you issue immediate instructions to your hair and nails to stop growing! I gather that after I left, she became a geography teacher at the school, which possibly indicates to what depths the school had sunk.

It was a harsh regime at the school with regular beatings from John Whately-Smith. Interestingly, Peter Whately-Smith seldom dished them out; it was always left to the younger one. He couldn't half whack you. Whatever you did, blotting paper down your pants, thin paperback novels, you would feel them. I speak from bitter experience as I was regularly summoned to the headmaster's study on the Monday morning. Six of the best was not uncommon, and we were always relieved to get to the sixth stroke, believing corporal punishment had a legal limit of six with the cane.

The slipper was worse as there were unlimited strokes with that, and I held the record! One week receiving twenty-four, the next thirty-six, all of them gleefully counted by other boys lingering outside the room listening to the cries of pain.

Boys so punished tried not to cry physical tears as it was not considered very manly, despite the fact we were only playing at being men. I must say, when the strokes went above fifteen, I would start quietly crying, which became an outburst when I could get somewhere private and clutch my bottom in agony.

Minus marks were issued for misdemeanours such as leaving your clothes lying around. Every time you left an item of clothing on the floor, you received a minus mark and anything above ten minus marks meant a beating. Teachers could also issue minus marks for many other transgressions which included poor work, not running fast enough or perceived laziness. In my case, poor work and leaving clothes lying around were my particular crimes. Diana Whately-Smith once said to my parents, "You always know where Anthony is, as you just have to follow his line of discarded clothing." Consequently, I was a regular visitor outside the headmaster's study door on Monday mornings, and the slipper beatings were a desperate effort to make me mend my ways. On reflection, some sixty years later, I think it worked; I am now very tidy!

As growing boys, we were always hungry, and school food in the '60s was terrible. The hunger was not helped by the fact they provided tiny portions of the terrible food! I liked their porridge (five spoonfuls) and tinned tomatoes on toast (two halves on half a slice of toast), but hated their tinned macaroni cheese (which has given me a lasting aversion to cooked cheese). The less said about their awful hot pot (bones and gristle of some indeterminate meat, possibly mutton, in a gravy) the better. To this day, I can't eat fat, finding it rubbery and chewy, disgusting to taste and impossible to swallow. Whether we liked the food or not, we were made to finish everything on our plates, which was no bad discipline to learn.

It was the yellow fish that was my bête noire. I do not think we ever knew it as smoked haddock; we just called it 'yellow fish' as it aptly described the colour of the food! No matter how hard I tried, I just could not chew it. It was rubbery, completely without flavour and certainly impossible to swallow. I used to stuff it into my pockets from my plate, take it out and throw it in bins around the school! For some months I got away with this, until one fateful day, I was stopped leaving the dining room.

"Empty your pockets, boy," came the thundering demand from Billy. Whereupon, bits of cold, solidified yellow fish came tumbling from my pockets onto the floor. Of course, there was an appointment with him Monday morning where there came a meeting between the cane and my bottom!

My cousin James Powell, the 'nickname perpetuator', who was slightly younger than me and therefore arrived at Hordle a year later, always tells the story of arriving at the school and, on his first walk-round of the grounds, discovering me being hung upside down by my feet from the football goalposts. My gang had lost a battle (but not the war). I had obviously been captured and was being interrogated by the Shorthouse gang, my rivals! Upon my seeing him, I said something along the lines of, "Oh, hello, James. Don't worry, old boy, this is just a temporary situation. As soon as I'm out of this, I must enrol you in my gang!"

There is a memory of that occurrence in my subconscious mind. I have little recollection of the following one, which he also tells with delight.

I am proud of my nose; it is the Inglis nose on my mother's side. I would describe it as on the large side and Romanesque with a hook. James tells the story of my angering Mr. John Whately-Smith to such an extent, he grabbed me by the collar and rubbed my face up and down the wall. Sadly for us both, the wall he chose was adjacent to the door and my nose came into contact with the light switch. Apparently, without either of us noticing, with every rub down, the light switch went on, and every rub up, it went off! James swears it's true and still laughs about it to this day!

In my opinion, one of the more sadistic pastimes Hordle used to organise were compulsory boxing matches between the boys, organised probably inevitably by the baited Mr. Lewman. One of these contests was arranged between James and me.

We met up beforehand and agreed we would not take this too seriously. No hitting in the face or groin area and no hard punches anywhere, just light taps. We agreed to confine these between the waist and the shoulders. We got in the ring and all that went out of the window. With his first punch, he shocked me into self-preservation mode. This mainly meant running to escape him, not a pastime I enjoyed at the best of times. When he caught me, he knocked the living daylights out of me, completely ignoring the gentleman's agreement upon which we had shaken hands. As he was left-handed, he was a southpaw as well, and I had no defence. Amid tumultuous cheers from the boys and masters alike, he won the contest by a unanimous decision; he was a popular boy! And this, after looking after him so comprehensively when he had broken his collarbone and could not do any of the most menial and intimate of tasks. Though, on looking back, I think he could have done them all. He just enjoyed having his own servant! I did not forgive him for several months.

Each summer term, the entire school would go to the nearby New Forest and have a picnic. We were either made to follow the New Forest Beagle Hunt or go on long walks as we couldn't keep up with the dogs. My only real memory of them was on one occasion being shot in the head, as I like to say! Ambling along in a clearing somewhere, I felt a sharp stab of pain on the left side of my head. Clutching my hand to the area, I saw I was covered in blood. I shouted out to nearby Matron who, quickly sizing up the issue, ran with me back to base camp! It was some distance and I was exhausted by the end. Very quickly, I sat down and had my hair around the area cut off and patched up with a large gauze. I do not remember any stitches so can only assume it was a pellet or maybe a stone that had hit me. What I do know is that I was not allowed to tell my parents in a letter home, nor were the police involved.

Every Sunday, we were made to write letters home. We would write about the mundane activities of the school and what we were doing. My father, though, had it in mind that teaching never stops; one is always learning, and it would be good for me to know any grammatical or spelling errors I had made in the letters written home. So, he sent them back with the mistakes underlined and corrections inserted! Years later, my mother told me she was furious when she found out and made him stop. She said he only did it once; I told her she only caught him once!

It was rather the same with comics. We were all allowed to be sent a weekly or monthly comic and most would get *The Beano*, *The Hotspur*, *The Dandy* or *The Eagle*, the popular mags of the day. Other boys would avidly read their comic cartoons and then swap their titles. Much eagerness was engendered in the second-hand market of comic magazines. However, in desperation to improve my academic ability, I was sent *Look and Learn*! This was a worthy British weekly educational magazine that found few takers in the second-hand market at Hordle House School. Hell, I did not enjoy reading it as the first recipient!

As said previously, the teaching was either not good, or maybe as I was not academically gifted, it needed more inspirational teachers like Mr. Howerd. One memorable week, my brother, who by now was in the same academic form as me, despite being twenty-one months younger, overtook me in the weekly class list. I shall always remember the huge cheer that went up from the school as the classroom achievement list was read out and Howard-Williams minor had gained a higher position than Howard-Williams major and was now ahead. I do not remember it bothering me very much!

Through no fault of its own, the school also left me with a confusion that has persisted to this day. I have a real issue with remembering whether the number one is higher or lower than the number two. For instance, manual gears in a car: do you go up from first into second, or down? What is top and what is bottom? This stems from the fact that at Hordle, the first form was above the second and therefore you went 'up' into the first form from the second, with the first form top and the fifth, bottom. I have a feeling it is the other way around in a car and if you go through the gears from first to fifth, you are going up rather than down! My mind has never been able to adjust from something learnt sixty years ago! Which is odd, as at my next school, the sixth form was the top form, with the fifth lower; you went up from the fifth to the sixth. Too late, the earlier schooling system has persisted to confuse me to this day.

What Hordle House did, and did magnificently, was foster my interest in music. This was in the shape of Peter Whately-Smith, who saw in me some interest and gift in music. He and his wife used to make me practise on their private piano in their house, Diana his wife shouting out from their kitchen, "No, no… do it again!" Something I later heard myself saying to my cello-playing son when hearing him practise!

I was partly able to repay that debt to the Whately-Smiths and, thanks to them, show them what I had achieved. When Peter and his wife Dorothy retired, they moved to Aldeburgh where Peter had become mayor. On 31 August 1994, I conducted a concert with the Royal Philharmonic Concert Orchestra in The Maltings in nearby Snape and was able to invite them both to the concert. By the time of this concert in 1994, Peter was in a wheelchair, and he died a short time later. Keeping in touch with Dorothy until she too died, I owe them both a lot.

John Whately-Smith may have had an even bigger hand in my future career because of one single incident. I didn't particularly enjoy piano practice, as it had to be done in my spare time and therefore took me away from my friends who were off playing somewhere. However, a comment John Whately-Smith made stayed with me when having a wobble and thinking of giving up music; it was another of those life-defining moments. He was talking to someone else, and I overheard him say he wished he could still play the piano. At that moment I thought, if he wishes that now, maybe I'll wish the same when I'm his age. From then on, perseverance and piano practice took on a different impetus.

I rapidly overtook the ability of the local piano teacher in the school, a lady by the name of Miss. Baker. Mark you, I don't think it helped when I once argued with her that there was no Bb in the key of F major (there is)! She brought her pencil down hard onto the back of my right hand whilst I was playing, breaking the tip – I still have the scar to prove I was wrong!

I also remember arguing with her about the timing of a piece of music and her screaming at me to count the beats of the bar as I played.

"You count!" I screamed back. She shouted at me to get out of the room. All I saw as I exited, was Miss. Baker with some smelling salts rocking backwards and forwards in her chair. What could she have thought I had said? Having outgrown Miss. Baker, or perhaps she refused to teach me, I was forced to travel out of school into nearby New Milton to attend lessons given by Miss. Edie Marr.

Scene 2: Show Some Small Talent at the Piano

Miss. Marr moved me on considerably, and I entered music competitions in Bournemouth and Ryde on the Isle of Wight, always doing well. I had a well-matched contest in the Isle of Wight music competitions with one of the Minghella daughters. The Minghellas were a famous family on the Isle of Wight as they made the fabulous local ice cream. One of the sons went on to be the talented film director Anthony Minghella.

Miss. Marr was a hard teacher but very fair, and with her, I progressed by leaps and bounds. Twice a week I would catch the bus outside the school gates into New Milton, a distance of some three and a half miles. Difficult to think of a nine-year-old boarding schoolboy, clutching his four old pence (now roughly one and a half pence), getting on a bus by himself and travelling by public transport. Doing that twice a week meant I never got into the first XI team at football.

I was a good goalie, though did not enjoy it as there was a lot of standing about in shorts and a football shirt. It was impossible to stay warm in the winter months when the wind came whistling over the Barton cliffs off the Atlantic. No one was allowed to wear gloves or double layers, even the goalies, and if you were in a good team, there was a lot of standing about in cold weather watching the game from the inactive end of the pitch.

I shudder to think what Mr. Branfoot, the excellent teacher and games master, would have made of modern-day football with pampered, overpaid Premier League footballers togged up in gloves, thermals, long-johns and headwear!

Practice for the first XI always fell on a Tuesday and Friday, yet I could never practise with them as they were the same days as my piano lessons in New Milton. So, Hutton became the first XI goalie, and I joined the second XI as they practised just once a week on Wednesdays. The seconds, however, were the champions of the local prep schools. There was one memorable year, when in five or six matches played either on a Wednesday or Saturday, we scored about twenty goals, against the one goal I allowed past me.

Whilst I was at the school, there was a cricket match that should go down in the Wisden annals of cricketing history. I was not playing but did watch. In the summer of 1964, the school first XI was a very good one, and by the time this match came around, were undefeated. We were playing at home against our arch-enemies Walhampton Prep School and were expecting a high score from our side. Having won the toss, we put the opposition in first so that we would bat second, which meant a run chase. What we weren't expecting was such a low total from the Walhampton team: five runs all out! Our opening batsman, a boy by the hallowed name of Keith Best (blessèd be the name of Best!), went in and hit a six off the opening ball, thereby enabling a victory in just one ball!

The story of Hordle House has a sad ending. There were too many local preparatory schools and, in the '90s, Hordle House went into sad decline. Finally closing its doors in 1997, it merged with the old enemy (and defeated cricket team in just one ball) Walhampton. Based at the Walhampton School premises, the two schools were renamed Hordle Walhampton. In 2018, the name Hordle was dropped from its title, and now my old prep school exists only in memories and aging books.

In the early 2000s, I took a walk with my family along the cliffs of Milford-on-Sea and stood transfixed as I came to the spot where Hordle House had existed. Quite by chance, the school was being demolished before my very eyes. Standing there, I couldn't believe the actual dormitory I had slept in, named Hamilton, was being attacked by a wrecking ball, and in its place would rise a new housing estate.

I couldn't raise a cheer. I may not have been happy there, but after the enforced boarding at Jean-Lou that was not the school's fault. I owe them a huge debt. Now, all evidence as to the existence of Hordle House was being expunged from the annals of history, something I might have wished whilst there. Nevertheless, sad to actually witness it happening.

As I stood there watching the ball and chain swing destructively against the dormitory walls, I recalled those sleep-filled mornings as one of the headmasters walked around the gardens of the school at 6.30am saying four words. To begin with, in our sleep-filled brains, the voice was soft, from afar, and all four words were indistinguishable. But we knew the last three: "Early morning swim." We were unable to tell whether the first word was 'voluntary' or 'compulsory' until he got closer. We all fervently hoped it was the former, but all too often as he went round the grounds getting closer and closer, it was the latter. In which case, all 110 boys in the school, supervised by just one headmaster, would get up prior to breakfast, dress into their swimming trunks and cross the fields before descending the cliffs into the cold sea at Milford-on-Sea.

I'm not sure how, on that shelved shingle beach, no small boy was ever lost at sea! As the surf went out, we would all struggle with the undertow. Apart from the danger of the entire event, I can tell you they were not much fun either. At that time of the morning, the sea had not had much of a chance to warm up. The sun, even if it was out, was at its lowest on the horizon and the shingle, which at night you could hear from your dormitory with the unmistakable sound of stones rolling against each other, was a very difficult surface on which to walk barefoot.

Walking along the Milford-on-Sea cliffs with my family, looking at what remained of the school, my eyes slowly followed the path taken from the school to the beach by us boys. Turning my head slowly towards the edge, the old path down from the cliff edge was barely visible. Over the ninety years the school had existed, the storms and spray combined with the tramping of thousands of small boys' feet had worn away the loose surface. Nonetheless, I was transported back to a time that had formed my life path's destiny. I stood there, engrossed by the memory, wanting to scramble down. No longer in the first flush of youth, I realised very quickly it was too dangerous to attempt a descent to the shoreline. Appearing to foretell my ultimate demise, which seems to be hurtling towards me with indecent speed, I realised nothing lasts forever.

Scene 3: Transport Fascination

Going back to school after the holidays was always tortuous. The drive from Cowes to Yarmouth, then boarding the ferry before crossing to Lymington where a taxi would be waiting to take us back to school. Occasionally, we would catch the ferry from Cowes and then the train from Southampton to New Milton. I always preferred this route as, though more expensive, the ferry from Cowes to Southampton took double the time of the Yarmouth/ Lymington route and delayed my return to school.

It also gave me the chance to boast I have travelled on a ship that took part in the 1944 D-Day landings. MV Norris Castle had been originally designed for that famous operation but, after the war, had been converted for the Red Funnel Line as a service from Southampton to Cowes. The ship was slow and not very luxurious, but the history! Taxis from the ferry terminal to Southampton Central Railway Station and New Milton to Milford-on-Sea all added to the length of the journey.

The most exciting part of the journey was very definitely the steam train! Yes, dear reader, I was only a child yet did catch the end of the steam era on the public network. Those huge Southern locomotives, belching great clouds of smoke and steam, whistling as they prepared to depart. Then, we hurtled through the Hampshire countryside, embers belching from the chimney stacks, flashing past the carriage windows. You very definitely leant out of the windows at your peril in those days.

Term was a huge anticlimax after that journey; nevertheless, it did feed my transport addiction. I love anything to do with travel; not necessarily the travelling, though I guess that's part of it. But the means of the travel; the machines that enable the ability of humans to travel. This includes the BEA tail-dragging DC3 I once flew in from Southampton Airport to Guernsey in order to spend a week sailing round the Channel Islands. This iconic aircraft was the workhorse of the British Army during the war and had probably been converted from military use. As in the 1940s, the pilots left the cockpit door open and, once in the air, we had a marvellous view!

Years later, I travelled up and down to Wolverhampton in 1975 to meet with the man who was helping me arrange the music for the pantomime that Christmas. There was one occasion I deliberately changed my route from the usual direct fast Euston service to a slow service to Paddington. Getting off the slow service at Didcot Station, I waited there for an hour or two for the brand-new experimental High Speed Inter-City 125, just to experience this new form of transport. It was running one service a day between Paddington and Cardiff, then back to Paddington. The public had never seen anything like it, with doors that slid open between the carriages as you approached them. I was late back home, but oh boy, was it worth it! The glossy brochure that was supplied in all the carriages about this bright new train of the future is still in my possession.

The 125 was supposed to be a temporary passenger train that would fill the gap while they worked out the many issues affecting the tilting mechanism of the Advanced Passenger Train before its entry into service. They never did solve the APT problems, and it now sits looking forlorn and unloved in the sidings next to the West Coast Mainline Crewe Railway Station, all part of the Crewe Heritage Centre.

The 125 had to remain in service and, as I write, they have just retired the last of them on the East Coast Mainline. I travelled on one in the last few months of their service, and it was a very tired example. It brought back so many memories of my wait at Didcot Station some forty-five years previously and my excitement at seeing this beautiful silver, sleek, gorgeous Kenneth Grange-designed machine approach the platform.

The journeys to and from Hordle were the formation of a

lifetime love affair with machines, especially the one home, when the time I loved best would begin: the holidays!

Scene 4: Holidays; Love Affair with Malta, Theatre and the Sea Begins

Occasionally, school holidays would be taken further afield, and this is where my huge affection for the islands of Malta and, more specifically, Gozo began. Situated just to the south of Sicily, these three islands, which include Comino, have a huge history and, due to the importance of Valetta as a naval base, a succession of powers including the Greeks, Romans, Arabs, Phoenicians, Carthaginians, French and, most recently, the British, have all had a go at ruling these tiny islands. They now have their own autonomy.

With my RAF family lineage, there was bound to be a free holiday there, thanks to various family member postings to RAF Luqa, now the international airport for the islands. In the 1960s in the old BEA Viscounts, it would take a long time to reach Malta as we would have to refuel at Rome Airport. With the arrival of the Vanguards, non-stop flights started.

Invariably, Dad knew the pilot who would be ex-wartime RAF, and we would be invited into the cockpit. Once, when flying over the Alps in a Vanguard, I sat in the captain's seat with my sister, not much older than six, sitting on my lap. She was asked by the pilot to push a button on the centre console and the aircraft then banked right. I was so jealous. Can you imagine doing that today?

My family often chide me for going back again and again. Yet I know all the secluded beaches like Slugs Bay (much better than it sounds), St. Peter's Pool (idyllic) and Xlendi Bay (marvellous) and all the great hotels of which, for us, the Kempinski is the best. The people are generous, very friendly and were incredibly brave to withstand the bombardment of their island by the Germans and Italians during the Second World War. Which brings me to a wonderful brain puzzle for those of you interested in frustrating and intriguing their loved ones in equal measure on a family holiday. I did this on one holiday to the islands and kept the answer for ten days, much to the intense irritation of my wife and children. The question I posed, which came to me whilst perusing the bookshop on board the ferry crossing from Mġarr to Ċirkewwa, was this: which letter of the alphabet do Malta and Gozo share in their name? It would seem at first glance that neither Malta nor Gozo shares a letter, but they do! Take a moment before reading on to see if you can get the answer!

I had a lot of fun with this question over a private dinner party on board the liner *Queen Mary 2* with some of the senior officers, including Robbie Howie the wonderful hotel manager and Paul O'Loughlin, the original and definitive entertainment director. I had to virtually give the answer in a series of clues at the end of the meal, before Captain Aseem Hashmi came up with the answer, which is the letter G. The Maltese were so brave during the continual bombardment in 1942, King George VI awarded the island the George Cross, with the words:

> *To honour her brave people I award the George Cross to the Island Fortress of Malta to bear witness to a heroism and devotion that will long be famous in history.*

The only time this has ever been done. So, the full and correct name of Malta is Malta GC.

I loved holidays at Cowes as well; it was a haven away from the spartan living conditions of an all-boys boarding school in the 1960s, away from masters and their tempers, tyrannical matrons and the gangs! The island in the '60s was, and to a certain extent still is, like stepping back in time. When we moved there, only one set of traffic lights existed on the entire island. They were just outside the capital Newport, and an exciting day out was a visit to see them working!

Holidays were a chance to get away and laze around with our bikes, race down Egypt Hill to Gurnard and watch the ships go by or go for a sail.

It was in Cowes that my love of both the sea and theatre started, though perhaps as regards the sea, not entirely smoothly. Dad thought if we were going to learn how to sail, we should learn how to get out of any difficulty we might encounter. For that reason, he would teach us how to right a capsized dinghy. He did this off the end of the jetty at the Island Sailing Club, the club his grandfather had founded, but reckoned without my capacity for screaming! I have never really subscribed to the theory you have to initiate something disastrous in order to learn how to get out of it. Just don't get into it in the first place!

I remember my son saying to me many years later when we were flying a Piper PA28 at five thousand feet, that he would like to practise a stall. I was incredulous! I said to him, "You mean you actually want to try and stall the aircraft, so you can see if you can recover the aircraft?" I went on, "You want to disrupt the airflow under the wings, so there's no lift and we fall out of the sky? This, while I'm on board?" By now, warming to my theme and completely unstoppable, I added, "I don't recall any B747 captain coming on the inflight cabin address system as I was about to consume my third glass of champagne and announce he was now going to practise a stall!"

"Yes," my son replied, and he did, and we survived. It was all very easy. He pulled the throttles back, lifted the nose slightly; the engine slowed down; forward motion slowed; the stall warning system went off (that was a bit unnerving); and he gently pushed the stick forward. The nose went down, and we picked up speed, an essential factor if you don't want to fall out of the sky! I threatened to get out if he wanted to practise anything like that again, though carrying out the threat whilst actually flying would have been quite a challenge!

It began the same way on the jetty of the Island Sailing Club. Dad pulled the mast over with the sails on; the boat went over; and this is where it was different: I screamed! Sad to say, he walked off, too embarrassed to admit ownership of this bawling ten-year-old at the club his grandfather had founded!

My love of theatre also began on the island. Well, not actually on the island as we had no major theatre on the island, and to my knowledge not many stars came over and performed. Everyone had to travel over to the mainland to see a show, though I vaguely recall going to see a wrestling match in Newport.

The first visit we made to the theatre was to see Charlie Drake at the Kings Theatre Southsea in the musical *Man in the Moon*, probably fresh from the Christmas 1963 season at the London Palladium. It was the first time I had seen anything so glamorous: the lights, the music, the real actors, everything so alive! Little did I know then that theatre would be in my blood for most of my professional life.

In Cowes, I first came across the curse of hay fever. Something I still suffer from today despite being semi-controlled by the simple method of taking a daily Benadryl one-a-day tablet. Back in the '60s, when my parents didn't really understand what was happening to me, there was nothing. Some days, my eyes would get so itchy, I would rub them so much they would swell up and I would not be able to see out of them.

I recall a lunch party my parents once threw and not being able to attend as I was under the covers of my bed trying to avoid the light, unable to see. Eventually, someone said to my mother, had she thought it might be hay fever? From that moment, I had hay fever and a daily Piriton tablet was administered. They must have been early days, as they were useless.

The water helped and, as often as possible, I would go out either in the Ratsey & Lapthorn Fairy Huntsman motorboat the *Blue Hunter* or, more often, the Dragon class sailing boat called *Blue Skies*. She was supposed to be a racing boat but was slow; she never did very well. During Cowes week and the class racing, we more or less made up the numbers!

However, there is always a sublime moment in sailing, almost as good as the moment an orchestra strikes up with a Mozart symphony.

Generally speaking, an engine is used to get in and out of a harbour mooring. Gently motoring away from the pontoon and out of the harbour, the sails are raised and then there is that moment all sailors know so well: with the yacht stabilised and heeling to the wind, the motor is turned off. It is that moment I am talking about; the beautiful silence as the skipper and crew harnesses the energy of the wind and peace reigns supreme over the boat until, that is, you go racing!

I have never really enjoyed racing as much as the rest of my family, preferring to saunter along, without any fuss, gently watching the world go by. I was and still am what is called a fair-weather sailor, never wanting to be hell-bent on getting round a buoy as quickly as possible. I have always desired a little round indentation in the wooden thwarts of a boat, somewhere for my gin and tonic glass to sit without sliding and spilling the contents!

In the middle of the Solent, which is a strip of water between the Isle of Wight and the south coast of mainland UK, there is a famous sandbank lying just below the surface called the Brambles. Sometimes, when the gravitational pull of the moon and sun is right, we have what are called spring tides. Very occasionally, if everything aligns, the sandbank rises out of the water like some enormous golden-backed whale, enabling boat visits. There is even a famous cricket match played when it does rise up. I'm not too sure of the match rules, as hitting the ball into the outfield sends it under water, so I would imagine the possibility of lost balls are quite high! I have seen this match played from the front at Cowes and a more bizarre sight is difficult to find!

The sandbank was guarded for many years by a lightship called the *Calshot Spit*, containing three men who maintained the light and made a note of passing ships. It had no engine, being securely anchored to the seabed, guiding the great ocean liners in and out of Southampton Water. Replaced by a buoy in 1965, it is now preserved at the Solent Sky Museum.

At normal tidal flows, the sandbank, usually invisible, lies just under the surface, ready to catch out any unsuspecting skipper. Some have famously not avoided it, the most famous being the arrival into Southampton of the Cunard liner *QE2* for her final departure to Dubai, where she would become a hotel. Stuck fast for forty minutes, some said she didn't want to go, unwilling to leave her life of ocean-going voyages.

Any ship with a deep, and sometimes not so deep, draft have to avoid it.

Approaching the Brambles, ships have to give an indication of their intention by a blast on their foghorn: either one for starboard or, if the tide was not in their favour and there wasn't enough depth of water, two for port, which would mean the long way round the IOW. I never heard three blasts at the Brambles as that would have meant astern and definitely a sight to see!

During the school holidays, those blasts on the ship's whistles became a contest between my brother and myself, which stood me in good stead later as part of my future pitch to Cunard. But wait, I get ahead of myself!

In the '60s, each ocean liner had a different foghorn sound, and if we were in our house, we became very good at telling the difference between the various ships by that sound. We would announce which liner (no cruise ships in those days) we believed it to be: *Queen Elizabeth* (my favourite), *Queen Mary* (my brother's),

Windsor Castle, then the exotics: *The United States*, the *Canberra*, the *Oriana*, the gorgeous *France* and eventually the even more gorgeous *Queen Elizabeth 2*. There were lots more we knew at the time.

If there was one blast, you have never heard such excitement from two small boys as we raced down Egypt Hill to Gurnard to see if it was the ship we thought it was. I once clocked 30mph on my new speedometer to see the majestic sight of one of the great ocean liners as they thundered down the Solent.

In the 1960s, they used to dredge the constantly shifting seabed of the Solent between the mainland and the island which would mean a turn to starboard (right) as they reached the Brambles, before applying power and travelling at speed through the narrow strip of water between Ryde and Yarmouth.

Now, without the dredging, cruise ships reaching the Brambles have to turn port (left), cruising slowly between Portsmouth and Ryde, before going the long way round the island, which of course means much more time and money in terms of fuel.

The 1960s was also the time of the invention of that great 'is it a ship, is it a plane?' quandary: the hovercraft. As children, we would see this extraordinary machine, the SR.N1, being tested by Sir Christopher Cockerel and his Saunders-Roe team on the roads of Cowes. The factory where it was made was in East Cowes. The slipway from the factory into Cowes harbour was huge but needed to be as the factory had also manufactured the world's largest all-metal flying boat, the Saunders-Roe Princess SR.45. The company would go on to manufacture the world's largest hovercraft, the SR.N4.

Opposite the factory on the other side of the river Medina in West Cowes, and facing Ratsey's where my father's new job was situated, they stored a Sunderland Flying Boat. We used to see this static aircraft every time we visited my father at work; she was beautiful. Sadly, it had to be moved when the Seaspeed hovercraft service from Southampton to Cowes started up as they needed the slipway, and I believe she was broken up.

After the demise of the passenger flying boat industry, the factory concentrated their efforts on helicopters and hovercrafts, becoming in the mid-'60s, British Hovercraft Corporation. I was an enormous aficionado of the latter, regularly travelling on the SR.N2 from Ryde to Eastney near Portsmouth. The service is still operating, though from a different terminal on the mainland (and different craft). When the factory in Cowes closed, it was converted into offices and units but, I'm pleased to say, still has the huge slipway in celebration of a famous company. If you go to Cowes, you will see it, as it sports a large Union Jack flag painted to celebrate HM the Queen's silver jubilee, still visible on the old hangar doors.

When my children were young, we used to drive down to Southsea, visit the Portsmouth Historic Dockyard, then over to the island on the hovercraft for lunch. Immediately, I became as young as the children as these majestic machines would slowly rise up in the air, slide backwards on land before hitting the sea at speed without the passengers noticing any difference. My wife suffered it reluctantly for a while, before deciding she was done with it. Then, we would drop her at Gunwharf Quays, an outlet shopping centre in Southsea, where she would quite happily spend the day doing some retail therapy, before visiting one of the excellent Portsmouth Harbour restaurants for lunch, while us children went flying on these incredible machines.

With a huge amount of pride in riding something so British, I am thrilled to have travelled on the SR.N2, N4, N5, N6, AP1-88, BHT130, BHT150, Griffons 2000 and 12000TD, plus the various hovercraft that traversed Hong Kong Harbour to Macau in the 1990s, in which I made a point of travelling.

I have also been a long-time member of the marvellous Hovercraft Museum at Lee-on-the-Solent, which was another frequent day out. My poor long-suffering wife!

Scene 5: Boarding School Ramifications

The holidays on the island from boarding school would come to an end all too rapidly and back to school we would go. We were allowed to see our parents three times during the term and only for the afternoon. In addition to these days there was an exeat, which was a half-term weekend, and it really was only a weekend, none of this full-week stuff as today. We were picked up Friday lunchtime after morning lessons, back Sunday evening. Going back afterwards, I would sob quietly into my pillow for a few nights so the other boys wouldn't hear me. However, I do not think I was alone, as every now and then, between sobs, others could be heard going through the same silent torment.

I'm afraid the homesickness went on into my teens. I did not cope well with leaving the comfort and security of our home. I am sure my enforced sojourn in Jean-Lou halfway up Mont Blanc at the age of four had something to do with it!

Unhappiness at spending long periods of the year away from home manifested itself in many ways, and I was a habitual bed-wetter until the age of ten or so, despite the headmaster's wife trying to bribe me with money. If the bed was not wet at night, I would receive one old penny. If it was, I would owe one. Always several shillings in debt, other boys at Hordle would tease me mercilessly, asking on a daily basis if I knew who had written the book *Rusty Bedsprings*. I would answer with a resigned sigh, "I.P. Knightly."

My mother told me much later in life that she had never wanted to send me away to boarding school, but my father had insisted we went to the same schools he had done. I wish he hadn't. I know it dramatically alters the relationship between children and their parents. Maybe it can be of benefit to some, but the boy or girl has to be of a certain mindset. Personally, it was not for me. I was forcibly taken away from my parents and made to live with people who don't love me and are only doing it for financial reward! Love is much more important than financial gain, and what you learn as a child you take through life.

Boarding school and parental discipline evolve through time, and we were at the end of an era. Sometimes it is for the better, sometimes the worse. I remember the one and only real hug ever received from my mother, and I'm not talking about a greeting at the front door. I'm talking about a heartfelt, arms-wrapped-around-each-other, committed hug!

I was about eight and on the right side of my jaw had just discovered a loose bit of bone or gristle under the skin that can be moved. I still have it and so does my daughter. It is round and very odd, especially as it gets bigger when we are about to become ill. I must have overheard a conversation about growths and how serious they can be, as I confided in my mother this 'growth' that could be moved. She attempted to find it and couldn't. Obviously seeing my distress, she gave me this huge cuddle. Even then, it surprised, and I'm ashamed to say rather embarrassed, me, until I gave in to the relief of emotion that there was nothing seriously wrong with my 'growth', or a cuddle. Yet another of those episodes in life one always remembers.

It is therefore all the more extraordinary that with children of my own, I should send the youngest of three to a boarding school. Alexander had shown signs of a talent in music and, like my own parents, we thought he would benefit from a thorough music education. To that end, we sent him, at the age of eight, to a choir school and chose St. George's in Windsor as it was the closest to where we lived. Because they supplied the boys for the Windsor Castle chapel choir, there was no option other than boarding as they were required for rehearsals and Sunday services.

Waves of déjà vu would come flooding back to me when I would go as often as possible and see him sing in the mid-week service at 5.15pm. I knew whether he was Cant(oris) or Dec(ani) (sides of the choir) and would sit the opposite. We were not allowed a demonstrative show of affection such as a wave before or during the service but were allowed eye contact. At the end of the service, parents would wait outside the vestry door, and the boys would come out. We would then take the hand of our sons and walk down the steps from the chapel to the school below. At the bottom, he turned left to go into the school and I to the right for Windsor and Eton Riverside Railway Station. Both of us would have tears in our eyes.

Unsurprisingly, neither he nor I settled. It was more difficult for him as he had two older siblings, neither of whom went to boarding school. One was at the excellent Tiffin Boys, the other the equally excellent Coombe Girls. One Sunday evening, in his third term, I was putting his cap and blazer on him to go back to school and he had tears streaming down his face. He was about to be driven back to Windsor while his two siblings were downstairs watching *Top Gear*. I looked at him and asked him quietly if he wanted me to do something about this.

"Please, Daddy," he pleaded. The next day I went and saw the headmaster at St George's and had the difficult conversation with him that Alexander was being withdrawn from his school.

Just as I hope Alexander doesn't, I bore no resentment towards either my mother or father for boarding me, as they came from a generation where boarding school for the children of service personnel was just something you did. They had been through a terrible war, where you could not get close to anyone, for tomorrow they might not be there. In turn, their parents had also come from the Edwardian age where demonstrative emotion was not considered normal; displaying sentiment was thought to be very 'un-British'.

To an extent, my generation suffers from this as well, and I am sometimes not sure how my wife has coped. She certainly thinks incidents in my childhood and boarding school have damaged me;

she may be right. I used to find it difficult to walk holding her hand and never showed affection towards her in front of her parents or, come to that, my own. Kissing, hugging, fist-pumping, any show of emotion; just give me a handshake as a formal greeting, and I am happy!

I hope I have broken that cycle with my own children.

Scene 6: Prep School Life Comes to an End

My brother and I spent the early half of the '60s at Hordle House boarding school with what felt like only occasional visits home. I can still remember that first day at home: the relief, the joy, the reacquaintance with the dogs, the utter exhilaration of being home with your family. Yet it was always tinged with the knowledge you would have to go back. With the winter and spring holidays it was four weeks, with the summer one, eight. I can so vividly recall the countdown to the end of the holidays and the last night in particular that I never wanted to end. I would try and stay awake for as long as I could, to remember the feeling of being warm and comfortable in a bed and not having to make a banana bed.

For those who had the 'misfortune/fortune' not to attend boarding schools, into the second half of the twentieth century, most school dormitories did not have modern facilities like heating nor, come to that, hot water too often. Cold weather at night and tepid water in the mornings were normal. At night in winter, we learnt to tuck the few blankets we were allowed, as tight as they would go, so the mattress would curve up in the shape of a banana and leave you cocooned between the two sides. It actually worked well! This, as opposed to playing a jape on someone, an apple pie bed, where the bottom sheet is untucked at the bottom end and wrapped over the top sheet and blanket (no duvets in those days). The bed then looks as though it is perfectly normal until you get into it and try to stretch your legs out. Of course, the bottom sheet was folded in half which prevented you from doing so. Such larks!

Unbeknown to me, at Hordle the next phase of my education was being discussed. As I had shown some signs of musical talent, it was decided I needed to go to a public school that had a good musical reputation. My father of course wanted me to go to his old school Felsted. In those days, music was not at the forefront of its prowess, so they chose Marlborough College in Wiltshire.

The school had a Hill, Norman & Beard chapel organ to die for, an excellent roster of music teachers and, being in the lower-middle part of the county, a fairly easy driving distance from the Isle of Wight. However, I had to pass the common entrance examination to get in, and Hordle had not exactly been the best school for academia. When it came to the common entrance exam, if the questions were difficult, we would cheat. There is no other way of saying it, we cheated to get into our next school of choice. My only excuse? It was not initiated by the boys. I did not look over the shoulder of the boy sitting next to me and copy out what he had written. Oh no, this was cheating on a much grander scale, and it came with the collusion of the school.

I vividly recollect the French exam and reading the paper for the first time. As we read through the paper, we all looked at each other and shook our heads in disbelief – it was hard. The word *escargot* had been written in an essay for us to translate and was obviously the key word. It was something about finding *un escargot dans la salade. Salade* we could all work out, but what on earth was an 'escargot'? Relief was at hand. Our French teacher came into the room, looked at the invigilator, who made his excuses and left the room, leaving the French teacher to go through the entire paper with us, making absolutely certain we all knew that the English word for *escargot* was snail.

You will not be surprised to learn, I passed the common entrance to my parents' school of choice and went to Marlborough College, considered one of the country's top fee-paying establishments and once again an all-boys boarding school, though that was to change before I left.

To help with fees, which were high, though not nearly as high as they are today, I went for a music scholarship. I had to go to the school the term before and perform on the piano and have an interview. I succeeded without cheating and was given a scholarship worth £150 a year.

The parting shot from Hordle was a much bigger boy than me beckoning me into the undergrowth on the pretext of wanting to show me something and proceeding to beat the living daylights out of me. The attack was so surprising and so out of the blue. He had obviously harboured a resentment towards me for some considerable time and, before we parted, wanted to make absolutely sure I knew it! I emerged some ten minutes later, battered, bruised and very bemused. I never saw or heard from him again.

Scene 7: Public School; Music Starts to Take Priority

Marlborough was and is an excellent school. There is no doubt when you pay for an education, you get a privileged and exclusive learning experience. I wish everybody in the country could have access to the facilities of a private school and the excellence of its teaching staff. Mark you, it did have some strange practices in the 1960s, hung over from the Victorian and Edwardian years, and one in particular I cannot imagine continues.

Upon arriving at the school, each and every boy aged twelve or thirteen would have a physical examination during their first term, and part of that examination was the doctor holding your testicles, asking you to cough while he did! We would all line up in the gymnasium (no privacy), lower our trousers, shuffling along at the word 'next'. Then, when we reached the doctor, he would grab our balls, tell us to cough and at the word 'next', we pulled our trousers back up and fled so the next in line could submit to the same humiliation. No explanation, no reason, no questioning!

There were also some outside lavatories, nicknamed 'The Woods', without doors and situated just as you came into the school on the left. They were rows of toilet bowls, and boys sat for as brief a time as possible, especially in the winter and spring terms, when snow and rain made it a more urgent case for doing your business as quickly as possible. They were demolished shortly after my arrival.

In 1965, most new boys would enter A House, either A1 or A2, living in one large house together centred around The Court, a bit of grass no one was allowed to walk on except prefects and beaks (teachers). I still had homesickness, though it was beginning to wear off quicker. Dad would generally drive us to the school, drop our things and drive away. I had learned never to look at the car as he disappeared out of the school gates.

For a couple of years, my brother and I were separated as he stayed at Hordle and I made new friends without forming a gang! Interestingly, and this is rather telling, as soon as I left all my schools, I never remained in touch nor saw any of those friends ever again. It was as though a door slammed shut while another opened. I have often wondered what happened to those faces that sometimes float in my mind's eye. We were such good friends at the time. It's as though I needed to shut that part of my life away. My brother, though, was completely the opposite and remained friends with a number of his old school chums.

At the same time as my move to Marlborough, Dad moved from Ratsey's and changed jobs to one in Southampton on the mainland and, much to my mother's relief, we had to move. We found a beautiful house called Hunter's Moon down an unmade lane called Brook Avenue just outside Warsash. It had a big garden that stretched down to the river Hamble. Everything about the house was big, and the only thing it didn't have was a swimming pool. But that was OK, as both houses on either side did, and we were given carte blanche to use either whenever we wanted.

The house had not been constructed well, with a part-flat roof which continually leaked. Shortly after we sold it, the house was demolished and another built in its place. Us boys had the upstairs to ourselves. It had a big playroom with the baby grand piano. This piano was to become the bane of my life as, back from Marlborough, trying to get a lie-in, if Dad thought we had been in bed long enough, he would play 'God Save the Queen' in F major with one finger but only using the white notes.

As we heard earlier, F major has a Bb in its key which, critically, is a black note. Playing it through, it's fine until you get to the word 'our' for the second time: in F major without that black note, it's a semitone sharp! This is followed by the short instrumental run-up which should have a Bb, but you're not singing. Then, the middle syllable of victorious is bad, and by the time he had got to 'long to reign over us', it was so painful to the ears I had to get up and close the piano lid – mission accomplished!

In the key of F major, 'God Save the Queen' starts on an F. I tried to show him where the note C was, because if he started on that note, no black notes were needed. I even showed him the note in relation to the key hole but to no avail. I even think I once stuck on the C an arrow saying 'here'! Dad, bless him, was tone deaf, which meant he sang tunelessly and could never sing the same note as the person standing next to him, which made carol singing at Christmas a nightmare. In this case, he knew what he was doing and, probably deliberately, would always play 'God Save the Queen' starting on an F, and therefore in the key of F major, but never playing a Bb, consequently always getting me up!

The house was lovely, and we had our bikes to get into the local village and could explore the banks of the river where there were lots of wrecks and history. Some of the pontoons for D-Day had been moored on the Warsash front and stone anchoring points still remained. Indeed, some of the troops had crossed to the Normandy beaches from Warsash and the river Hamble. There were wrecks, and I seem to remember an old nineteenth-century three-decker on the opposite bank that was used as a training facility.

We would walk the dogs into the woods, and with idyllic holidays at home, it really is no wonder the return to school was not eagerly anticipated. However, back I went each term where my burgeoning music ability was blossoming. There was so much to do at Marlborough: chapel choir, orchestra, recitals, glee clubs, visiting orchestras and soloists, external concert trips, plays and chamber music, the latter two sometimes at the same time!

The school had no girls, so rather like the renaissance era, boys would take the role of girls. In the renaissance it was because if the female sex appeared in a public performance, it was a sure sign of their immorality; in our case it was simply because there weren't any! When we performed *Julius Caesar*, I was therefore cast in the role of Portia.

The director had decided to stage the play in modern dress, and I was costumed in a flower power miniskirt, long blonde wig and tights with lots of make-up! This, at an all-male boarding school with teenage boys either approaching, going through or just after puberty! I can't remember who was playing my husband Brutus, but I'm pretty sure he must have been confused, for even I knew I looked extremely interesting for a single-sex male boarding school!

Unfortunately, the performance date of the Shakespeare play was also the evening I had agreed to perform Beethoven's piano trio in Bb opus 11, and for some reason, no one had seen the clash until too late. Not wishing to let anyone down, it was decided to perform the Beethoven at a time Portia was not onstage and I could nip over to the Adderley, play the Beethoven and be back in time for my next stage appearance. The Beethoven concert, however, was a dinner jacket affair. With no time to get out of my miniskirt into dinner suit for the concert and back into miniskirt for the play, I performed on the piano as a full cross-dressing 1960's flower power female hippie, in front of a packed audience, clarinettist and cellist who were all in black tie! There is a strange memory of rather enjoying it too, as I refused to take my wig off for my piano performance. My claim was that I was 'in character', but whose, I could never answer!

As an organist, my services were used at services in chapel, the big voluntaries being my speciality. I could perform the Widor Toccata and Bach's Toccata and Fugue in B minor at will. I played percussion and violin in the orchestra, though was never any good at the violin. My main claim to fame with that instrument (boasting about it) was that I never practised, passing my ABSM grade five violin exam without ever once picking up the instrument between lessons! I also began to learn the bassoon, my thought process being, if conducting was going to be my career, there was a need to learn a bit about as many instruments in the orchestra as possible. I left school before getting to the brass section!

Should I tire of practice on an ordinary upright piano in the practice rooms, there was a real concert grand Steinway. The school was fortunate enough to own two of them. One was in the memorial hall where concerts, lectures and school gatherings took place, the other in the Adderley, conveniently located on the ground floor of C3, my senior house and the room of my Beethoven/Portia triumph.

In its early days, it had been the school's dining room before becoming the library, now ending up as a function room. In it, I had permission to strike up on this magnificent piano whenever I wanted. It was a gorgeous room, sumptuously decorated with a real Gainsborough portrait taking up most of the wall on one end. One of his largest paintings, it was a landscape portrait of the George Byam family standing under a tree on a windy day. What stimulus to play Rachmaninoff and Brahms under this famous painting. No wonder I gained distinction in both grades seven and eight in this room; the examiner was truly inspired and not by my piano playing!

The painting became too expensive to insure and protect and in 1987, fifty-five years after being given it by the great-grandson of the little girl in the picture, the school had to sell it. In its place there now hangs a copy.

We had a certain amount of freedom given to us and were allowed into Marlborough town, though not the pubs. We could go shopping and visit the Mop Fair, which happens once a year in the second widest high street in the UK. We could also go on bike rides, and the furthest we ever got to was Stonehenge in the days that people were allowed to walk round the stones and touch them. On the same trip, we also visited Woodhenge and Silbury Hill.

I was taught by two directors of music while at Marlborough. The first was a man by the name of Robert Ferry, who was inspirational. He floated between Sherborne School and Marlborough College, never quite making up his mind where he wanted to stay. Years later, when he had retired, I tracked him down to a little house in Sherborne and invited him to a concert I was conducting in Poole with the Bournemouth Symphony Orchestra. Believing he would like to know he was part of a process that led me to a wonderful career, standing in front of great orchestras, making music, I told him my name and invited him along. Sadly, from his puzzled side of the conversation, I am not entirely sure he remembered who I actually was. Out of the hundreds of pupils he had taught, why should he? The clincher came though when he told me he couldn't stray too far from a lavatory and turned down the invitation!

When Robert Ferry left Marlborough for the second, or maybe third time, a man by the name of Graham Smallbone took over.

Graham gave me lots of opportunities and indeed I performed the first movement of the Beethoven *Piano Concerto No. 3* under his baton with the school orchestra. One of my first ever reviews said of the performance that I had played it with 'gusto, feeling and considerable accuracy'! When he left Marlborough, he went on to become headmaster of Oakham School in Rutland.

I think you will all have worked out that academically I am not the brightest pebble on the beach, and at Marlborough I had all this much more enjoyable stuff to do! Something had to give way to my music and of course it was maths, geography, history, English, English literature, biology, chemistry and a myriad of other subjects. I knew I was never going to need them as I was going to be a conductor. But it seems that message had not got through to anyone else, even my parents!

They and the school were so concerned, they sent me to a company in London who, after a series of tests, would tell them where my abilities lay. I spent the whole day at these rather swanky offices in the middle of London being given lots of verbal and written tests. I came away thinking, *that was a complete waste of time*, and how right I was! When the results came back, they said 'Anthony would be an excellent floor walker at Harrods Department Store'! I am still not entirely sure what a floor walker does! Is that Captain Peacock from *Are You Being Served?*

My parents and the school, realising I was never going to be a high achiever at academia, decided they should push my music as I had desired ever since conducting at the age of six. Acknowledging my exam results might affect their position in the published results table, Marlborough suggested an early end to my school life and an attempt at the entrance examination to both the Royal College of Music and the Royal Academy of Music. Accordingly, in October 1968, at the age of sixteen, I journeyed up to London and sat the entrance examination at both music colleges a year early.

Scene 8: Reflections of Public School Life

I recall very clearly the morning of the journey to London, as my alarm went off in the school dormitory at an ungodly hour. I really did think, this is terrible. I don't want to get up at 4.30am; I'll just turn over, go back to sleep and pretend to never have heard the alarm. Even at the age of sixteen, boarding school mentality kicked in and I thought it pretty extraordinary everything had to be done by me. Not to be woken, checked, supervised and cleared to leave school for an outside journey during term!

I eventually got up as quietly as possible, so as not to disturb the other sleeping boys, and collected my breakfast that had been left out the night before, before going into the town of Marlborough to catch the bus up to Swindon Railway Station for the journey into Paddington Station.

It was just as well I did, for though I failed to get into the Royal Academy of Music, at my Royal College of Music audition I was sent to play for Sir Keith Faulkner, the director of the college, which meant definite entry with the possibility of being awarded a scholarship. I didn't get the scholarship but had got into the college, and my schooldays were coming to an early end.

What has an expensive and private education done for me? I had privileges beyond compare and tried most of them. Facilities included an outdoor swimming pool which was always freezing as it continually leaked, topped up with fresh cold water. It was part of the old moat of the Marlborough Mound, a Neolithic monument in the school grounds and reputed burial ground of the Welsh bard Merlin. It had a sporting reputation with an excellent record in rugby, cricket, hockey, fencing, athletics, beagling, plus a host of other sporting activities, none of which were ever pursued by me, mainly because I disliked standing around sports fields of any description!

For one fleeting term, I played fly half in rugger and, upon seeing these huge upper sixth formers bearing down on me, looking as though they were intent on tearing me limb from limb, I made sure to never play again by screaming and throwing the ball as far away in any direction I could. I remember wanting to shout, 'fetch' as I had so often done to our dogs when throwing a stick! It's odd, as now I absolutely love the games of rugby and cricket and will make any excuse to visit Twickenham, The Oval or Lords.

There was also a game called Bagger which would be held on the water meadows at the beginning of certain terms. There were no rules, probably because there was no referee. The object of the 'game' was to get the ball from one end of the waterlogged pitch bounded by the road, to the other which was the river Kennet. The whole school took part, and it just seemed an excuse for the older and stronger boys to physically assault the younger boys. It was finally stopped after too many limbs were broken and parental complaints made!

Many important people came and lectured in the memorial hall, one such being the inventor and designer of the bouncing bomb and Wellington bomber Barnes Wallis. I wish I had known he was great friends with my great-uncle Sir Victor Goddard, as I would have gone up to him and introduced myself.

The school had a tradition that sons of the clergy and army, navy and air force, were given handsome discounts, and these were provided by various charitable funds. Therefore, the Combined Cadet Force, a sort of mini army for youths, was given a huge weekly Wednesday afternoon parade, though if you wished you could do social work instead.

With all my RAF pedigree, surely there was only one branch of cadet service life I should join? Accordingly, I went into the army signals section!

I hoped I would not have to do much marching, running and walking. I reasoned I would be held in reserve to transmit messages from headquarters to boy cadets running about all over the place. I mean, why send a runner when you can send a radio signal? In reality that was a false hope and I ended up doing as much running and walking as everyone else but with a ruddy great radio strapped to my back! Having been first used by the regular army in 1947, the Wireless Set No 88 with which the CCF were issued may have looked fairly small and light, yet the heavy-duty battery ensured it wasn't!

The cadet force had trips away (I remember spending some time at Blandford Forum) and overnight camping treks. Forced marches were the worst, and I shudder at the memory of the week we spent with the real army on the Brecon Beacons!

I learnt to read Morse code and, in my spare time, would transmit either by Morse or voice over the public schools' radio frequencies to other similar establishments. I can still remember the Morse for calling all stations: dah-dit-dah-dah, dah-dah-dit-dah, which of course means CQ (calling all stations)! I made some good friends over the primitive forerunner of Skype and WhatsApp.

What Marlborough did leave me with was an independence of spirit, probably more so than is healthy. But I get on with myself and would be fine on a desert island. Yes, I would miss my family and friends hugely. However, solitude for a while does not alarm me.

It has also left me with a deep conviction of faith. My parents brought me up to attend church on high days and holidays and a belief in a God 'up there' and a devil 'down there' and, whilst realising it's not as simple as that, I do have my faith and attend church when possible. I think that evensong is the jewel in the Church of England's crown. Not for me, Holy Communion and all that shaking of other people's hands and saying, "Peace!" What is that all about? If ever I do attend Holy Communion, when we come to the 'Peace', I stand there with my arms resolutely folded, daring anybody to come up to me and say anything.

I love the King James Bible, disliking the modern services and preferring Hymns Ancient and Modern! The college chapel was and still is a magnificent building, and to take part in a service there, or where I currently worship, Kingston Parish Church, both with great choirs who sing some of the fantastic Victorian and Edwardian anthems I love, can still bring tears to my eyes. It's the magnificence of the buildings, the language and the spiritual conviction that there is a purpose, and we will know it when we give our final breath.

It could also be said that Marlborough saved my life. In May 1969, Group Captain Peter Helmore DFC AFC, married to my maternal aunt Wendy Inglis, was still in the RAF. He had just been diagnosed with PTSD, though in those days it wasn't called that. During the war he had carried out 102 Pathfinder operations which is the joint-highest number of sorties carried out in the Second World War. Pathfinding was considered to be one of the most dangerous wartime missions. The number eventually caught up with him, and as a result, instead of taking over as station commander of RAF Scampton, he was dispatched to the British Embassy in Ankara. As he knew he would want to sail his boat *Caperer II* on the Bosporus, he decided to set out from the river Hamble to Malta as a halfway staging post, before sailing on to his new posting. He needed additional crew for watch-keeping duties as he only had one other person going with him for a fairly lengthy non-stop journey. He first asked my father, who could not take time off work. He then turned to me and asked if I would like to accompany him as crew. Also unable to go as still at school and term had started, I regretfully declined the trip of a lifetime, which maybe ensured my survival.

During the trip, on a dark night somewhere in the Bay of Biscay, *Caperer II* was hit and run down by a tanker which, by an awful twist of fate, was carrying a malfunctioning radar.

For whatever reason, neither my uncle nor the person crewing for him spotted the approaching tanker, nor did anyone on board the tanker see the sailing boat. The first the tanker bridge crew knew of the collision was seeing a mast scrape down the side of the ship. It took a while for the big ship to stop and turn round. By the time they returned to the location of the incident, despite conducting an intensive search, there was no sign of wreckage or survivors.

The families were devastated as two fine men lost their lives. If either my father or me were on board, would we have seen the approaching tanker and changed the course of family history? Or would we too have drowned at sea? It was one of the big regrets of my father's life as he believed either Peter or he, both equally experienced sailors, would have seen the approaching tanker. Whatever the answer, every time I cross the bay in one of the Cunard Queens, I raise a glass to my uncle, a life lost far too early.

In the 1960s, despite my protestations that as a conductor, I was never going to need them, education was all about getting at least five O levels, the equivalent these days of GCSEs, and three A levels. Most boys got at least eight, nine, even more Os and three or four As. Having started at Marlborough in September 1965, I left in July 1969 with the frankly astonishing total of three O levels and one CSE (Certificate of Secondary Education). I know music was one; English may be another, though ordinary or literature I couldn't tell you; and I have no idea of the third. What is more, no one has ever asked me!

Maths, after two O level attempts and fails, was considered unachievable, so after trying CSE, a different exam board, and gaining a grade three, which was not considered equivalent to an O level, we called time! At one of my previous maths O level attempts, I had attained an amazing 0.25%, and that for guessing a true or false question correctly. There were three true or false questions, and I got the others wrong! That is a 33.33% accuracy rate. See? My maths is not too bad!

I was just not interested, though did not have the magic five that everyone said you needed to get on in life. The school had even decided to try and get me there with scripture O level. They said to me that most people get scripture O level in one term but that I was going to get two! I remember being rather insulted at that so, determined to do well, I settled down to study and revision. At this point, I would love to say I passed with the highest marks anyone has ever achieved. However, I'm sorry to say I can't; I failed dismally. I seem to recall someone called Japhet who begat Jophat, who begat Jiphat, who probably begat someone else beginning with a J and ending with a phat, though I may be wrong with the name! There is an awful lot of confusing begetting in the Bible!

The teaching was of a considerable standard, though it was not until recently I discovered the dark history of a teacher prior to his arrival at Marlborough. His name was Kenneth Keast. During lessons at Marlborough in the 1960s, he used to extol the virtue of his visits to Germany in the 1930s, all the time knowing he was responsible for this awful tragedy, forgotten in the UK but known to this day in Germany as Engländerunglück (Englishmen's misfortune).

On 17 April 1936, at the age of 27, he was the sole leader of a group of twenty-seven boys aged from twelve to seventeen who were on a hiking trip in the Black Forest region just outside Freiburg im Bresgau. The group of boys, were engaged through Keast's own private company rather than the previous school. On that morning, the boys were in summer clothing as the weather the day before had been very springlike. He ignored warnings from the locals as they were about to set out, that the weather was unpredictable and could change. He also ignored warnings from local forestry workers they met along the way, who were returning home due to the snow now starting to fall, who said they should do the same. As the snow fell heavier, they continued climbing the mountain. He pressed on, determined to reach his destination of a youth hostel in Todtnauberg, a distance of some twelve miles from Freiburg. It was only when the younger boys started collapsing from exhaustion he decided to seek help. He abandoned those smaller ones and split the remaining group. After travelling in circles, three boys heard the bells of Hofsgrund church and staggering towards the sound, hammered on the doors raising the alarm. At great risk to themselves because of the blizzard, villagers went up the mountain to rescue the party. There, they found four small boys dead, and a fifth who died after they had brought him down. The rest were in a serious condition.

Adolph Hitler, chancellor of Germany, saw the opportunity for some propaganda and decided to elevate Kenneth Keast to hero status for saving twenty-two boys. Herr Hitler lied that the Hitler Youth Movement had played a vital part in rescuing the English boys by going up the mountain. They were in the locality, but had not taken any meaningful part in the rescue. Keast was quickly feted in both the British and German press. On subsequent investigation, the local Freiburg prosecutor compiled a report that laid the blame solely on Keast and recommended prosecution for manslaughter. This report was conveniently mislaid by the German authorities, but not before Stanley Baldwin, prime minister of Great Britain, had seen it. One can only assume that like his successor Neville Chamberlain, Baldwin wanted appeasement with Hitler at all costs, and not wishing to call the chancellor of Germany a liar, he recommended that Keast should be quietly forgotten. He was however, disallowed from ever taking boys on foreign trips again. Kenneth Keast was my German teacher at Marlborough!

Considering the amount of money spent by my parents at all the various schools versus academic attainment, the cost was a very poor return. My father once calculated what each O level had cost him, then promptly tried to forget it out of sheer horror and disbelief!

Although I failed most of my exams and cannot tell you the third O level or what kind of English I gained, my schooling was incalculable in terms of life's education.

Having complied with the school's correct advice not to stay, in July 1969 I travelled home from Marlborough College for the last time in my school life, before in September of that year going up to London all by myself. Finally, despite everybody from my teachers to my parents telling me I needed the option of an alternative career path when my conducting ambition did not materialise, I was off to do what I had always known from the age of six I was destined to do: conduct!

Act 3

Scene 1: The Royal College of Music and London

Being on my own in London, without knowing anyone, was a novel experience. No dormitories and no brother, eased somewhat by being resident in the new male-only student hostel at the Royal College of Music which opened the year I went.

The female students already had one called Queen Alexandra House opposite the Royal Albert Hall and very close to the college. In my first year, straight out of all-male establishments, I was to get to know QA House quite well, especially one evening when sneaking out of the building well after the curfew hour of 10pm at which all visitors had to leave. I could hear the female warden coming up the stairs as I was going down. In order to evade detection, I quickly climbed into one of the empty alcoves around the circular staircase and froze still, imitating one of the many statues adorning the hall. Bless her, the warden of the building, pretending not to see me, walked right by.

The new male student hostel was named the Robert Mayer Hall after the man who had put a lot of his own money into the building. I recall Sir Robert very well, as he came and took a look at his legacy during our first term. Overwhelmed to hear he had actually performed and sat next to Johannes Brahms, means I have shaken hands with a man who has shaken hands with Brahms! How amazing is that? Exclusively for music students at the RCM,

Robert Mayer Hall was a halfway house between school and home and the freedom of living on your own.

This was just as well, as having boarded from a very early age, I was not what is now called streetwise. A few months after arriving, I was in a car with a new friend of mine travelling down the Portobello Road and saw a man slumped in a doorway with all his worldly goods around him. He was looking around, obviously awake, conscious and in some degree of distress. I could not believe this man was in such a state and, despite the protestation of my London friend who had seen this all too often, insisted he stop the car while I got out and asked him if he was alright.

Another major bafflement confronting me in London for the first time were the signs on the top deck of buses that said 'Do Not Spit!' Why would anyone deliberately spit in public? I could not comprehend the request and actually had to ask what it meant. Now they've given up with the signs on the buses and it appears compulsory at football matches! I still find it a disgusting habit.

In my first term at the RCM, there was an incident I still regret above all others. On leaving for London, my father had given me his old flying jacket, the one that had kept him warm at night while he was in the skies defending the country. For a few months after I arrived, the weather was decent enough not to need it, and because there was little space in my shared bedsit at Robert Mayer Hall, I kept it in the college's cloakroom underneath the entrance hall, every now and then, looking and admiring it. One day I went to see it and it had disappeared. I could not believe that anyone would steal a flying jacket, until some years later I saw the prices real jackets were fetching. At the time, the theft was reported to the college which, sadly, was not taken too seriously, and I chalked it up to experience. How I wish I still had that jacket.

There were house parents at Robert Mayer Hall who looked after you and the building, and there were other boys living alongside you. We had a communal area, and two shared a bedroom. My companion was not someone of my choosing, but we got on well enough. He was an organ student from the Isle of Man. I don't think he lasted long at the college, and we only lived together for one year.

The walk from Evelyn Gardens in South Kensington up to the college in Prince Consort Road, which is adjacent to the Royal Albert Hall, a building I was to get to know extremely well, was via Queen's Gate and would take twenty-five minutes each way. This we would do on a daily basis in order to attend lessons, practise and generally spend the day amongst like-minded students at the RCM.

Sir Keith Faulkner was the director and a kindlier man difficult to find. In his performing days, he had been a very distinguished bass-baritone, before deciding to branch out from just giving concerts. He had also been a flyer in the First World War and an officer in the RAF Reserves during the second. More than that, he was a keen cricketer, and in 1969, the RCM had a net where us boys would go and get batting practice from the spin of Sir Keith. No wonder I liked him! He had lots of contacts in the musical world and once got the veteran Edwardian conductor Sir Adrian Boult to come to the college and conduct.

Sir Adrian watched some of us students conducting in the same concert as he was, and the only thing he said as he advanced towards me with his dazzling white moustache bristling was, "Dear boy, you're going to get arthritis of the wrist!" It hasn't happened yet, Sir Adrian! Fingers? Yes! Wrists? No!

His style was very much that of Arthur Nikisch: long baton which he held between thumb and forefinger and would flick for the accuracy of the beat or long sweeping gestures for legato passages. Everything was dedicated to the point of the stick; that was where musicians were supposed to look for an indication of what he wanted. His followers included Vernon Handley, who was one of my teachers at the RCM.

I got on with Tod (as Vernon Handley was universally known), so much so that I went on holiday to his Welsh cottage just after his first child was born. Tod was a keen ornithologist, and we spent two weeks birdwatching. I hadn't been interested in birdwatching before those two weeks and, by the end, I knew I was never going to be interested in birdwatching. Two pairs of trousers, three pairs of socks, countless jerseys and coats still couldn't keep out the cold, all for the sake of catching a glimpse of some bird who hadn't the sense to keep still while I trained a pair of binoculars on it.

Shortly after coming home from the holiday, I was distressed to learn that his new-born baby, who he idolised and called Baby Glue, died of SIDS (Sudden Infant Death Syndrome). I can only imagine how that must affect parents who have children die of this terrible syndrome, and it must have affected Tod in a horrible way. He became a fanatical hypochondriac, and rumours abounded of his addictions and requests to orchestra managements that he had a doctor on standby to prescribe him his (legal) painkiller drug. He was a superb conductor and a real champion of British tonal music, and forgotten British music at that. When it was unfashionable to conduct music from his own country, he thought nothing of programming an Arnold Bax symphony, something no one else was doing.

Conversely, William Glock, BBC controller of music in personal charge of the Proms in the 1960s, was a huge supporter of atonal contemporary music. Music that became known in the trade as 'squeaky-gate' music, because when you played it, it sounded as though a gate was slowly swinging on rusty hinges! Most musicians hated playing it. The audiences were tiny and indeed the composers having their music performed appeared grateful for this, as to them it meant they were ahead of their time and misunderstood. Convinced they would have their moment of fame in the future, they competed with each other in requiring strange, weird and unnatural sounds from an orchestra. All this funded by the taxpayer via the BBC. British composers who still composed tonally, such as William Lloyd Webber (father of Andrew and Julian), Arnold Bax, Edmund Rubbra and Havergal Brian, were ignored and most took other jobs to help with their commitments.

Personally, I think William Glock did a huge disservice to music in general, and the BBC Symphony Orchestra became an orchestra you took a job in only if you couldn't get one anywhere else, or enjoyed contemporary music, or wanted the pension and employment perks that came with the job. Morale slumped and standards fell dismally.

Glock must have so hated traditional music and all it stood for that he tried to ruin the Last Night of the Proms, so they wouldn't have to do it again. The element that made the Last Night popular with people who would not normally listen to an orchestra was the traditional singing and hand-clapping and general shenanigans of the final section of the concert: the hornpipe, 'Land of Hope and Glory', 'Rule, Britannia!', 'Jerusalem' etc. That was the bit he hated the most. He reasoned, if you stopped that, there would be no cause to have the concert. I had the misfortune to attend that concert in the early '70s, the only BBC Last Night I have ever attended.

In previous years, much fun was had by all, as the sea shanty, written in a rollicking and accelerating 2/4, was accompanied by the audience clapping along, as they desperately tried to keep up with the music, sometimes successfully, sometimes not so much! However, Glock decided to commission a version in 5/8, making it impossible for the Prommers to clap along as the rhythm was now an uneven two-and-a-half and not two. As Glock wanted, this was impossible for the general public to accompany, so we all gave up. What he was not prepared for was the huge backlash from the audience and TV viewers. The experiment only lasted the one year and was never repeated. I am happy to report Glock did not last much longer either.

Regrettably, I think there have been one or two BBC music controllers since who have agreed with him, as they repeated this mistake in 2020. Of all times to shoot oneself in the foot, the year 2020 was not it. When the majority of the UK needed security, tradition and escapism through the awful period of Covid-19 we were all experiencing, the BBC once again decided, in the name of wokeness, to attack all that was best and end the singing of 'Rule, Britannia!' and 'Land of Hope and Glory' at the Last Night. Presumably their thinking was these tunes and lyrics celebrated Britain's colonial past; however, nobody of any intelligence thought that, and they were merely great tunes with words that celebrated a great country. After the outcry from senior politicians, including the prime minister, and most of the country, they had to do a complete about-turn and rescind the decision, though not without commissioning a new arrangement of 'Rule, Britannia!'. To me, the arrangement ultimately sounded as though no one performing was in agreement as to the same bar of music they were supposed to be in.

Sir William's legacy lived on for a few decades as, in 1988, at a very modern music concert – broadcast live on the BBC, with the desultory applause 'ringing' and the airwaves still tuned in – the principal cellist of the orchestra stood up and stamped on his (borrowed) modern cello, smashing it to pieces. Contemporary music had sunk so low that the few fans in the audience thought this was a deliberate act and part of the composer's instructions for performance. Afterwards, when asked why he had done it, he replied that 'the composer was asking him to make sounds on the cello it was never intended to make, and he was simply finishing the job for him'!

My other conducting professor at the college was a man by the name of Harvey Philips, who had been an excellent cellist yet wanted to conduct. It was rumoured he came from the Harvey's Bristol Cream sherry family so had money. Certainly, he took the chamber orchestra, the college's top orchestra at the time, on a European tour and paid for it himself. I can see him now, sitting on a stool in the concert hall of the RCM, cigarette hanging out one side of his mouth as he airily wafted his hands about in 4/4 time. His favourite comment to the orchestra was, "And at this point I'll drift into two." Then he did!

When I arrived at college there was no conducting course and you had to enter with two studies. I started with the piano and organ, giving up the organ in the first term and substituting it for conducting. I never looked back.

Scene 2: Girlfriends and Best Friends

It was this first year that I began to make friends with people with whom I have been in touch ever since. One of them was to be very influential on my career, however, it did not have an auspicious beginning. Upon arriving at college, almost immediately I discovered there were people not built as us boys! They had bumps, lumps and curves in all the right places and even smelt better than my male friends.

My only experience of girls up to this point had really been in my final year of Marlborough. John Dancy, headmaster of the school and a progressive, decided the all-male school needed to admit females and, in the summer of 1968, admitted about nine to the school to settle them in prior to beginning their academic life. Apart from meeting one or two during the holidays, those Marlborough girls, plus my mother and sister, were the sum total of my communication with the female sex.

At college, I soon began to go round with a girl called Christine and thought I was getting on well with her. No, we had not got much further than petting, as it was called then, but I was hopeful.

One day she delivered the awful news that she was going with someone else to the midnight premiere of the new film *The Virgin Soldiers*. His father was someone high up with the Warner Film business and had got him two tickets. He was looking for someone to take and had invited her. 'Would I mind,' she asked me? Well of course I would, but being public school and magnanimous, I said of course not, secretly seething inside with jealousy.

On the day of the date, I had walked from my hall of residence into the foyer of the RCM ready for practice and there, leaning nonchalantly against the statue of the old Prince of Wales in the entrance hall of the college, was this opportunistic lounge lizard talking to my girlfriend. There was a hurried conversation between the two of them; the boy stood up straight, probably because he was a lot bigger than me, and so did Mike Reed enter my life.

The result, dear reader, was probably as you expected, and Mike and Christine became an item. Years later, he claimed she had told him she had to get away from me as I was sex-obsessed! Yes, probably so. I had been at male boarding schools for all my life and was a late arrival to the swinging '60s! The only thing that surprised me was that Mike wasn't, as he had also been at another all-male public school called Malvern College. I must have been a generous chap as forgiveness came quickly, and we became the best of friends. He has remained an overriding, important and huge constant in my life ever since.

An enormously talented musician, he is one of those people who is brilliant at everything he does. His sight-reading was (and still is) phenomenal. We used to take out piano duets from the college library, mainly concertos with the orchestral parts written out for the piano. We once took out the Ravel *Piano Concerto in D major* for left hand. Written for Paul Wittgenstein, who had lost his right arm during the First World War, I watched Mike play the whole concerto *and* cadenza with just his left hand! It was incredible! I used to feel privileged to witness these amazing feats of sight-reading. There I was, struggling with the orchestral part, and he was literally tossing off the solo part with consummate ease.

The only time I ever played the solo part was the Grieg *Piano Concerto*, and that was because it was in my repertoire! He claimed it was good. I like to think it was better than Eric Morecambe! However good or bad, he remains the only person ever to have heard me play the Grieg *Piano Concerto*!

Scene 3: First Real Efforts at Conducting

After the first year, it was time to move out of the cosy world of a hall of residence, to leave my warm, friendly, safe environment and head into the wide, wide world. In the 1970s, the local government where your parents lived supported university students and paid the study and accommodation fees of all students. Your parents were expected to pay your living expenses, and my father gave me the princely amount of £16 per month to live on – in London! I had to feed, clothe and water myself for this sum of money, and I succeeded, despite spending an inordinate number of hours each day round at the Queen's Arms in Queen's Gate Mews.

The Queen's Arms was blissfully known to the music students as the ninety-nine, as there were ninety-eight practise rooms in the college! Mike and I would arrive at opening time, 5.30pm, and stay until closing time, 11pm. We could make a pint of Worthington E last a long time in those days. Worthington E was so awful there was really very little incentive for actually drinking it!

By the time of the 1970 summer holidays, I had nowhere to live when term restarted in September. Extraordinarily, my parents did not seem overly concerned and left me to find somewhere. For all they knew, I could have been sleeping on the streets.

As it turned out, I very nearly was. In some desperation, I looked up the address of hostels in London and chanced upon one just round the corner from Euston Station that had a vacancy. Yes, it was a bit of an awkward commute, but it was somewhere to rest my head.

The hostel was full of itinerant travellers passing through London for various nefarious reasons, none of which should have been looked into too carefully. I was by far the youngest person there and felt very vulnerable. The owner was friendly enough and, knowing I was a music student, used to say to me that he wanted tickets to my first appearance at the Royal Albert Hall. I have always felt a guilt at not seeking him out and giving him some complimentary tickets to that first performance. He had kept an eye on me, a posh, very green public schoolboy in a rough, tough world.

I stayed there for a while until my new friend Mike Reed, along with a pianist friend of ours called Richard Meyrick, decided to rent a flat together. Mike already lived in North London but wanted to leave home. As he and I were already best mates, we shared one room with two single beds of a two-roomed flat at 45 Blenheim Crescent in Notting Hill Gate. Richard got the single room at the front, which was also the sitting room and kitchen. The entrance door was through our bedroom.

It was a fun, very much bachelor, pad, directly on the 52 bus route to and from the college. The only issue being our sex lives had to be conducted very discreetly at night with the lights very definitely out and hopefully while the other was asleep.

This flat arrangement lasted about a year. I do not think I was easy to live with, particularly when locking Mike out of the flat for coming back after curfew time – an hour set by me! I also found his alarm clock tick far too loud and hid it for the duration of our flat share. Should you read this, Mike, it was in the gap behind the shower! Unsurprisingly, from our flat in Blenheim Crescent, he decided to move back home, and I was left looking for another place to live.

A few years later, Mike and his first wife divorced, and he moved in with me for a few weeks until he could find himself a place. After a short time, he stated he had forgotten what I was like, and I nearly drove him back to his wife!

After the flat share, I knew a friendly Canadian horn player at the college by the name of Dan Emond, and he told me there was a room next to his in Notting Hill Gate available for rent. I jumped at the chance and went and saw the landlord Mr. Crisp, immediately moving into a room on the second floor of 53 Colville Gardens at £4 a week. There was a toilet for the whole house halfway down one flight of stairs and a bathroom at the bottom. But it was my own room! Always grateful to Dan for thinking of me, I returned the favour years later, when he became principal horn of the *Phantom of the Opera* orchestra and he had some difficulties of which I was probably too tolerant.

Dan had a girlfriend who had a daughter, and at one of her very early birthday parties, I must have misread the invitation which said fancy dress. My girlfriend at the time and I decided to go as Prince Charming and Cinderella but with a twist. I would be Cinderella and she would be Prince Charming. We actually walked down Notting Hill Gate dressed like this, to ring the doorbell and find we were the only ones, apart from the children, in fancy dress!

Misreading invites would appear to be one of my strengths. Years later, two of my friends got married and invited my partner and me to their wedding in Biggin Hill. We both turned up and, as we entered the church grounds, were asked whether we were with the bride or groom. There was a bit of difficulty with this as the bride was an old girlfriend and the groom a colleague. I said bride (well, I did know her better!), so we had our names and photo taken, given a sprig of flowers and sat on the left side of the church.

We settled ourselves down and looked around for some friends to whom to say hello. The more we looked, the more we realised we could see no one we knew. What's more, when we looked at the order of service, we realised we didn't know the bride or groom either! We had to get out of there before the service started. We smiled sweetly at everyone, before asking our neighbours to keep our place as we had left our spectacles in the car and exited upstage left.

We rang our friends to find out which church we should have been at, only to be informed we had turned up to the right church but on the wrong day – we were a whole twenty-four hours too early! Apparently, they had to get married on the Sunday as there was another wedding on the Saturday. We knew that! We had to make the same trip at the same time the following day, to much hilarity in the groom's wedding reception speech!

We often wonder what the couple who had married on the Saturday thought, when they saw two people neither of them knew in their wedding photos at the start of the day, but not at the end! I hope my announcement of knowing the bride did not spoil a beautiful life together!

My memory of important events has also been called into question once or twice, illustrated no better by the following story. In the early days of our marriage, one of our sons, learning the cello and playing around with his brother, broke the instrument which required a visit to the workshop of a well-known repairer. Just as I was about to pick it up, I received a phone call from the man tasked with the job of putting it back together, and he informed me that his daughter-in-law had been involved in a terrible car crash and had subsequently died of her injuries. He asked whether I would mind delaying the pick-up until later in the month. Of course not, I said, how awful for him, and told him to ring me whenever he was ready.

Some two or three weeks later, after a very busy period of

concerts, events and shows, I received the phone call to come and pick it up. Driving to his workshop to pick it up, I had completely forgotten the reason for the delay but had remembered it concerned his daughter-in law. As soon as he answered the doorbell, I immediately enquired about her health. "She's still dead," he replied. Aghast, I'm afraid I paid him the money, picked up the cello and fled!

In the winter of 1970, I had made my student solo conducting debut with Nicolai's *Merry Wives of Windsor* overture in a concert with lots of other conducting students. But I had ambition, and my ego was telling me I had shared my conducting debut with other students; I needed to do one on my own! My new abode in Notting Hill Gate freed me up to concentrate on my conducting, and in 1971, I thought I was ready.

The RCM had three orchestras plus a chamber orchestra: the first orchestra and chamber band were considered the best; the second orchestra was OK; and the third was for new students studying orchestral instruments as their first study and older students, such as pianists and singers, who had orchestral instruments as their second study.

As all the orchestras were unavailable, I decided to form my own, calling it the Student Association Orchestra, which meant rehearsals were not compulsory as they were for the college's own four orchestras. Attendance in my new orchestra by the students was at best sporadic, occasionally non-existent and only completed with bribery, corruption and, towards the end, sheer desperation.

Yet for my solo concert conducting debut, I still chose to tackle one of the classical repertoire's most fearsome compositions: Ravel's *Daphnis and Chloé*. *Daphnis* is not a piece of music to be tackled lightly, and being young and immortal, I did not tackle just the second suite, the popular movement quite often performed on its own, but the complete one-hour ballet! This meant it had to have a chorus. The second suite does not need a chorus and is often performed without (though is much better with one). The whole piece, on the other hand, which lasts an hour, very definitely requires one. It has a section for unaccompanied choir in the middle, and unless there was to be three or four minutes of silence, I would have to find one.

Getting an orchestra of eighty students was hard enough; finding a voluntary chorus of one hundred voices of students at the Royal College would be impossible. I wrote to the only chorus whose reputation I knew, the Royal Choral Society, in the shape of the secretary Phyllis Dabbs who ran it and had been the PA to my idol Sir Malcolm Sargent. She agreed to send a choir to the college.

I sometimes wonder whether they had actually rehearsed the piece before I got to them. It is an incredibly complex piece to sing, with lots of semitones and resultant tuning difficulties in the unaccompanied section. When we came to the concert, Mike Reed had to accompany them on the piano, in order to keep them in pitch. Nothing is worse than, at the end of an unaccompanied section, the orchestra entering in a completely different key to the chorus! The performance was a powerful experience and, I thought at the time, a great one. There is a recording of this performance, but just in case my memory is fallible, I have never had the courage to listen to it!

Not content with doing a piece of music that was seldom performed, I decided to do an unknown piano concerto in the first half as well! A fellow student by the name of Howard Shelley, now a well-known pianist and conductor, was keen to perform my suggestion of the Khachaturian *Piano Concerto*.

He and I have since performed professionally together a few times. Not least the memorable occasion when, at the Royal Festival Hall with the Philharmonia Orchestra, the stage crew moving the piano into position on the concert platform forgot to tighten the brakes on the instrument. Every time Howard played a crashing chord in Rachmaninoff's *Piano Concerto No. 2* (and there are a few from the very beginning!), it moved towards the edge of the concert platform and the audience sitting a few feet away. The only way to stop it was for Howard, during the orchestral tutti passages, to bend down and tighten the wheel brakes on each piano leg. However, the orchestral passages were not long enough to tighten them in one go, and it took several tuttis before the audience were safe!

What a wonderful piece of music the Khachaturian is, utilising a rare percussion instrument called a flexatone. It works by shaking in your hand two round metallic objects attached to a cradle. By bending a small strip of metal in the middle of the two objects, the performer can alter the pitch of the notes, making a strange haunting sound. The player tasked with playing it was a student by the name of Gary Kettel, who, in later years, from co-principal percussionist of the BBC Symphony at the age of twenty, became the go-to percussionist for anyone wanting a prodigy on percussion.

Because the flexatone was so rare and difficult to obtain, we only had it at the final rehearsal, and we were all looking forward to a special treat: an opportunity to hear a unique-sounding instrument. Reaching the slow movement, Gary raised his hand… and the most awful clanging issued from where he was standing. I looked to see an enormous grin on his face. Stopping, and with the whole ensemble of the elderly ladies and gentlemen of the RCS sitting there, I asked him, with a good deal of trepidation as he already had a huge character, what on earth the noise was.

"Sorry, mate," he said, "one of my balls is missing!" Sure enough, only one of the round metallic objects was there, causing the horrendous caterwauling from the instrument. I am sorry to say, he played it like that in the concert!

It can't have put the RCS off though as, a year later, they accompanied the same orchestra and me down to Sandhurst

Military Academy, where my honorary uncle Brigadier George Powell was commanding officer and where we performed the Verdi Requiem. I gather the bar bill at the end was legendary. The student orchestra discovered they could sign MOD chits for their drinks, and the chits were never looked at by the bar staff. George later told me, as commanding officer, even he had some explaining to do when chits were presented to him signed by Mickey Mouse, Field Marshal Montgomery, Winston Churchill and General Erwin Rommel! I have since conducted the RCS about 150 times. None have compared to that performance for sheer effrontery!

Another fantastic best friend who remains with me to this day is a chap by the name of Vaughan Meakins. We met when we were both on what was then playfully called the conducting course and have kept in close touch ever since. He married another student called Magda Hamblin, becoming house parents of the Robert Mayer Hall of residence, before work took him to head of music at the Arts Educational Trust School in Tring. We saw each other as often as we could whilst he lived in Aston Clinton, especially playing tennis together which we both loved. Upon retirement, he moved to the beautiful hills of Wales.

Now, sadly, we only meet up when driving from a concert in Manchester or Liverpool to one in Cardiff. When visiting them in Wales, I take the opportunity to either stay the night or pop in for lunch before driving the sensational A438 and A470 over the Brecon Beacons.

He formed a choir at college called the Parry Choir, into which Mike and I contributed a sizeable part of the tenor section and have never forgotten the fact that he used to call us Pinky and Perky. Popular TV characters at the time, they were pig puppets who used to squeak their way through the dialogue with voices recorded by actors, played back at double speed.

Vaughan ended up with one of the most pleasant jobs in music. Whilst director of music at the Arts Educational School at

Tring (a ballet school), he formed a choir from the senior girls in the school, and they became very good. Indeed, they entered the BBC/Sainsbury's Youth Choir of the Year and habitually reached the final round, before, rather scandalously in my opinion, just as habitually, never winning. They were usually miles ahead of the other competing choirs, but the judges, none of whose names I recognised, failed to recognise this. The choir's standard was astonishingly high, solely trained by Vaughan. When they reached the final round, they caused a sensation as these beautiful young ladies, watching Vaughan conduct, sang their hearts out with passion and commitment.

Scene 4: The Life of a Student; First Encounter with Royalty

Never having had a serious long-term girlfriend before, during my first year I had started to hang around with one in particular. Nothing serious, just to go out and have fun on a regular basis. Her name was Christina Reid, and though she was betrothed to another, he lived overseas, which meant we could go everywhere together in a perfectly innocent relationship. We had a lot of fun and became quite well known at the Royal Festival Hall, attending as many concerts there as we could. Having performed in the hall a great many times since, I have always wanted to get back in touch and invite her to one of my concerts at the hall, where we had spent some wonderful evenings together, listening to the great musicians of the day, but have never been able to trace her.

Christina was the daughter of Major Pat Reid, the escape officer at Colditz Castle during the Second World War. He was a fascinating chap and indeed one of the few British people to actually escape from the castle. A short, round little man with a white moustache, looking not unlike the actor Richard Todd, though John Mills had portrayed him in the film *The Colditz Story*. He was very aloof with me, probably because he liked Christina's fiancé and did not wish to encourage any interloper. He need not have been. His daughter and I were students together for the first time in London, enjoying the sights, sounds and smells of a great city and, as two single people with the same sense of humour, naturally gravitating towards each other. Apart from his wartime heroics, he was to have some fame post-war, as he became the technical advisor to the 1972 TV series of the same name, with Edward Hardwicke playing his character.

Some of those famous soloists and conductors that stick in my conscious memory from that time include Otto Klemperer who, by the time I saw him, conducted sitting down and gave a terrible performance of Mozart's opera *The Marriage of Figaro* with the New Philharmonia Orchestra. It was so slow I am not sure we weren't still there the next morning. Jascha Horenstein, who would galvanise his orchestra (the LPO) during performances of Mahler symphonies and Artur Rubinstein, who played three piano concertos in one concert: Saint-Saëns *No 2*, Grieg and Beethoven *No 5 (The Emperor)*. Carlo Maria Giulini had a small repertoire but everything he did with the New Philharmonia was sensational. Bernard Haitink I remember as a young firebrand, who conducted the London Philharmonic with verve and passion. I particularly recall his *Rite of Spring*, an incredibly difficult piece to conduct with different time signatures every single bar at the end, yet he performed it from memory; now that's impressive. There is another. But he so special he is being kept for later.

There were many wonderful musicians available in the early '70s, with the London orchestras all working flat out to a full London concert hall. There was really only one dedicated concert hall and that was the Royal Festival Hall, which was the reason the Barbican Hall was built in the early 1980s. The ability of the four London orchestras to perform in their home city was limited by the one hall, and it had a different concert seven nights a week, fifty-two weeks of the year with nearly all sold-out. Yes, there was the Royal Albert Hall, but until the current iteration of the mushrooms was installed, the sound delay precluded too many serious classical events apart from the BBC Proms taking place there.

My second year of RCM life saw me with my first serious girlfriend, Michelle. This was quite a coincidence as, after Jean-Lou, I had fled so quickly I had forgotten to pack my teddy bear. However, not wanting to go back for him (maybe I thought I would be left again), a replacement was bought. Still speaking French, I immediately named him Michel. But the bear was not female, he was French for Michael, probably so named after my best friend in the TB sanitorium, though I have no recollection of him or anyone else there.

Michelle's parents had a house in Somers Crescent in Bayswater before moving to Somerset, always retaining a scenic holiday cottage in Llangrannog on the west coast of Wales. The relationship between Michelle and me was volatile, with moments of arguments interspersed with long periods of growing up. I must have been a very difficult boyfriend coming from an all-male society, grappling with the difficulties of relationships that at boarding school were intense for only three periods of the year, to one that now had to survive throughout the year. We remained together for three years. It was not to last of course, and in the end we both moved on, but not before the incident with one of our dogs!

My mother and father had two dogs, one of whom was called Maxwell and he was a Heinz 57 type, a mongrel, not that we ever called him that when he was within hearing distance! The other, a yellow Labrador called Damon, we had rescued from an owner who could not control him. In all honesty, he was a bit of a handful, especially in the presence of smaller dogs who he would savage! One of our neighbours had a small Terrier and it made for an uneasy relationship with them after Damon had chewed him up and spat him out a few times. However careful we were on walks, somehow, he could get through the small openings of his muzzle.

I took Michelle down to meet my parents for the weekend, and in the '70s, there was still some decorum in sleeping arrangements at parents' houses, or there was in ours. My father considering himself 'in loco parentis' ensured we had different bedrooms separated by a staircase! To ensure probity, she was down; I was up. On the first night, my father woke up in his bedroom, opposite Michelle's room, and was shocked to hear a gentle knocking against the wall of the long corridor towards the stairs which led up to my room. My father, thinking she was on her way up, shouted out very loudly, "Michelle? No!" This actually woke her up, and getting out of bed, both she and my father poked their heads out of their respective doors at the same time to see the dog Damon padding down the corridor on his way up to see me, his tail swishing against the wall.

Having entered the college so young, I stayed on for longer than the standard three years. In fact, I stayed five, though in the last year I wasn't there a very great deal of the time. I attended lectures whenever possible, and there were some memorable ones: Nadia Boulanger, the legendary teacher who had taught such diverse composers as Aaron Copland and Michel Legrand amongst others. There was a story doing the rounds that Gershwin had asked her for lessons, and when, after he had played some of his pieces to her, he had said he wanted to compose like Ravel, she had asked him, "Why do you want to be a second-class Ravel when you are a first-class Gershwin?"

Another fabulous speaker was Eric Fenby. He was the amanuensis of Frederick Delius, which meant that when Delius became so incapacitated through syphilis and couldn't write,

Fenby would physically write the notes onto the manuscript. The glorious ten-minute *Song of Summer* is one such piece, composed entirely by the composer singing the notes of every single instrument to Eric Fenby, as memorably portrayed by Christopher Gable to the Delius of Max Adrian, in Ken Russell's film *The Song of Summer*.

I won the Sir Adrian Boult conducting scholarship three times and the Ricordi Conducting Prize, which in broad terms meant very little but did give me some much-needed extra pocket money: £50, which was just about three months' subsistence!

I even ended up on the student committee where I had been co-opted by the president of the student's union, my friend Mike Reed.

During the year of our tenure, we had a visit by the college's president who was Queen Elizabeth the Queen Mother, and her visit was meticulously planned and a huge success. The day went well, and she listened to a number of concerts and toured the buildings. The end of her visit was marked by some tea to which some of us had been invited. All went well, until by some invisible sign, it was time for her to leave. Gradually, everyone moved to one side except the man to whom I was talking. I said to him, "I'm not sure what's happening. Perhaps we ought to step back?"

"No," he replied, "I never do at this point; there's plenty of time for that later." She then started to climb the stairs from the basement where tea was being held up to street level, and he followed, beckoning me to do so as well.

"Should we do this? I think we should stop now," I said.

"No, I always attend these events and follow her up," he replied. So, we carried on. I had grave misgivings and knew something was wrong when, as HM the Queen Mother, her lady-in-waiting, the director of the Royal College of Music Sir Keith Faulkner, this man and I ascended the wide staircase, people lining up each side were bowing and curtseying to the entourage as we processed by.

"We should not be here," I whispered to the man, by now with some urgency.

"Nonsense," he said. "Come on." We got to the entrance of the RCM, and she turned to say goodbye to the college representative.

She shook Sir Keith's hand, and I was next. She sort of looked at me with a very puzzled expression and said, "Er… goodbye… nice to have… met you."

Then blow me, as she turned to get into her car, accompanied by her lady-in-waiting, this man also turned to me and, with a wink, said, "Well, goodbye then," and got into the car! Of course, he always followed her upstairs: he was HM's personal security officer! I can only imagine the humorous conversation that followed in the car, probably much more humorous than the one I had with Sir Keith!

My friend Mike Reed was a very enthusiastic student and used to invite his friends to partake in some of his extra-curricular concerts outside college, particularly in his local church of which he was music director. There was always something fraught with interest when we went to one of his shows. This included the time he was performing the *Christmas Oratorio* which had an instrumental movement called the 'Pastoral Symphony' for four solo oboes. This was a step too far or, to be more accurate, two steps too far for Mike's performance, as only two oboes turned up for the performance. Unhappily, the rehearsal plan was abandoned as both oboists in the concert forgot which part they had agreed to play, striking up with the same one. With a squeak and a squawk and much confusion, they ground to a halt. I have no idea why at that point he also did not stop. Possibly because at the college, we had been drummed into keeping musical performances going at all costs. We watched aghast as Mike valiantly attempted to sing all four parts on his own for the rest of the movement, instead of stopping, which, in my opinion, would have been the better option!

At another concert, a friend called Chris Tingley and I had been recruited by Mike to sing the tenor line in the chorus of the Fauré *Requiem*. For some reason, we couldn't make the preliminary rehearsals, probably because they were held during opening hours. This meant neither of us had looked at the part, so we sight-read the music and Latin text at the final rehearsal. Unfortunately, there was a word in the chorus we had never come across before, and which had to be sung, and that word was *pœnis*, which, as everyone knows, is the Latin word for pain!

When we came across this line in rehearsal, first we looked at it in disbelief, then at each other, unable to believe what we saw. A faint snigger began at what we thought was a misprint, which built to a crescendo of uncontrolled guffawing! There was a lot of tutting from the more elderly members of the church choir, and I subsequently learnt some awkward explaining to the more junior members. I regret to say Chris and I never managed to sing the word that day, giggling in the performance like the silly students we were. I have never conducted the Fauré *Requiem* since without thinking back to that day.

But perhaps the most memorable evening was Tchaikovsky's *1812*. At the end of the piece, in order to recreate the bells of Moscow ringing out the triumphant victory of the Russian Army over the French at the Battle of Borodino, he decided, without completely thinking it through, to rig up a sort of washing line of pots and pans and other assorted metallic objects between the pulpit and a column of the church. At the appropriate moment, they were to be banged and bashed as a substitute for the tubular bells he should have had yet were too expensive to hire. All had gone well in the rehearsal and indeed the metallic sounds had adequately replicated the cathedral bells. When it came to the big finale moment in the performance, the person charged with striking them hit them so enthusiastically that, after the bashing they had had at the rehearsal, with his first blow in the performance he broke the line, setting up the most awful noise you have ever heard as dozens of pots, pans, ladles and other metallic objects hit the stone floor of the church. Not content with lying there, they proceeded to roll around, not helped by the fact that the person who had caused this then tried to stop the noise by stamping on them, but only succeeded in getting the string caught up in his foot, thereby substantially increasing the overall effect. It was not so much the bells of Moscow ringing out in celebration, more like the gates of hell opening, and we were being dragged unwittingly in, which was probably very much like the battle itself!

I was the first student to invite a well-known conductor to the college and persuaded the then chief of the London Philharmonic, Bernard Haitink, to conduct my student orchestra in Tchaikovsky's *Symphony No. 6* which we were performing later in the term. No one could quite believe it when he turned up. He was completely wonderful with us students, taking the rehearsal without payment and giving his time freely.

A few students were also picked to interview Leopold Stokowski for American TV, of whom I was one. There was a heavy rumour, even then, that he was born Leonard Stokes in North London and had changed his name to give himself an air of Russian mystique for all those Hollywood ladies! Whether he really was slightly dotty or was putting it on, it was certainly a bizarre encounter, with his favourite question, 'where am I?' reverberating continuously round the room.

Our venerated director Sir Keith Faulkner was in attendance and sat next to him, while we students sat further down the table. We solemnly asked him questions about his life and meeting Mickey Mouse, to which he mumbled a reply until, suddenly perking up, he looked at Sir Keith and, in one glorious phrase, said to him, "And who are you?" However, the whole thing was a complete waste of time as the sound man had forgotten to switch on his tape machine and was only reminded three minutes before Stokowski got up from the table and left!

Scene 5: Student Life Finishes

College was an incredible place to be for someone who had only ever been around other boys in quiet, sleepy villages/towns, such as Sevenoaks, Cowes, Milford-on-Sea and Marlborough. London was, even then, a bustling, thriving, 'happening' place in the early '70s. Carnaby Street, BIBA and flower power were places and events that had meaning for students, well at least for most students. I took very little interest in such things, except once trying to impress a girl by walking around London in bare feet. On and off buses, through the underground, down Park Lane, it didn't matter; bare feet were the dress of the flower power generation and as she was one, so for a few days so was I. After a while, realising what the streets were doing to my feet, and as the girl was not overly impressed and despite the Royal College of Music being surrounded by Imperial College where these things mattered more, I stopped.

Maybe being 'square' and a music student also had something to do with it. I was quietly content to visit the 99, do my practice and attend lessons, one of which was music theory.

This used to be quite an event as it was run by a composer called Alan Ridout. Alan liked a drink with his students, and if his lessons were after lunch, they could be quite lively. I once witnessed Alan playing a Bach Two-Part Invention on the piano which, considering the alcohol intake he had consumed, was itself impressive enough. But Alan went one further and used to do it whilst standing on his head. No one could ever work out how he did this and still make the inventions recognisable.

I finally came towards the end of my student years. I had

spent five years at college and had grown up. I was leaving with much more self-confidence and had begun to pick up the art of being streetwise and caring for myself, as well as other people. I was starting to learn about the female sex, something that had eluded me while I was at school, and I was beginning to learn about the profession I had always wanted to do: conducting. I had also gained a degree!

Yes, I am entitled to write the initials ARCM after my name, with the initials standing for Associate of the Royal College of Music. In 1972, there were two versions of the diploma, teaching and performing, and the difference between the two is obvious, well, to everyone except me! It was decided that as I was spending so much time on my conducting, neglecting the piano-playing element of my studies, I would take the teaching version.

Accordingly, in my third year at the college, I took the exam and, on the first attempt, promptly failed it! I had failed to understand that the teaching diploma was not just about the ability to play the piano but also to teach it, which meant answering questions from inquisitive students, some obvious, some not so. Therefore, when one of the examiners, pretending to be a pupil, asked me why a piano keyboard wasn't alternate white and black notes all the way up, I cried, "No idea, but that's a brilliant idea! So much simpler." No, the answer of course was geography. As they told me, if they were not grouped as they are, the player would not know where they were by touch alone. Of course, so obvious when explained like that! Trouble was, I should have told them the answer!

By the end of the exam, knowing I had failed, when they asked me what the middle pedal on the piano was for, I quoted Victor Borge and said, "It was there to separate the other two!" John Barstow, one of the teachers examining me, later told me that it had given them a much-needed laugh!

After achieving the degree at the second attempt, my parents were the only people who ever wrote letters to me with the initials

ARCM after my name on the envelope, presumably because they wanted to see some tangible return on their financial outlay for privately educating their son. Now they are no longer with us, similar to the exam itself which no longer exists, almost no one knows I have initials after my name and am entitled to wear a hat and gown at certain events. Those four initials are gradually disappearing into the mists of a few people's memory.

Act 4

Scene 1: Beginnings of Professional Career

In my fifth year of college life, I was away quite a lot starting to earn my living.

We students were occasionally booked to provide a cheap chorus for films and other enterprises and one such film was *The Wicker Man*. A group of us were recruited to a recording studio, handed some sheet music and asked to sing badly, as if drunk. That we could do! If you watch the film, wait for the pub scene; the high tenor singing along is your scribe.

Around the same time, I was picked to assist a man called John Forsythe who was to be the music director for a new Ken Russell film. Russell had previously made the films of Elgar and Delius which were very successful for the BBC. But he had become rather too quirky for the BBC and, truth be told, some of the public too. His particular style of storytelling was deemed more suitable for the large screen in the cinema, where they could be rated.

My first day introduction to his world of shooting films was down at Shepperton Studios, playing the piano for a rehearsal of the dancers in the film *Mahler*, while they worked out their routine on top of a horizontal nine-foot erect phallus! An extraordinary introduction to the film world; it would not be my last.

I was also in the music department for *Lisztomania*, Russell's biopic of Liszt, and very envious entering a recording studio and seeing a large professional orchestra, hearing John conduct the *Prelude* and *Liebestod* to Wagner's *Tristan and Isolde*; oh, how I wanted to conduct that piece myself!

Another on the music staff for that film was the Yes keyboardist Rick Wakeman. He and I shared a common fact. He had attended the Royal College of Music a few years before me, both taught by the same piano teacher, a wonderful lady by the name of Eileen Reynolds. We naturally bonded as we discussed the college and our respective times. I do not know whether this is what he said about all conductors he met, but he went round asking everyone if they knew the difference between Anthony Inglis and Dr. Scholl's sandals. Eventually, he gave the reply that 'one bucks the feet, the other....'. I thought that was rather good, especially as he had never seen me conduct!

In the middle of all this I did my first theatre show which was *Cinderella* at the Sybil Thorndyke Theatre in Leatherhead, now The Leatherhead Theatre, with Stacey Dorning as Cinders. She had just come out of the successful TV series *Black Beauty* and was extremely popular. I was on piano two with the married couple Jean (music director and piano one) and Rex Lear (on drums). Jean was later to become the pianist called Ramona at Maplins Holiday camp in the very successful BBC TV series *Hi-de-Hi!*

It was here I learnt that having a relationship with a person in the theatrical world could be a transient affair. It was almost as though when you moved shows, you moved relationships. My girlfriend Michelle was no longer around, so I went out with someone in the show, a beautiful dancer by the name of Carys.

At the same time as *Cinderella*, Mike Reed was the pianist in the stage show of *West Side Story* at the Collegiate Theatre in Euston, now The Bloomsbury. Ed Coleman, who was the music director, was going to leave, and the natural progression was for Mike to move up to conduct, leaving space for a pianist. The timing was almost perfect. Mike asked me to fill his very large pianistic fingers, and I went from *Cinderella* in Leatherhead to the Collegiate Theatre.

West Side had an extraordinary orchestra, not for the first or, I regret to say, the last time, fuelled by alcohol.

In those days, there was a huge problem of alcoholism amongst musicians, now largely eradicated. I suppose it's not really too much of a surprise. Music should be a creative process, not a recreative process. Yes, in opera or concerts you're recreating a moment of inspiration by the composer and lyricist, but it is of the moment, recreated then left. When you're doing a show that is on eight times a week, six days a week, fifty-two weeks of the year, it becomes a repetitive recreative process. The art is completely different. You have to remember what you did the previous night and do it again! After a while, for some people, that becomes monotonous, and when that happens, they should leave. However, if you have a partner and children to support, the attractiveness of a steady weekly salary in a profession that at any one time has a great many people unemployed, is very tempting. Too tempting for some, and musicians stay for the money. Then, they turn to drink to forget that what they are doing is boring and unsatisfying.

That is now a problem largely solved, as at *Phantom of the Opera* in London, we had musicians who stayed with the original orchestra for the entire thirty-three-and-a-half-year run. To allay the repetitiveness of the job, there was a very generous deputising system, which meant if you wanted to go and play somewhere else, you could! There are tight rules in place, so the patrons and cast (and conductor) do not notice any difference in quality. It is essential for the mind of the various musicians within a long-running show that they are able to do this. It refreshes their artistry.

It is very similar to being a virtuoso and natural musician. Yehudi Menuhin was one such example. I met him at his Eaton Square house when accompanying another great chum

Christopher Warren-Green, at that time a violinist and leader of the Philharmonia Orchestra, now a very fine conductor, who went to play to Mr. Menuhin. He was a man of such humanity and sensitivity, and a naturally gifted violinist for so much of his life, he did not need to know how he did it, he just could. When, towards the end of his playing career, things started going wrong and his technique needed some help as things were not working quite as they had, particularly with his bowing arm, he did not know how to help himself as he had never needed to know how he did it. Oddly, he could diagnose others as he was a wonderful teacher. Self-diagnosis, however, was not his strength. Attending a recital of his at the Royal Festival Hall when he played the Brahms *Violin Sonatas*, it was rather sad as his right arm let him down badly; it had always been so natural for him.

Alcoholic musicians (and the teetotal Yehudi was very far from alcoholism) are the same: when they have to remember how to do it, they can't, so they drink even more to forget. The *West Side* orchestra was one such example. With the fumes emanating from the pit, you dared not strike a match anywhere near them. Yet so many of that orchestra were in their prime.

One of the first to be produced by the *Crossroads* actor and subsequent Everton Football Club chairman and mega-producer Bill Kenwright, it was wracked by bad behaviour in the pit. During the show, the orchestra used to chain the music director Ed Coleman to the handrail so he couldn't conduct; they'd put pornographic pictures in his score which he would hold up and show the actors while they were singing 'Gee Officer Krupke' to the audience at the front of the stage; he would drop his trousers at all opportunities. Yet, all this went unnoticed by the audience, and the band was one of the very best in which I have ever played. The cast were superb, all choreographed by Bob Arditti who had been the first British Baby John in the original London production.

It was not without its incidents. One night, early in the run when understudies were not rehearsed, a broken foot took out Riff, one of the leaders of the Jets. It was decided Bill would act it, however, as he couldn't dance, Bob would do the dance routines. At the end of a dialogue scene containing Bill, the lights dimmed for a moment while the two actors swapped over. When the lights went back up, Bob, in the same position as Bill when the lights had dimmed, would be onstage ready to dance. At the end of the dance, lights went out, Bill would come back on, lights went up and we'd carry on with the dialogue. Bizarre! At least they wore the same costumes. Mike very ably took over this bucking bronco ride of a show, and I tried to fit in as pianist.

When the limited season of *West Side* finished, I played the piano for a chum who was conducting a show on tour. I had met Trevor York during the production of the Ken Russell films, and we were to remain friends. He was later to become the rehearsal pianist for *Phantom* and one of the deputy keyboard players, but in 1974 he was the music director for a tour of *Peter Pan*. It starred Anita Harris as Peter and John Gower in the important role of Mr. Darling and Captain Hook. The show was fabulous and glamorous with quite a large cast and orchestra. When it ended, I met the star of the show, John Gower, at the offices of the Department of Health and Social Security in Lisson Grove for the brief time both of us were unemployed. So odd seeing star and humble pianist in the same dole queue!

Around this time, I worked with the actress Nyree Dawn Porter, a very well-known actress, largely as a result of playing the character Irene Forsyte in *The Forsyte Saga* of 1967. For the life of me, I can't remember why we were working together, but she gave me a piece of advice that I can almost quote word for word. It was in the press that she had just married a man fifteen years younger than herself, and in the mid-1970s, that was unusual enough for it to be front-page news in the more salacious pages of some Sunday newspapers.

With the rudeness of youth, I asked her whether she was concerned that no matter the age difference now, did she not think that would play a part in their relationship in the future?

I can recall not only her words, but that we were travelling in a taxi along the Old Brompton Road in South Kensington just by Queens Gate when she uttered them. She turned to me and said that she and her first husband had gone to bed one night and gone to sleep. In the morning, she woke up, and he didn't; he had died in the night aged thirty-six. She went on, "From that day, I have lived for the moment, without worrying about tomorrow or the day after. We never know what the future will bring, so I live for the now, not the 'morrow." She was absolutely right and I have never forgotten it. Oh, the wisdom of experience!

Sad to say, I was also right, as eleven years later, she and her second husband divorced!

Scene 2: Touring

The finish to these short runs was the offer by John Forsythe to assist him as assistant music director on the 1975 six-month tour of *Rose-Marie*. With music by Rudolf Friml, it starred John Hanson and the Welsh actress Margaret Williams.

Like a lot of shows around that time, such as *The Student Prince*, *The Vagabond King*, *The Desert Song* and *Rose-Marie*, all originally produced between the years of 1924 and 1926, the plots and characters were largely interchangeable, which made them so suitable for a young, dashing leading tenor in the 1960s.

Enter John Hanson, a tenor whose signature role had been as the Red Shadow in the stage show *The Desert Song*. A difficult man, not given to much warmth towards the junior members of the cast. Years of improper singing every night had caused his throat and vocal cords to be so raw, he had to gargle with a strange concoction before every entrance. To our knowledge, it was non-alcoholic but possibly contained a strong antiseptic that would numb the pain he may have been experiencing. In addition to the gargling, he had this disconcerting habit of turning to face upstage (away from the audience) and coughing up a lot of phlegm into a handkerchief before belting out the hit numbers.

He did, however, have a huge following amongst ladies of a certain age which gave him a very good career singing these roles, even appearing on a Morecambe and Wise Christmas special. Maintaining this position, he made sure he was not outshone by other dashing young men who shared a stage with him, though by 1976 and at the age of fifty-six, he was probably past the time when he could be described as young or indeed dashing! In *Rose-Marie*, there was a wonderful front cloth, downstage, unaccompanied number sung by the men of the Canadian Mounties. Each performance by the male chorus brought the house down when beautifully sung. It lasted about a week, before John had it cut and I had to write an arrangement, which of course was not nearly as good! On the last night of the tour, the men in the chorus arbitrarily put the original back in!

The tour lasted about six months and was a number one tour put on by Humphrey Stanbury, erstwhile producer and general manager of the Wolverhampton Theatre. A number one tour meant you visited the major theatres in the big cities. We would finish the evening performance in one city on a Saturday, travel on the Sunday, have a dress rehearsal on the Monday afternoon in a new city with the new local orchestra ready for the first performance Monday evening. The itinerary was poorly organised, with several long journeys on the Sunday to cities which were very adjacent to cities we'd been to recently but not the previous week! We could easily do Glasgow, Southsea, Newcastle, Southampton in consecutive weeks, all done by coach on our one day off!

The show also featured a young Sue Pollard who was to achieve fame a short while later as the character Peggy Ollerenshaw in the BBC series *Hi-De-Hi*.

The transient life of a single young guy on tour kicked in, and I began a relationship with a girl called Patti. She was a dancer and singer in the show, and we kept each other amused, happy and warm on a six-month bus journey, interrupted by evenings of performing a musical, at least that's how it sometimes felt! There was never a chance to settle anywhere. We were always looking for digs and had to get in quick, before other itinerant performers in all the productions in town grabbed the best ones.

Actors and musicians used to jealously guard the names and addresses of good-quality digs. If you were new to the game, you would have to go into the theatre on the Sunday when you arrived, look at the noticeboard at the stage door, then ring round the various places that were advertised or had been put up by the theatre management. The new theatre was always open of course, as the set had been struck as soon as the curtain had come down on the Saturday night in the old theatre, so it could be transported overnight and set up on the Sunday in the new theatre, ready for the dress rehearsal on Monday.

At least the search for digs in 1975 was not as difficult for an unmarried couple as it had been only a couple of years previously.

When Michelle, my girlfriend in 1973, and I had gone looking for her university digs in Leeds, we tried to book into a small, private hotel. When the owners asked our names, we told them, and they gave us two rooms which of course cost more money. We enquired whether we could share one. They told us, not unless we were married as it was against the law. There was a moment's pause before I lied and said we were. They immediately asked us why we had not said that before and gave us a double. Even then, the long arm of the law reached out to preclude any illicit unmarried fraternisation in hotels and boarding houses.

With *Rose-Marie*, I began learning my craft. Yes, I mainly played the piano but was given conducting opportunities on the show, beginning to learn how to lead and how to accompany; I began to learn how to listen, yet be listened to; I began to communicate with my fellow musicians. It was not easy. I was in my early twenties, yet the average age of the musicians was probably in their fifties/sixties. They'd seen it all and done it all and were not appreciative of a young, keen and green youth in charge. In those days, the pay was not as good as it is now, and playing in the pit was the place you went towards the end of your career. When all else failed, you would go into a theatre pit where you could drink and not be noticed! Playing was not that important either. The stars were on the stage not the pit, and providing you were not too outrageous, you could keep your job!

Now all that has changed. The pay in the pit of a West End theatre pro rata is the best paid regular job in the music industry. You can be well into four figures per week for twenty-four hours' playing! In addition, there is sickness benefit, holiday pay and, as seen, the opportunity to take performances off and earn money elsewhere.

After *Rose-Marie*, I had one last throw of the dice before finishing with the touring life. For ten weeks I was music director for *Jack and the Beanstalk*, the 1975 Christmas pantomime at the Wolverhampton Grand Theatre. Ten weeks was normal in those days, some even longer. Nowadays, pantos are lucky to reach the second week of January, though most start a little earlier.

Our production of *Jack and the Beanstalk* starred a double act, popular at the time, called Little and Large. Syd Little (the straight man) and Eddie Large (the gag man) were an interesting couple, continually bickering, as do quite a few double acts. I was amazed they stayed together so long, though I heard after the act finished, they didn't talk to each other for a number of years. They were both extremely likeable, neither having any airs nor graces. If memory serves, Syd married one of the dancers in the show. They are both still together.

As Jack we had a singer called Susan Maughan. She had first come to the public's notice with a song called 'Bobby's Girl', before appearing with Morecambe and Wise at the Royal Variety Show.

For me, the memorable fact about the panto in Wolverhampton was making the music quite orchestral. For instance, we did some chase music where I arranged Paul Dukas' *Sorcerer's Apprentice* for a band of eight or nine which included a rhythm section. The piece is normally played by an orchestra of eighty which does not have a rhythm section! It must have sounded awful. I have a terrible feeling there was also Wagner's *Ride of the Valkyries* in for the chase music; well, at least it saved on PRS! It was a baptism by fire as we would regularly do two performances a day and, on some occasions, three.

The third performance used to be on a Saturday morning and was put on by the council for the benefit of the local toughs: cheap or free tickets for those who were not able to afford them. None of them really wanted to be there; they'd have preferred terrorising the local neighbourhood. However, they were made to go, and what the hell – it was free!

We were warned there could be trouble, and they were right. Catcalls, boos, wolf whistles and general mayhem throughout the show. It became so bad, it was the only time I have personally stopped a performance. During the second act, coins started raining down on us from the upper circle, landing in the pit. Expecting this as they had previous, so did the local orchestra as most had brought hard hats. The toughs were not stupid and only used lower denominations of coins. Two pence thrown from the gods was still heavy enough to do damage. Upon realising they had quite a supply, I stopped the show, turned round and shouted to the upper circle that if this continued, I would take my musicians out of the theatre. For some reason, this did the trick and halted the metallic shower. We finished the show without further incidence.

After this, or maybe because of it, it was time to stop travelling for weeks at a time, and I obtained work in London so could live at home.

Scene 3: West End

In the summer of 1976, I began my West End career in *Irene* at the Adelphi Theatre on the Strand.

It was produced by the legendary impresario and showman (he liked that expression) Harold Fielding. He was a diminutive man with a lopsided face and had been a child prodigy on the violin, studying with the legendary violinist Joseph Szigeti.

After starting to tour as a violin prodigy at the age of twelve, he had in his twenties turned to concert promoting, before eventually producing musicals.

A popular misconception is that he retired from concert-giving in his twenties due to a failing memory. However, probably as we shared the same disease, he confided in me that he gave up violin playing when he got tuberculosis. What is not commonly understood, is that, having had the disease, it lies dormant in a part of your body for the rest of your life. In Harold's case, it was his wrist which affected his playing.

Harold and his wife Masie ran the operation with a rod of iron, risking his own money and, in the process, making and losing fortunes several times. After the flops of the musicals *Ziegfeld* (based on the life of the Broadway impresario Florence Ziegfeld Jr, after whom he modelled himself) and *Someone Like You*, he had to go into voluntary liquidation so ending the career of a legendary West End producer.

In the 1990s, Harold had a number of strokes and was put into Galsworthy House, a nursing home in Kingston-upon-Thames, just around the corner from where I now live and to where I would take my family for a visit. He was a sad sight, this powerhouse of a man who, in earlier years, had been a dynamic, vibrant force, able to chew people up and spit them out, now sitting shrivelled up in a chair in his room, unable to speak and dribbling from his mouth. I think he enjoyed the visits from my family. When they seem to hand out honours like sweeties, it is extraordinary to me that this man, who had given employment to so many and pleasure to so many more, should never have been recognised with a single award. Maybe it was for comments such as his response to the following story.

The musical *Cats* is a song and dance show with music by Andrew Lloyd Webber set to the poems of *Old Possum's Book of Practical Cats* by T.S. Elliot. At the New London Theatre, now the Gillian Lynne Theatre, it had the gimmick of a revolving piece of scenery which was not the set but part of where the audience sat. With the overture, some of the seats in the auditorium would turn and end in a different position.

At this particular performance, there was a lady who had a very upset tummy. Realising she should have visited the ladies' before taking her seat, as soon as the revolve had finished its movement, she got up to search for the toilet bowl she now desperately needed in order to complete her own movement. In her agitation and weakened state, the revolving of the auditorium led to some confusion and she lost her bearings. Finding a darkened corridor, and with no alternative solution, she went to the end and squatted.

Unfortunately, this cul-de-sac was above the musicians who were hidden from the audience's view. Worse, the floor only had grating, acting as the musicians' ceiling to aid ventilation. The resultant mess descended on the heads of the unfortunate players sitting beneath, bringing the performance to an undignified halt, accompanied by yells of horror from those who were affected.

When Harold heard this, he was reported to have said, "I've been trying to do that to musicians for years!"

Irene was all about an immigrant New York shop assistant (Irene) hired to tune a socialite's piano, and with the aid of a flamboyant male artiste (Madame Lucy) who pretends to be from a famous French fashion house, she falls in love with her son (Donald). It played at the Adelphi and starred an unknown Australian girl called Julie Anthony as Irene, along with Jon Pertwee as Madame Lucy. He had been an excellent Doctor Who. I remembered him more from *The Navy Lark*, a radio show I adored and still listen to on BBC Radio 4 extra. As Donald, we had from the BBC mini-series *Ivanhoe*, the handsome and dashing Eric Flynn.

Mike Reed was beginning to forge quite a career in the West End, becoming the music director of choice for Harold Fielding. He was therefore music director for *Irene*, inviting me to be the pianist in the large orchestra.

West End shows always made a cast recording to sell, and *Irene* was no different. We made one very early, upon which I played a number of keyboards including piano, organ and celeste. The album was produced by the very famous gay record producer Norman Newell who, when preparing a track, asked me over the studio talk-back system to the recording floor which instrument I was going to play next and how loudly I was going to play it. Thinking for a moment, I blurted out, "My organ, and it's going to swell quite a bit!"

There was a moment's pause before, with the faintest hint of a leer in his voice, he said, "Oooooh, lovely."

The show was my first real West End intro, and my friends and I behaved appallingly. Nowadays, with the professionalism involved, performers could not get away with what we got up to in the pit during the show. Once, drinking a bit too much, I was late back for the second half of the show. No one knew where I was, and the call went out over the backstage tannoy system to 'find Anthony'!

In the end, a singer called Sue James found me in the downstairs gentlemen's toilets, looking into a mirror and mimicking a parrot with the phrase, 'who's a pretty boy then?', before answering my own question with, 'Anthony's a pretty boy' over and over. With some gentle persuasion, I was led back into the pit, and Madame Lucy (Jon Pertwee) could continue his seduction of the various ladies in his fashion house.

There was a scene in the show where Julie Anthony had to go to the piano and mime an ascending arpeggio, doubled of course by me playing it in the pit. If feeling a bit bored, I thought nothing of doing a descending arpeggio instead. Eventually the joke, such as it was, wore thin and I was made to stop.

During the first half of the twentieth century and well into the second, orchestras in theatres were quite large, so there was limited room in the Adelphi pit, and we had to put the organ on top of the piano on a fairly Heath Robinson wooden-type contraption. I was seated immediately to the left of Mike Reed the conductor and, during the dialogue, he would read or do a crossword. During one such sensitive dialogue moment, I was obviously bored, so unsighted, left my seat and crawled under the front row of the stalls to the back of Mike's position. To this day, and I don't know what made me do it, but I grabbed the back of his legs and pulled. This necessitated a forward motion by Mike who, out of sheer self-preservation, grabbed the nearest thing to him, which happened to be the organ.

As said, it was not very secure, certainly not secure enough to be grabbed and, sure enough, the organ fell with a clatter. Unfortunately, I had left it switched on and the force of the organ hitting the ground pushed the casing at the back of the instrument onto the black notes of the keyboard. This then caused a sound such as you've never heard before, certainly not during a live performance of *Irene* at the Adelphi Theatre. Horrified, I rushed back to my seat as fast as crawling under an auditorium would permit, in order to stop this awful noise from the amplifier that only I could reach! Mike, though, had the presence of mind to pull the lead out of the back of the organ before the sound engineer, Eddie Fardell, who was probably writing his magazine, could react and stop the noise that had interrupted the performance!

I thought that was it, I would quite rightly be fired, but had not reckoned with the guile of Mike Reed. When summoned to Jon Pertwee's room to explain the noise, Mike used attack as the best form of defence. He immediately complained how he had tried to draw everyone's attention to the perilous state of the organ perched on top of the piano, until now, without success. I gather he was quite vociferous, ending with, "It was lucky no one was killed!" Jon Pertwee was immediately concerned, enquiring after everyone's well-being, and I learnt an important lesson: behave myself!

For the London revival of *Irene* fresh from Broadway, the young Mike Reed had written a couple of new songs: 'If Only He Knew' and 'Up on Park Avenue', two of the best songs in the show, and yes, I know 'Alice Blue Gown' was in it! 'If Only He Knew' was a powerful ballad sung by the star of the show as she pined for her lover, and 'Park Avenue' was a ballsy front cloth variety number for two girls. Both wonderful and well worth seeking out. I still play them today.

As previously discussed, in those days there was a huge culture of drinking in the pit; well, not normally in the actual pit but in the local pubs, and *Irene* was no exception. Before the show, during the interval and after the show, plus any extended dialogue breaks in the musical, the musicians would be in the local hostelries downing as many pints as they could in the short time available.

Due to the exceptional quality of the Young's Directors beer, the favourite pub to drink in was upstairs at the Marquess of Anglesey, which was on the corner of Russell and Bow streets by the Drury Lane Theatre. In the twenty-minute interval, and despite the Peacock pub next door, we thought nothing of running to the Marquess from Maiden Lane, downing two pints of beer and being back in time to play the entr'acte to Act 2!

Matinee evening performances were to be dreaded, as the musicians had been there all day! As a player, I would never get aggressive through drink and never got so drunk I couldn't play (well, not that I noticed anyway). With others, that was not always the case.

After a while, Mike left the show, and I moved up to lead the production as music director, and this was where the work began and where I really started to learn the trade. College and touring shows can teach you many things, but it can't teach you the tricks, the tensions and the tantrums of actually conducting live professional musicians! Some of those musicians were hard work.

With many mistakes and great advice from the fixers who managed the band on a day-to-day basis, orchestral managers Chick Norton and Alan Franks, I moved from being a pianist in a show to being musically in charge and began to learn how to deal with situations. At the same time, I was conducting! It may not have been the Mahler, Tchaikovsky and Beethoven I craved, yet I had a real live orchestra under me, and nothing can replace that for experience. I also learnt to control my alcohol intake. Don't get me wrong, I was nowhere near being an alcoholic, but it might not have taken me many more years to become one.

From the moment of actually becoming a conductor full-time as a living, I very seldom touched alcohol before a show and, for the past forty years, never! My judgement is impaired if there's even half a glass of wine in my bloodstream. This is why I don't drink a drop before driving either. There's a rule before a concert or show I stick to rigidly: no drinking of any alcohol. It's simple and easy.

For the first year of *Irene*, I commuted door-to-door from 9 Delorme Street in Fulham, which was where I lived, to the Adelphi Theatre on the Strand by the number 11 bus. After a while, I desired the nightlife, and that meant buying a car so I could get home after the buses and tubes stopped. Night taxis were scarce, and there were few private hire car companies.

The car I bought was a Triumph Spitfire, which somehow lasted the run of *Irene*. The car was a dog, and three engines had to be put into it in the space of two years.

In 1979, I went with a show to Australia for six months, which meant selling it. Unbelievably, my bank manager Mr. Fox expressed an interest in purchasing it, asking me to take it round so he could view it. On the way to him in South London, the car broke down and the AA had to be summoned. This put me in the unenviable position of having to call my bank manager from a telephone box on the side of the road, while a breakdown engineer had his head under the bonnet of the car he wanted to buy. The excuse used for not completing the journey to him was that I had been called at the last moment into the West End to save a show, as the music director had been taken ill at the last moment. It worked!

A week later, I took it to him. My heart was in my mouth as his son pointed out the temporary fix by the AA of an electrical bypass of wires from the thingy to the thingy, but Mr. Fox dismissed his perceptive son's observation and bought it!

The Spitfire was followed by an assortment of cars including a TR7 (another Triumph!), Ford Escort (an aberration), Porsche 924 and 944, followed by one of my favourites, a red Mitsubishi 3000GT: three-litre V6 twin turbo, four-wheel steer, four-wheel drive, active spoilers front and rear monster or, as others called it, a poor man's Ferrari!

My wife claims that I bought the Mitsubishi at the same time as the birth of our second child and sent pictures of the car to all my friends rather than the new baby! I have an awful feeling she might be right!

With a growing family, we subsequently had a Volvo, Galaxy, S-Max and then smaller cars for the children to learn on as well, Daewoo Matiz and a number of Ford Fiestas, before my current steed, a Jaguar XF normally aspirated five-litre V8... grace, space and pace!

With *Irene*, I formed a very close relationship with a girl I still speak to on an almost daily basis: Sue James. Yes, the girl who had found me in the gents' urinal talking to myself in the mirror! She was in the chorus of *Irene* and will always be one of my closest friends. A singer and understudy of the main character Irene O'Dare in the show, she eventually gave up the performing side of the business and became an extremely successful agent.

She began by working in the agency of the famous drama school Italia Conti. At the time, Conti managed an all-girl singing and dancing group called Sam's Set, and Sue, working in the agency during the run of *Irene*, asked me to come and do some musical direction with them. It was like inviting a chocoholic into a sweet shop! I was a twenty-five-year-old single man with money and a car, being asked to help an all-female singing and dancing group in their late teens and early twenties. I hesitated for a millisecond, maybe less, and certainly needed no second invitation. She then took me on as my manager and has looked after my commercial work for more than forty years.

In Sam's Set was a beautiful young blonde lady called Alison. My relationship with Antionette, who had been one of the dancers in the Wolverhampton panto, had ended as she had gone to a holiday camp called Bobbenjaanland in Belgium forming a relationship out there, and Alison and I started going out with each other. I would pick her up in my new sports convertible (new to me anyway), from her house in Lavender Hill where she lived with her mother and father, and off we would go on the open and uncongested roads. She always said she fell for me when, picking her up from outside what used to be the department store Arding & Hobbs in Clapham Junction, I arrived in an open-top car and had Wagner blaring from the speakers as opposed to the Rolling Stones!

She became a TV presenter for a local regional TV station, changing to another before becoming one of the first presenters for the newly formed Sky TV News. Eventually, she left that and moved to Los Angeles where she is now a senior TV producer for Fox. She and I are still in touch, and in fact she is godmother to my eldest child and I, godfather to her eldest son.

At this time, my parents had their twenty-fifth wedding anniversary which they celebrated at the Royal Southern Yacht Club on the river Hamble, a stone's throw from where they were living in Warsash. All their friends from a long time ago, their newer local friends and family came from far and wide to help them celebrate their big day. It was a fantastic day with lots of friends and family greeting us and making gracious speeches about my parents. Shortly afterwards, they announced they were to divorce! I mean, it was so quick they could almost have announced it at their twenty-fifth and avoided the pain of having to tell everyone separately!

My mother stayed in Warsash, and my father went to Park Street near Radlett, close to where he was now working as editor of Adlard Coles, a nautical division of Granada Publishing.

Dad had a big, booming voice, and his new job meant he had to make a lot of overseas telephone calls. When he was on one of those calls, people would say, "Come and hear Jeremy talking to America without the aid of telephone!"

The divorce was to have a happy denouement. Having lived apart for a few years, much to the amazement of the family, my mother and father solemnly announced they were going to remarry. Accordingly in July 1992, the mother and sister of the bride, plus myself, attended South East Hants registry office where Mum and Dad were married to each other – for the second time!

They asked me to be a witness and appointed me the official photographer, an opportunity I was determined to enjoy and celebrate. My mother was a reluctant participant in the day, though not the idea, and did not enjoy me asking them both to pose signing the register for my camera; nor me insisting on throwing confetti over them outside; nor the masses of photos taken! I was very pleased with myself, until getting home and opening the camera to take the film to be developed (no digital cameras then). I discovered, to my horror, I had forgotten to load the camera with film. An essential job for any photographer.

Ah well, Mum was happy. They were to share a house and bedroom for the rest of their lives.

Scene 4: More West End Shows

I was always very fortunate, and unemployment never lasted long.

When *Irene* ended in 1978, I was recommended by Harold Fielding to a new, young and upcoming theatrical producer called Cameron Mackintosh. He was looking for a replacement music director to take over his 1977 production of *Oliver!* at the Albery Theatre, which had been called the New Theatre and is now called the Noel Coward Theatre, coincidently the same theatre where it had opened. It starred Roy Hudd as a superb Fagin and Helen Shapiro who had been a child pop star and was a raunchy Nancy.

It was directed by Peter Coe, the man who had directed it originally. Peter was a man at war with himself, constantly pacing about cajoling actors onto even greater efforts, sometimes in a bullying manner.

In the theatre, he was hugely respected but not much liked by cast members, which probably explains the reason why, upon hearing of his death, one of them cried out, "Good God, which actor killed him?" He was a very self-confident man and sure of his own abilities, expecting others to attain his own heights. This may partly explain his unnecessary death: he tried to do a U-turn on the newly opened M25 and died in the subsequent accident. For the record, I thought he was a brilliant director and much underused.

Oliver! is a musical by Lionel Bart based on the Charles Dickens novel of the same name. Many, including me, like to think of the author as a Victorian reformer. From his own experience of the debtor's prison (his father had been incarcerated in one), his novels were thinly disguised attacks on the unfairness of Victorian society during the nineteenth century. Dickens wrote first-hand of the horrors of being kept in prisons and poor houses. Poor houses, also known as workhouses, were institutions where those too destitute to look after themselves would be kept. The buildings themselves were divided into sections of boys under fourteen, able-bodied men between fourteen and sixty, men over sixty, girls under fourteen, able-bodied women between fourteen and sixty and women over sixty.

Orphans were a prime ingredient of the boys and girls under fourteen in the workhouses and were kept in appalling conditions. This is where the 1960 musical *Oliver!* Opens: the young Oliver himself, confined to a workhouse, hungry and being egged on to ask for more food by his fellow incarcerated inmates. Not the most entertaining way of opening a musical, you might have thought. Yet, with Lionel's music, book and lyrics, and the set of Sean Kenny, it was a smash hit success. With songs such as 'Consider Yourself', 'As Long as He Needs Me' and 'Oom-Pah-Pah', it's of little surprise.

What perhaps is more of a surprise is that Lionel could not read or write a note of music. In that sense, he was a bit like Frederick Delius. As already discussed, at the end of his life, Delius was incapacitated by disease and Eric Fenby had to physically write down the notes for him. In Lionel's case, he could not read or write a note of music, so he had to have the composer Eric Rogers imitating the role of Fenby throughout his composing career! Eric Rogers had composed the music for twenty-two of the *Carry On* films, consequently the perfect amanuensis for Lionel as he sang the tunes for one of the greatest English musicals.

Strange facts in music are not uncommon. For instance, Irving Berlin could only ever play in one key, so he commissioned a specially built piano with a sliding mechanism which, when you moved a lever, shifted the whole piano action to the left or right. This meant, while Berlin was playing in the only key he knew how to play in, I believe in Db which has five flats, his audience were listening in another!

Oliver! is an astounding show and conducting it with the original Sean Kenny set in the original theatre was a huge privilege; the Albery Theatre even had the original sepia London skyline painting of the original show, though somewhat faded, still existing on the back wall. The set had a revolve that could form the backbone of many different scenes: one moment Fagin's den, the next the streets of London, the next Tower Bridge. Revolutionary at the time of the first performance, even in the late '70s, it still had the ability to amaze and dazzle. You had to be careful not to get caught when the set was in motion, but it was incredible how simple yet effective it was.

Then there was Bill Sykes' dog called Bullseye, who did not seem to care that she was actually female and called Bonny; she answered to both.

Generally speaking, she was a well-behaved dog and would perform superbly every night. She had her role off pat, especially the end of the show when, after killing Nancy, Sykes gets his comeuppance, and it is Bullseye who leads the hostile crowd to where Sykes, holding Oliver hostage, is hiding.

She did this every night by following a pre-determined trail liberally dotted with portions of her favourite sausages which had been placed in the interval, so she would always know to take the same route.

Every now and then, while stopping to greedily gobble a bit of sausage, the Londoners chasing Sykes would have to wait while she finished her morsel, so the chase would sometimes become more of a saunter. Occasionally, she would forget one, causing havoc amongst the cast as she hurtled back to the errant sausage she'd just remembered. To make up for this and fill in the time, the cast would cry out, "I think he's picking up the scent," or "Wait, he's lost," before another would cry out, "Again!" She was looked after by one of the actors and was a much-loved member of the cast with her own bow at the end. Running from one side of the stage to the other, she would come down to the footlights just in front of me for one last sausage/bow.

Not having an understudy, if she was ill, she did sometimes misbehave onstage and, in one unforgettable performance, the poor animal had a very upset tummy. Whilst leading the crowd, Bonny/Bullseye let go of her entire stomach contents in one long, never-ending stream of diarrhoea; a sort of 'defecate-while-you-run'. This was exacerbated by the sausages she still stopped to consume en-route, which only succeeded in making the already appalling situation, even worse. This time, the actors and actresses did not need to follow the dog by sight but by the trail of runny poo she left.

It was one of the funniest moments I've ever seen on a stage, as all the actors, supposedly chasing Sykes in anger, slid about the stage, clutching at any adjacent piece of scenery or person to keep themselves from falling over.

A replacement Fagin came in for Roy Hudd with the actor

George Layton, who I thought was his equal. George was one of the student trainee doctors in the ITV show *Doctor in the House*, based on the very funny Richard Gordon books.

We also had an actress by the name of Joan Turner playing the role of Widow Corney. She had once been a very famous star, becoming the UK's highest paid female entertainer and topping the bill at the London Palladium. However, I am sorry to say, taking to drink, she imbibed rather too often and for rather too long.

In her inebriated state, she used to open her dressing room window at the Albery Theatre and hurl her empty bottles at any passer-by she didn't like the look of. Of course, we could not tolerate this, and she had to go.

For five years, she became homeless in Los Angeles living on the streets, before moving back to the UK in 2001 to sheltered accommodation. She died in 2009 at the ripe old age of eighty-six.

Scene 5: The Two Ronnies – Responsible for Everything!

After my time at the Albery Theatre, I followed Mike yet again! Whilst conducting *Oliver!*, he was musically in charge of the stage show for one of Britain's greatest double acts, *The Two Ronnies*. They were not really a double act, more two actors playing opposite each other. They were huge on TV in the '70s and '80s and different from Morecambe and Wise, Canon and Ball, Little and Large, Mike and Bernie Winters and other partnerships of the time in that they could and did perform without each other.

Ronnie Barker, known by everyone as Ronnie B, who had also appeared in the BBC radio series of the '60s and '70s *The Navy Lark*, starred in such well-loved TV comedies as *Porridge* and *Open All Hours*, as well as other, more serious, stage roles.

Ronnie Corbett, known as Ronnie C, starred in the sitcom *Sorry* but had started out in musicals such as Lionel Bart's ill-fated show *Twang*. Ronnie B and C were famously put together by David Frost in *The Frost Report* and were a match made in heaven.

Their stage show, premiered by Harold Fielding at the London Palladium in 1978, was once again MD'd by that musical director of choice, Mike Reed.

Of course, with the busy schedules of both Ronnies, it had a limited season at the Palladium, and it closed all too soon but was not ended! In 1979, Fielding decided to take the show to Australia and, Mike being unavailable (so wanted!), I was given the task of taking the unaltered show to Sydney and Melbourne.

The show came at a good time for both Ronnies, who needed to vacate the UK and the oppressive taxation of the then Labour government under James Callaghan. The UK Government was charging higher paid citizens 83% tax, which meant for every pound earned above a certain figure, eighty-three pence went to the Treasury! Of course, on 3 May 1979, Margaret Thatcher won the general election, reversing some of the higher rate taxes that had been levied and increased over the preceding years by successive UK administrations.

Both Ronnies had already planned to spend a year with their families in Australia, and in early summer 1979, along with them, one or two support artists, some technicians and Harold Fielding with his wife Maisie, I flew to Australia for the first time.

It was a long, hot journey, and we had to land twice. Bahrain and Singapore were our stopovers as there were no 747-400s in those days, just the basic three flight-deck crew standard 747s. I was better off than my parents' and grandparents' generations as, back then, it took a few days just to reach Singapore, travelling in the flying boats, as they were then called. It was a very glamorous journey though, as nights were spent ashore in first-class hotels, and jet lag was a curse yet to be discovered.

I very quickly settled into Aussie life. Even though it was winter there, it was not bad when you are used to UK winters, and I was made to feel very welcome.

Although the content of the show stayed exactly the same as the Palladium show, the majority of the cast were of course changed. The dancers were Australian; the singing support act was an Australian act called Jada; the juggler was Hungarian and he had appeared at the Palladium, as had Omar Pasha, a puppet act. The lead male dancer was Australian, though residing in the UK, and had also appeared at the Palladium.

In 2021, the lead male dancer – ninety-year-old Fred Evans, who retired back to Sydney – and I, still maintain contact, regularly ringing each other to gossip about the latest goings-on in the world of show business!

The show soon settled into a routine and was enormously successful.

On *The Two Ronnies* show was that great actor, Sam Kelly. He found fame in the BBC TV sitcoms *Porridge* and *'Allo 'Allo!* as the German Captain Geering, who greets everyone with the expression 'clop'! In Australia, he was his character Bunny Warren in the *Porridge* sketch and could make me laugh on and offstage.

In the stage show, Ronnie B took a segment of the TV show and, with Sam and the Australian actor Peter Ford playing the role of a prison warder, had the audience laughing uproariously every night. What a privilege it was to watch from up close, Ronnie B in one of his finest comedic creations as written by Ian La Frenais with his sidekick, the straight-faced Sam Kelly.

Being one of the UK's greatest actors, Ronnie B didn't seem to take long to get from one character into another and, aided by a costume, he could morph into a singing hillbilly, Norman Stanley Fletcher or a member of an all-girls singing group with consummate ease.

He was never comfortable showing his private side in public

and once said to me, he needed a moustache, a wig or the make-up to get the character of the person he was portraying, then he could hide the real Ronnie B behind the mask of that character.

I seldom saw the private side of Ronnie B. Whereas the opposite was the case with Ronnie C: what you saw with him was what you got. He hid nothing, exactly the same in public as he was in private: an extrovert and a bon viveur. I liked them both immensely, and in terms of audience entertainment, they were hugely influential on my career.

One excerpt that must be mentioned from the Ronnies' show was the famous *Four Candles* sketch which they performed out there. I must have seen that sketch at least two hundred times, and I'm here to tell you I laughed every single time. It was even better live than on TV. Being on the conductor's podium and so close, you could see every nuance and every bit of acting brilliance those two great actors employed to get maximum effect. The way Ronnie C would take one or two steps to get a tin of peas, give a look, then move back to Ronnie B, about to say something but not doing so, before getting the tin of peas. All the while, Ronnie B would just stand there doing very little, contributing so much. They taught me the secret of comedy: play it for real; never find anything funny yourself, let the audience find it funny... timing is everything. Do not speak over the audience applause, but do not leave it too long so there is an uncomfortable silence. Wait for the laugh which, if you have done your job correctly, is coming, then carry on just as you feel it has reached its peak. Timing is the secret of comedy. What gold to learn from two ordinary people offstage, yet comedic geniuses on.

Ronnie B actually wrote that brilliant *Four Candles* sketch himself. He started writing for the show quite early on but never wanted his writing to be accepted because of who he was. He wanted them accepted on merit. So, he wrote under a pseudonym. If you look at most *Two Ronnies* TV programmes, you will see in the rolling credits at the end that one of the script writers is called Gerald Wiley.

The story goes, having submitted the scripts anonymously in the name of Wiley, everyone began to wonder who on earth this great writer was. They recognised the talent behind them, but no one had ever met him. Lots of famous names, such as Spike Milligan, were mentioned, yet no one knew.

After a while, Ronnie B thought with so much speculation, he should come clean. He booked a table at a local Shepherd's Bush restaurant in the name of Gerald Wiley, with Mr. Wiley inviting all those involved in the making of the series to dinner. Both Ronnies were there, producers, directors, script writers etc, all looking round to see who was the odd one out. All, that is, except Ronnie C, as Ronnie B had told him beforehand. They started their meal, and still no Gerald Wiley. They all assumed a no-show on his part, until Ronnie B stood up and announced that, in fact, he was Gerald Wiley.

When we flew back to the UK from Melbourne, I flew with Sam Kelly on Malaysian Airlines in a hard-worked 747. We were late leaving the airport and sat on the plane for ages, before the captain came on the intercom and explained that the cause of the delay was due to a ground support vehicle crashing into the wing tip, and we were unable to take off without having it checked. He did not make it any better when he added, "Fortunately, the wing tip is only a secondary structure, and we should still be able to take off!" I do not know a whole heap about aerodynamics but do know that the wing of an aeroplane is necessary to create lift and that it is curved on top to make the air flow faster underneath which creates that lift. Presumably, that includes the tip! Resolving to tell him of this fact, when later he walked down the aisle doing his best to reassure passengers, he only looked about twelve, so I thought better of it.

Eventually, we did take off, and the plane took an absolute age rolling down the runway. It was shaking from side to side, obviously struggling to get airborne, and both Sam and I thought we were going to run out of runway. I remember him looking at me with that famous look and just saying the one word, "Fuuuuck!" When we staggered, groaning into the air, we all breathed a sigh of relief.

The explanation for that very long take-off: we were a full flight and had an extra engine tucked under a wing going back to Kuala Lumpur for maintenance. I am sure we were either near, or on, the limits of weight. I've certainly never had such a long take-off roll since.

Some people have said that, when talking to an audience, I have a comedic gift and timing, especially when dealing with members of the public who I occasionally invite to the stage. If I do, and I am not saying I do, I learnt from the masters. Anything I say on that stage comes from them. If I have a fiftieth of their ability, I'm doing well! I was very privileged to witness their performances so many times, and when the Australian production reached the end of its run, I am happy to say, I was not finished with them yet!

Prior to leaving the UK, my girlfriend Alison had given me an ultimatum: "If you want to come back to me, we had better make our relationship more permanent!" I knew what that meant and so asked her to marry me. Very happy, though with a slight feeling of foreboding, as two hours after asking her to marry me, I was going to get on a plane to Australia for six months. Experience had taught me parting for so long was never a good portent! So indeed, despite the fact that she came out to visit me during the break between Sydney and Melbourne, when I got back to the UK, she was seeing someone at her TV studio. As I had been seeing one of the girls in the singing group and one or two of the dancers in Australia, there was not too much complaint from me! The reunion between us didn't last, and when Alison and I met after I got back, hoping to pick up where we left off, she was sensible enough to end it.

Back in the UK, I moved back to the Adelphi Theatre and *My Fair Lady*. I was earning decent money by now. My first conducting job at Wolverhampton Panto had earned me the princely sum of £95 per week plus some expenses, good money for a young single lad in the mid-'70s. Now five years later, I was on a salary of £345 per week for eight performances of *My Fair Lady*; even better wages for someone still single and only in their early thirties.

Our production starred Tony Britton as Professor Higgins and Liz Robertson as Eliza Doolittle, plus the highly eccentric Peter Bayliss as Eliza's father who, when he died, had his ashes flushed down a toilet. Also in the production was another actor from *The Navy Lark*, Richard Caldicot as Colonel Pickering. Completing the principals were Peter Land as Freddie Eynsford-Hill and Dame Anna Neagle as Mrs. Higgins. Dame Anna was a lovely, dainty actress and, coincidently, one of the artists booked by my grandfather at the New Opera House Blackpool on Sunday, 5 October 1941. I did talk to her about him, and she remembered him well and with affection. Sadly, he had died ten years previously so was unable to reunite them.

My Fair Lady was responsible for a number of marriages, most notably that of the lyricist Alan Jay Lerner to the leading lady Liz Robertson when she became his eighth wife! The marriage survived until his death parted them. The show was directed at the Adelphi by Robin Midgely, then taken over by Alan when we toured to the Royal Alexandra Theatre in Toronto.

Alan Jay Lerner is a legend in the world of musicals both on Broadway and in film. With his partner and friend Fritz Loewe, who Alan told me spent most of his later years in a psychiatric hospital they had written the music, book and lyrics for musicals such as *Brigadoon*, *Gigi*, *Paint Your Wagon*, *Camelot* and many more. For heaven's sake, Alan had written the film *An American in Paris* with music by George Gershwin and starring Gene Kelly,

Leslie Caron and Oscar Levant. I was a huge fan, and he became a friend and guru to a young West End conductor.

He had by now fallen in love with our leading lady, and we would often go out in a foursome for an evening meal after the show or dine at their flat at the back of Harrods in Knightsbridge. He was a wonderful human being and many an evening was enlivened by his company, listening to his fantastic stories of the scurrilous times in the golden age of Hollywood and Broadway. I just wish I could remember them, but as the evenings also contained a fair amount of alcohol, sadly I can't... except for one as it was so shocking!

Alan claimed that the orchestrations the young André Previn did for the film *My Fair Lady* were so awful that the whole lot had to be junked and another orchestrator engaged to do the film. However, the deal was that Previn would still get the credit. If true, it would not be the only deception of that film, as the public were not informed that Marni Nixon was the singing voice of Audrey Hepburn!

Alan died in 1986, and therefore it was all too brief a friendship. I was incredibly honoured to be asked by his widow to play the organ at his memorial service in St. Paul's Covent Garden, the church where, under the colonnades at the back, Eliza Doolittle had her first encounter with Professor Henry Higgins.

As the congregation piled out at the end of Alan's service, Liz and I chose that, fittingly, they should walk out to the overture from *My Fair Lady*. I knew it would sound slightly strange played on the organ but had not reckoned with the tracker action of the instrument. To make an organ sound good and loud, you couple keyboards together, which increase the sound by transferring that sound from one set of pipes and adding it to another. Normally this is done by an electro-pneumatic system. At St. Paul's, they still had the old-fashioned system of a tracker action. This does indeed couple one keyboard, or manual as organists call them, to another, but does so mechanically. By pressing a note on one keyboard, it also forces down the note on the coupled keyboard, and at St. Paul's, there were three! Having decided to make it good, loud and joyous, they were all coupled together!

About halfway through the first page, I realised my error. A tremendous amount of effort was required to press down three notes simultaneously, and the opening to the overture consists of fast quavers. As the overture progressed, my fingers tired quickly. I rapidly gave up all attempts to use the pedals, saving what flagging strength I had for my fingers. By about midway through, the pace started slowing, then the wrong notes appeared.

By the end, the piece was almost unrecognisable. Fortunately, most of the mourners had left, but in case Liz or anyone else was still lurking, I took a long time to switch the instrument off, get my breath back and slowly make my way down out of the organ loft. However, it was not long enough and I was horrified to see the widow Liz Robertson at the church door, waiting for me. Deciding there was no other option but to confess and apologise before there was a chance for her to say anything, I went up to her and said, "I'm so sorry, Liz."

She looked at me and, without missing a beat, replied, "I know, he was a wonderful man!" What a lady! No mention of the unrecognisable music emanating from the organ loft.

The show was also responsible for the marriage of the incredible choreographer Gillian Lynne to Peter Land, our juvenile lead. They were to remain married until her death on 1 July 2018 at the age of ninety-two and, with her passing, we lost one of the great creative minds of *Phantom of the Opera*. She and I had our moments; what conductor and choreographer hasn't? She would choreograph fifteen steps to the beat and then complain the music was too fast for her dancers to dance. I am a huge admirer of her work, which included *My Fair Lady*, *Cats*, *Phantom* and numerous ballets for well-known ballet companies. What staggers me is that she had a raging affair with Errol Flynn whilst they were filming *The Master of Ballentrae* together. She always said that Flynn was a very well-made man, and I knew she was not just referring to his looks!

I have never known anyone with such energy. Even at the age of ninety-one, she was coming to *Phantom of the Opera* and taking a class onstage followed by a day of rehearsing.

Mark you, we were always nervous when she did come in; she had this habit of falling into orchestra pits. She became so engrossed in what she was doing, she forgot she was on a stage and not a rehearsal room, invariably stepping backwards into thin air.

She fell off stages at the London Palladium, one on Broadway and, finally, Her Majesty's Theatre. I watched the final moments of the last one unfolding. As my attention was momentarily distracted elsewhere, I turned just in time to see this blonde hair descending into the pit! I was the second person to reach her behind Bjorn Dobbelaere, our music director, which was better than our resident director who immediately fled in the opposite direction and out of the building! But then, a whole series could be written about Geoff Ferris, a man adored by everybody and who had a hilarious story for every occasion. Gillie was by now in her late eighties, and having had hip replacement surgery, there she was after her fall from the stage, lying ominously silent amongst the music stands and chairs.

We summoned an ambulance, though all she could say was she didn't want an ambulance, just her hip doctor. Amazingly, she made a full recovery, possibly so she could do it again somewhere else! At Her Majesty's, whenever she came in, we placed someone between her and the front of the stage whose sole job it was to keep her from falling into the pit. She did get awfully impatient with whoever it was, but we felt happier! Gillie was one of those people who had a force, and if she wasn't working on a stage somewhere, you had to feel sorry for Peter, her husband! All she wanted, apart from Peter, was a stage.

My Fair Lady was a huge commercial success for Cameron, famously produced with Arts Council backing, which received criticism from some quarters at the time as they were funding a commercial organisation, not what the critics claimed they were there to do. However, the Arts Council must have earned back their original investment several times over, enabling them to finance ever more worthwhile productions. Still, the concept of gambling by the Arts Council on a commercial production was not universally approved.

At the Albery Theatre with the show Oliver! meanwhile, there was some concern with my replacement, a man by the name of Dick Leonard. The cast were not happy with what appeared to be his indifference and lack of energy. Cameron told me to go and conduct the matinee performance and show him how it should be done; embarrassing all round, especially as he had a reputation as an excellent music director. What was unknown to us at the time, as he had not told us, was that he had cancer and he was sadly to die a short time later. I went in and conducted the afternoon show of Oliver!, heading off afterwards to conduct the evening performance of My Fair Lady, surely one of the few people to conduct two different major West End shows in one day.

Never will I forget the awful wailing set up by Dick's children at his funeral a few weeks later. One of the saddest and most terrible sounds I have ever heard.

I hugely enjoyed conducting My Fair Lady despite not having much to do. It is what is called a 'book' show rather than a sung-through show such as Phantom. That means there is dialogue, followed by a song, and it's the dialogue that generally moves the plot, and therefore the show, along. Plenty of breaks for us musicians, and while some would leave the pit to drink in the pub or sit and play cards in the band-room, I never left the pit. That was far too dangerous. Suppose someone had a memory lapse and skipped a few pages of dialogue. It has been known to happen! If they did, then I would be able to start the next song with the remaining musicians!

The orchestra was a very reasonable size for the West End, and we made a good show of the music, though I'm not sure at one performance an audience member thought I personally was up to the job.

At the end, we were playing the play-out, which is an up-tempo bit of music reprising all the best tunes from the show, during which the audience could walk out of the theatre with the show tunes ringing in their ears. Some, though, would stay and gather round the pit rail to watch and listen. On one memorable occasion, a gentleman remained. He stood in the auditorium just to my left, staring at me intently. We came to a flourishing end and stood to take our bow from the audience members who had remained. As the musicians packed up their instruments and I was still on the podium talking to anyone who wanted to say hello, this foreign gentleman came up to me and said in a thick accent, "Vuuunderful show, vuuunderful music. Tell me, 'ow many musicians are zer in ze pit?"

I beamed with pleasure and said, "Twenty-three," before swelling even more with pride and adding, "twenty-four if you include me."

He looked me straight in the eye and, very deliberately, said, "Ah, twenty-three!"

Scene 6: My Wife Enters My Life; Explanation of the Title

When *Fair Lady* closed at the Adelphi, we did a UK tour, and this was where I met my wife.

Actually, I had seen her while still doing *My Fair Lady* at the Adelphi. I saw this beautiful vision in the Peacock pub (now a restaurant) in Maiden Lane which was in-between the stage doors of the Adelphi and Vaudeville theatres and opposite Rules restaurant. Discovering she was at the Vaudeville appearing in Bill Kenwright's production of *Joseph and the Amazing Technicolor Dreamcoat*, I thought she was wonderful. Being shy and persistently fearful of female rejection, I could not summon up the courage to ask her out. This shyness is probably another of the downsides to having spent my youth at all-male boarding schools! In the end, our company manager, a man by the name of Roger Bruce, volunteered to take a note on my behalf to the company manager of *Joseph*, asking her out. She rejected the note (quite rightly), and both shows closed shortly afterwards.

Fast forward a few months, and we were holding auditions for the *My Fair Lady* tour, when this ravishing woman who had rejected my note, walked into the audition room and into my life. In the end, it was a straight choice between the singing talents of this beautiful young lady, who had something indefinable, or another, who to me appeared very ordinary. In the end, I persuaded everyone else that this talented actress Jan Revere should get the job, not that they needed much persuading.

The 1981 UK tour was a happy one, though there were tensions between Tony Britton and the subsequent actresses who played Eliza Doolittle. He adored Liz, and no one ever quite measured up to her. I am afraid he sometimes detested her successors so much, he would not even look at them in their scenes which, to be fair, for most of the show was in character!

We played Manchester during Christmas 1981, which was one of the worst for weather on record. By then, my mode of transport was a Triumph TR7, which was definitely not built for the snow or ice, nor, come to think of it, the road. It was a Triumph so, being British Leyland in the '70s, was probably not built at all, merely banged together with nails and a bit of glue. Mine was also probably stuck together on a Friday afternoon!

A trip up to Manchester from my flat, in Fulham, took eight hours in the snow instead of the usual four. We, along with everyone else, were skidding about all over the place.

Christmas Day was spent in front of the fire in our digs, watching television, eating a Christmas dinner and madly feeding coins into the insatiable electric meter. We were very happy and very much in love.

Again, the tour was successful, so in 1982, the production went overseas, this time to Canada and the Royal Alexandra Theatre in Toronto.

In my downtime over there, I took flying lessons from Toronto Island Airport and shall never forget one glorious day buzzing the CN Tower and doing some cloud-based exercises, unfortunately making Jan, who had elected to come up with me, sick in the back of the Cessna 172! I still have my logbook which has the sum total of 4.4 hours of flying. For a long time, I would proudly show this private flying off to my children. Even when my eldest son began in the Air Cadets, I would boast of the hours I had done. Now, with our eldest son in the RAF and many hours both on rotor and fixed wing, I can no longer bring it out with a flourish and declare myself a pilot!

You will be familiar by now with my fondness for all things mechanical that transport people: hovercraft, boats, trains have all entered my conscious, and probably subconscious, mind and stayed there. To that list must be added aeroplanes.

My flying lessons in Canada were a dream come true, following my father and his father, my mother's father and various uncles and great-uncles. Although stopping when I came back to the UK as work, money and family precluded the time and expense of continuing, I can often be found at air shows, luxuriating in the noise of a jet engine or two. I went to Farnborough in 1974 when the Blackbird SR.71 made an appearance. That aircraft is so fast, with an admitted top speed of Mach 3.3 and maybe more, that the story I heard from a pilot was, when it came over from the States to Farnborough for that air show appearance, it was going so fast it overshot England and had to turn round over the North Sea!

I said earlier I had not finished with Messrs Barker and Corbett, and after Canada and *Fair Lady*, I came back to the UK and another season of a brand-new *Two Ronnies* show. This time to the London Palladium, but not before trying it out for the 1982 Christmas season at what was then called the Gaumont Theatre, now the Mayflower Theatre, in Southampton.

The choreographer was the same one who had done the original *Two Ronnies*, a man by the name of Paddy Stone, who, if not at war with his dancers, was another one at war with himself. He would pull clumps of his hair out and tear at the skin of his face in frustration if what he said was not picked up straight away, or if he thought his dancers were taking too long to grasp his choreography. His rages at himself and his dancers were terrible to behold, yet they adored working for this virtuoso of the dance. He would throw chairs around the rehearsal room and have to take himself outside, as he wasn't ultimately sure of what he was capable. Nor, I confess, were we. His choreography was sublime, and dancers would kill to work with this tortured virtuoso of a man. His routine to *Money Makes the World Go Around* in the first *Two Ronnies* has never been bettered.

You can actually see Paddy dancing with Julie Andrews towards the end of his life in the Blake Edwards film *Victor/Victoria*.

It was at this Southampton theatre that the famous story, which eventually reached the ears (and pages) of *The Daily Telegraph*, occurred, which is the explanation for the title of this book.

There is no centre aisle at the Mayflower Theatre; whoever sits in the middle of the front row is immediately behind the conductor. Nowadays, these are called restricted seats and sold at a discount, but not in 1982. At the end of the overture, there was a fairly complicated routine where I would turn round to the audience, take a bow, turn back, put my headphones on and press the button to start the click-track. This is a means whereby the conductor can play live music to pre-recorded voices, a necessity given Paddy Stone's energetic choreography!

At this performance while conducting, I could sense a man sitting immediately behind me getting more and more agitated. We finished the overture and, as usual, I turned to the audience, took a very deep bow, acknowledging the applause, noting that the agitated man was not joining in. Turning back to the orchestra, I had got the headphones within an inch of my head, when he tapped me on the shoulders from behind and said, "Excuse me, would you mind sitting down?" I made the mistake of engaging him in conversation and began to explain the job of a conductor. Whilst this was not going to take long, it was obviously too long for the stage manager who, by now, was wondering why, at the end of the applause, I had not pressed the button to start the tape so they could open the curtains. Green lights for 'go' on my podium started to flash, and I knew both Ronnies were waiting at the top of the staircase behind the curtains and dancers were holding a pose. In the end, I had to say to the exasperated man that I was sorry, but I was going to have to start the show. To which, his astonishing reply was, "Well, if you won't sit down, would you stop waving your arms about; it's most distracting!" Maybe there have been one or two musicians who have agreed with him since.

In spring 1983, we did a short season at the London Palladium, again sold out. Then, that was it. No more stage shows for the Ronnies. Ronnie B had had enough, and inspiration was running out. Four years later, he retired, and the much-loved team was broken up.

Oliver! was revived by Cameron for a 1983 tour, and I was available to take over as music director in Birmingham on a salary of £400 per week which, considering the equivalent in 2021 would be £1380 per week, was good money for a thirty-one-year-old. All I really remember about this touring production was having Jimmy Edwards playing the part of the beadle.

Now there was a wonderful and unique character! He was larger than life with a moustache and whiskers to match and would occasionally, if he had imbibed a bit too much, and there's no doubting he enjoyed a tipple or three, get his trombone out and start playing it mid-scene, mid-performance. None of us ever knew why. He would give us his version of 'My Way' completely uninvited at any stage of the plot! We would just have to wait until he had come to the end; the audience would clap; and on we would go!

This was fairly prevalent in the old days. I went to see *Charlie Girl* at the Victoria Palace Theatre and, for no apparent reason other than she could, Dora Bryan, in one scene, brought her xylophone onstage and proceeded to play it, all part of her one-woman act! It was in her drinking days. Nevertheless, I must confess, very bizarre!

Birmingham was followed by Manchester, which was followed by the 1983 Christmas season in London, and when it moved to London, it was going to star the original Fagin: the utterly wonderful Ron Moody. This production was to be the last time he recreated the role in the UK. He took it shortly afterwards to Broadway for seventeen performances, before it prematurely closed due to poor audiences.

Ron was a fabulous actor, typecast by this one role. He should have had a great and glittering acting career, but every time you looked at Ron Moody, all the public and producers saw was Fagin.

Every night at the Aldwych Theatre, I would accompany him in 'Reviewing the Situation', and every night I could see him reviewing the situation of his life: if he could live it over again and foresee what he now knew, would he have accepted the role of Fagin when originally offered to him? I have a feeling he would not. He had an enormous chip on his shoulder about the fact that because of *Oliver!*, the Royal Shakespeare Company and the Royal National Theatre had never beaten a path to his door.

He was right – they should have done. Like all national institutions that hold their traditions dear, they would have thought it too populist to engage the great Ron Moody. They couldn't see beyond their own narrow perceptions and realise he was a very good actor. To them, he was Fagin: popular, successful and commercial!

There is no doubt he would sometimes go through the motions of a performance at the Aldwych, perhaps more often than not. But there were those occasions when he took off; then we all flew with him.

After all this West End work, appearing at one of the world's greatest theatres, the London Palladium, and musically directing some wonderful shows, where else could I go but sideways? To avoid that, I needed a change.

Scene 7: Change of Scene

I decided to step down from accepting any further West End work and see what would happen.

Due mainly to financial reasons, there were a couple of exceptions. The first being, in the summer of 1984, I accepted the offer of musically directing the George and Ira Gershwin musical *Oh Kay!* down at the Chichester Festival Theatre. It was very adjacent to where my parents lived in Warsash on the river Hamble, so I could get cheap digs, though in the event I mainly commuted from Fulham. Plus, the book was by P.G. Wodehouse and Guy Bolton.

Wodehouse is my favourite author of all time, and I can reread him time and time again. If ever I was invited onto the radio programme *Desert Island Discs* – and having done the celebration concert *Desert Island Discs at the Symphony* in 2014 with one of the programme's interviewers Kirsty Young presenting, perhaps I should – the book I would definitely take with me to the island would be an anthology of Jeeves and Wooster. Since first reading him at Marlborough in the '60s, I can still pick up any one of his books and reread him all over again. I also quote him at various times. My favourite is, having had my car serviced at a garage, asking the service manager, "Are all the sprockets now running true with the differential gears?" No one has ever recognised the quote from Bertie to Jeeves as he's about to get on a bicycle. I'm always greeted by a very puzzled expression.

Oh Kay! starred actors mainly from the subsidised theatre and was directed by Ian Judge. Coming from RSC and National Theatre background, Ian and his team had a very odd outlook on casting musicals, as indeed do most people in that world. I was not involved with casting at all which, considering it was a musical, I thought at the time strange. On getting to the first rehearsal, it was apparent why. It appeared music was secondary to the acting, and it did not matter if one or two of the actors could not sing that well. It was the acting performance that mattered. I banged my head against a brick wall thinking, as I still do, that if they couldn't sing, then the overall performance was compromised!

Ned Sherrin was the instigator/producer of the musical, and he wasn't much help either. The musical was old and tired, and our updated treatment did not really work. Most people who came to see *Oh Kay!* thought the best thing about the show was the interval, when the orchestra pianist Gareth Valentine, now a very popular and much-used music director in his own right, came onstage and improvised around tunes by George Gershwin. He was brilliant at this and quite rightly became a huge interval hit in his white tie, white tails and white piano, centre stage.

This show, more than any other, persuaded me that I was not cut out for musical theatre. If they wanted to cast people in singing roles who were not singers but actors who could sing a bit, then I was not going to conduct it.

Chichester Festival Theatre did give me a chance to play some tennis, finding a worthy opponent in the shape of Geoffrey Hutchins, a very good actor and singer of the Royal Shakespeare Company, later going on to become a household name in the ITV series *Benidorm*. We would regularly spar across a net and, just as regularly, he would beat me.

The other exception was the London Palladium pantomime of 1985. The pay was good, and I was not going to be music director. I would just guest conduct *Cinderella* every now and then, and a fascinating experience it would prove to be. It had some of the top TV personalities of the time with Des O'Connor as the rather aging Buttons and Paul Nicholas as Prince Charming, with the double acts Hope and Keen as the Broker's Men and Lambert and Ross the ugly sisters. Sarah Payne was the beautiful Cinderella. Space was also found for John Junkin as Baron Hardup and Dame Anna Neagle as the good fairy.

I remember nothing of the music, the prime interest being the onstage romance between the fifty-three-year-old Des O'Connor and a new, young actress called Sarah Payne. It was dealt with very decorously, with a slight send-up of the age difference. Glamorous, popular and fun.

I also conducted for the ballet. Now that was getting closer! An orchestra of more than twenty-five with proper classical music. I had first conducted the art form in 1983 with Festival Ballet (now English National Ballet) and their Christmas season of Tchaikovsky's *The Nutcracker* at the Royal Festival Hall. It was more of an audition as there was a ballet conductor vacancy on their staff. I did not get the job, with one of the rehearsal pianists telling me, probably with her tongue firmly in her cheek, that I was far too good for the ballet.

In September 1984, I conducted Sadler's Wells Royal Ballet (now Birmingham Royal Ballet) in a tent on Jesus Green in Cambridge. I had a full symphony orchestra and the glorious scores of *Sleeping Beauty* and *Swan Lake* but the ignominy of having to follow a leg!

For instance, the white swan solo in *Swan Lake* is a beautiful piece of music. If the dancer can hop gracefully and slowly across the stage (and I am sure there's a more technical word for what she does), then she wants the music to reflect the pace she is hopping. This sometimes meant taking the music agonisingly slowly, and Tchaikovsky never wrote his music to go that slowly. I found it unacceptable. I have actually attended a live performance of it going so slowly, that the famous run-ups in the violin solo have to be repeated for another octave higher up the violin string, otherwise they run out of time. That's crazy! If Tchaikovsky wanted that, he would have written it. Finding the constraints far too restricting, I knew I was not going to last long in the ballet world!

At Her Majesty's Theatre, we did a ballet gala and had one of the greatest ballerinas onstage, Sylvie Guillem. How she got that leg up to where she did and held it there was a complete mystery to me and I suspect others as well! Be in no doubt, she was one of the greatest female dancers of all time. However, when we performed the Bach *Violin Concerto* for her to dance, we had to take the slow movement very slowly. It still wasn't slow enough as, with the orchestra upstage and behind her, when she came past me, she hissed, "Slower, maestro, slower!"

So, with some sadness, I left that as well because, let's face it, the music written for the ballet world is glorious, and when the two worlds meet, it is an incredible experience. Music and dance must be equal partners, not one sacrificed at the cost of the other; both art forms are sublime and, once again, must not be an example of one serving the other. Like musical theatre, music should never be subservient; equal partners yes, subservient, never!

Conducting for the ballet did have one major influence on my life. Some of the more observant amongst you will have noticed a disparity in names: my father's side of the family Howard-Williams, my mother's Inglis and my name. The clue lies in the opening sentence of Act 1, Scene 1: I was born Anthony Inglis Howard-Williams.

For the early part of my life, I conducted as Anthony Howard-Williams. However, at the Royal Ballet, there was another conductor, unbelievably called Howard (given name) and Williams (surname), without the hyphen. He was at Covent Garden; I was on tour. He was, and is, the more senior to me by about ten years, and confusion was rife. Howard-Williams and Howard Williams... far too confusing. I decided to drop my surname and just conduct as my two given names, and Anthony Inglis is how I am now professionally known.

Having struggled with the discipline and inequality of the ballet world and actors who were not necessarily singers and deciding neither was for me, I headed, I hoped permanently, for the exit of the pit door and an uncertain future.

That is, until an irresistible show arrived which would shape my life and career forever.

Walking out of Kingston Parish Church on 9 September 1994 under a parade of batons held by Mike Reed, Kevin Amos, Vaughan Meakins and Jan's brother Mark Wernham

With my beautiful wife. One of us has aged a lot better than the other!

At the wheel on the bridge of RMS
Queen Mary 2, giving it a bit of the old
'left hand down a bit', whilst Captain
Hashmi looks on

by permission, Cunard

Not 'Three Little Maids from School
Are We' from The Mikado, *but about
to perform the Malcolm Arnold March
from St. Trinian's at Symphony Hall
Birmingham, with Lincoln Parkhouse
(centre) and Malcolm Hicks (right)*

*The picture my father would have been most proud of:
with Dame Vera Lynn CH DBE*

IN THE COCKPITS OF...

Top: Rolls-Royce Spitfire PS853 at Biggin Hill
Middle: Typhoon at RAF Coningsby
Bottom: The Thames Clipper,
Hurricane

*Apache at AAC
Middle Wallop*

*Chinook at RAF
Odiham*

*PA28. Author
in temporary
command with
son*

EARLY PUBLICITY PHOTOGRAPHS...

John Gilbride

*Nigel Shipway Timpanist NSO,
demonstrating his mastery
of the cymbals*

Fritz Curzon

Katherine Jenkins and author demonstrating their dancing technique on the stage of the Royal Albert Hall

LCO
Mayflower
Theatre

Paul Sanders

NSO Rose
Theatre,
Kingston

By permission

Conducting
LCO Royal
Albert Hall

Paul Sanders

*Conducting LCO
Barbican Hall*

By permission

*NSO with author
on bow of Queen
Mary 2 as she
crosses the Atlantic
at twenty-five
knots*

Cunard

*Sunset Parade.
Combining my
two favourite
passions: music
(NSO) and flying
(RAF Marham)*

*Christopher
Howard-Williams*

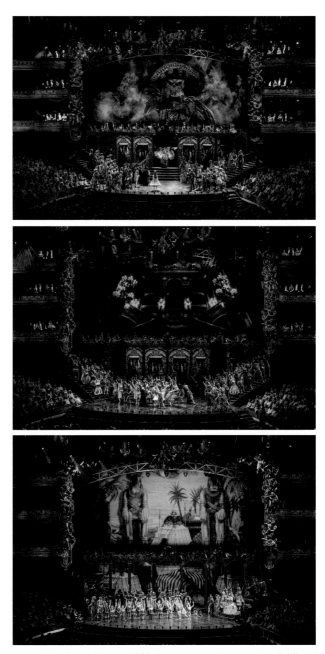

Phantom of the Opera Twenty-Fifth Anniversary Concert, Royal Albert Hall
Jonathan Driscoll

CHILDREN

Eleanor on a film set

West Side Story

Dominic flying us from RAF Scampton to Duxford.
Now, where's that sugar factory?

Alexander leading the cellos of the Thames Youth Orchestra in their Barbican performance of Mahler No.2

Act 5

Scene 1: *Phantom of the Opera*

I will admit that, for a while, work was slow and sporadic. Therefore, when a show opened that had not had an opening like it since *West Side Story*, I was intrigued by a suggestion. In December 1986, I was invited to watch *Phantom of the Opera* at Her Majesty's Theatre, which had opened some three months previously on 9 September 1986 and was asked if I wanted to guest conduct it.

The story of the show, which was directed by the legendary Harold Prince who had produced *West Side Story* at the same theatre on 12 December 1958, is well known and does not need retelling here. Suffice to say the enormous buzz around it was the stuff of legends, and the producers Cameron Mackintosh Ltd and the Really Useful Group (RUG) could not have asked for better publicity: hiatus hernia from the star; delayed opening night; visits by royalty; the wife of the composer with a lead role; ticket touts fighting outside the theatre for impossible-to-get tickets, all contributing to the hype.

During the rehearsals, the music director was substituted at the last minute by, and I bet you can't guess who, or by now you probably can, Mike Reed, who conducted the opening night. He had worked for Cameron Mackintosh even before I had, as music director of Tony Hatch and Jackie Trent's musical *The Card* and knew the star of the show Michael Crawford well as the two of them had done *Barnum* together for Harold Fielding. Crawford had recommended Mike, and he in turn had recommended me when they decided they needed a guest conductor; yet another reason to be grateful to this man I have now known for five decades.

Sitting in the stalls on the left side of the auditorium of Her Majesty's Theatre at the beginning of 1987, I can still remember falling in love with the drama of the piece, thinking then, as I do now, the final twenty minutes is perfection. What goes before is wonderful, but those final twenty minutes are completely driven by the conductor. There are the occasional pauses. To me, even those pauses contain music; the music of our thoughts within that silence and what that is saying to each and every one of us. If conductors pace it wrong, get the pauses wrong, hold some notes too long, it's ruined.

Watching the show that December evening and immediately adoring it, I became the guest conductor, agreeing to conduct the production once or twice every ten days or so.

I had a week in which to learn the show and conduct my first performance (January 1987) without the benefit of any rehearsals, or even a rehearsal with the company. My opening night, even if I say so myself, was a triumph, except for one passage!

In the Il Muto scene halfway through Act 1, there is a recitativo sung by Carlotta and Piangi, and at one point on my first night, I gave the harpsichord player an indication to play a first inversion chord a bar too early. It wasn't a disaster, and we soon sorted it. I gather Michael Crawford, watching the monitor in the wings, playfully raised an imaginary gun to his shoulder, aiming at me on the screen! He was right of course, a silly and unimaginative mistake. I never conducted that scene afterwards without thinking of my first performance all those years ago.

I had a marvellous time as guest conductor. No responsibilities, except getting it right and the kudos of conducting the hottest ticket in town. However, after nine months, Mike wanted to leave. He and I had such a great relationship and understanding with this brilliant musical that I did not want anyone else becoming my boss. Accordingly, in June 1987, I agreed to step up and become the music director of the smash hit West End show *Phantom of the Opera*.

Princess Diana was a regular visitor to Her Majesty's, as were all the Hollywood A-listers. I was once conducting a performance when the Duchess of Kent was a visitor and started the National Anthem before she had got to her seat. Giving the down beat for the drum roll, she had to stand still in a frightfully awkward place: the narrow gap between a person and the dress circle front rail. I hope the person was someone she knew well!

There was an incident early on in my tenure as music director of the show that taught me a valuable lesson. I needed a haircut and, deciding I could now afford somewhere fancy, I went round the corner from Her Majesty's to The Ritz and the salon of a well-known hairdresser to the stars who had a branch within the hotel. I sat there and had my golden locks trimmed. At the end, I was presented with the bill which amounted to £90 – in 1987!

I had timed the cut with the matinee so walked the five hundred yards from the hotel in a bit of a daze, straight into the pit at HM's. The musicians in the orchestra saw the look on my face and asked what the matter was. I replied, "I have just paid £90 for a haircut!"

One of the original grizzled old boys looked at me and, mishearing, said, "£19? That's an awful lot of money for a haircut!"

"No, not nine*teen*… nine*ty*!"

We couldn't start the show for five minutes whilst the members of *The Phantom of the Opera* orchestra recovered from laughing.

Moral? Always ask before receiving, and never go somewhere too posh for a service not associated with the location!

I also nearly died conducting the show. At the end of Act 1,

I don't think I am spoiling anything for anyone when I say the chandelier drops from the ceiling of Her Majesty's Theatre's auditorium, crashing onto the stage. It is an iconic moment and one that, over the years, as technology improves, has gradually sped up. I used to judge the moment to synchronise the final four notes to end the act with the stage flash and lighting cues by crouching down, so it was easier to look up. When I saw the chandelier immediately above my head, I would give the beat to indicate the final crash.

Right at the beginning of the run, something went wrong and one of the guide wires got caught round the bottom of the chandelier, tipping its axis, so it came down at an angle. This meant the bottom of the one-tonne stage prop was now lower than normal, and as it swung onto the stage, it hit the front, taking a great chunk out. If I'd been standing up as normal, it would have hit me and I would not be here now. Fabulous publicity for the producers: 'Phantom Phights Back!'. Not so fabulous for me!

For ever after, there was an assistant stage manager standing in the prompt side upper box over the stage, with an emergency stop button that was subsequently installed to prevent a reoccurrence! Mark you, it did not stop the fact that at every show I conducted afterwards, I still made absolutely certain to crouch down at the end of Act 1.

There was another occasion when we set fire to a conductor. As an experiment one year, in assistant music directors, I appointed two: one was David Firmin, at the time music director for Victoria Wood, and the other John Owen Edwards, both hugely experienced musical directors.

John was a tall chap and had been music director of D'Oyly Carte at the end of its existence. At the very beginning of *Phantom*, just after the opening dialogue, the chandelier – positioned about eight feet away on the stage immediately in front of the conductor – is revealed from beneath a muslin cover with light, smoke and pyros emanating from within, to the music of the famous overture. On this evening, one of the pyro sparks went further than it should and landed in John's hair.

I was standing in the corner, observing curtain up on the monitor, and the first we noticed anything amiss was when we saw wisps of smoke emanating from his head. John, who was completely unaware, carried on conducting with smoke, which by now had turned to flickers of flame, rising from his head. Just as I was thinking of going down there myself with a fire extinguisher, a viola player looked up (which in itself was a miracle!), saw what was happening, patted his head and put it out.

I personally believe *Phantom of the Opera* is one of the greatest pieces of music written for the theatre in the last fifty years. That includes opera, light opera, musical theatre, everything. I know there are a lot of serious people in high artistic organisations who will scoff at me, probably one reason they do not take me seriously! I honestly believe that, and it was a huge privilege to be involved with *Phantom* for a little over thirty-three years. Andrew has often described how it is the one piece of his that came together almost instantly and needed little altering from the first preview to the opening night. If a piece is right, it's right from the beginning, and *Phantom* certainly was.

Take 'Past the Point' which makes up the bulk of the final twenty minutes of the show and, for me, the most fantastic music of the show. It's sung three times, first as a solo by the Phantom, followed by a solo from Christine, ending as a trio when the three leads of the show sing it together. All three sections must be paced exactly right and, most importantly, different, so subliminally it reinforces the story onstage.

The first section is Phantom's solo and is contained, dangerous. With a cloak over his head, we do not know who he is, so the pace is very slightly under tempo: dangerous, measured, it doesn't feel quite right. Christine's version is the second and is innocent as she believes she is singing not to the Phantom but to the Italian tenor Piangi. In her innocence, it is absolutely normal; it feels the correct tempo for that piece of music, brilliantly supported by the Verdi ostinato figuration from the orchestra underneath. The third version, the trio, is all three passionately singing of their love and anger for each other: Raoul for Christine (love), Phantom for Christine (love), Christine for Phantom (hate), Raoul for Phantom (hate) and Phantom for Raoul (hate). This last verse is therefore passionate, violent and the fastest of the three. Surely this section brilliantly proves that if you drew a circle with love and hate side by side at the top of the circle, the two emotions can slide independently round the circle, overlap and tip into each other. It depends on how much the two sides of that circle overlap, and where on the circle they meet, as to the relationship and how much one either loves or hates.

At the end of the trio, Christine sinks exhaustedly to her knees and appeals to the Phantom's human side. The Phantom tells Christine to choose, either himself or Raoul caught upstage in the hangman's noose. There is then that silence! To me, that silence is hugely significant as we see Christine struggling to decide what she is going to do; which man should she choose? I used to love holding that silence for as long as I thought the audience could sustain it, before starting the music. Christine would slowly rise to her feet, singing 'Pitiful Creature of Darkness', and, in her humanity, and the first act of love ever shown to the Phantom, she would kiss him on his grossly extended lips, followed by his disfigured head. He repays this act of kindness by setting free both Christine and Raoul to a future life together, thereby demonstrating his own humanity.

Unless the conductor understands all that, and the subtle but oh-so-important little details, including the final moment when Christine hands back the ring the Phantom has given her and he makes a final justification of all that he has done – "Christine, I love you," – it will not make people weep, as they will not have understood the previous two and a half hours. It's all in the detail.

I had a wonderful eighteen months in charge of the hottest ticket in town. But, those eighteen months, with the previous six as guest conductor, made two years, and I hit that barrier. Despite earning good money, making many friends and having a wonderful time, I knew it was time to leave.

I was not conducting very well, and the smallest things were becoming really big things for me. I could not work out how to solve passages going wrong in the music. Nothing major and nothing an audience would notice, but I did! So, perhaps more pertinently, did the musicians. On a personal level, some of my relationships with actresses and dancers had not worked out, and there was a terrible time when I was having affairs with two of the leading ladies at the same time, yet still watching them onstage every night. So, I asked the management to leave.

They were very understanding and said that was fine, however, they were going to create a new position for me: music supervisor. Through Sue James my agent, we agreed that I would be responsible for the music side of the production, though they could not expect me to appear at the drop of a phone call! By now, there was a career outside of Her Majesty's Theatre and, if abroad conducting a concert, or even on holiday, they could not demand I return.

I was also not going to be a supervisor that never conducted their show. I was at heart a conductor and adored conducting the show. Therefore, I would go in and occasionally conduct, maybe once or twice a year. As other people have said, this rare show I conducted to the end of my tenure would always end up being a very special evening, not just for me but also for the cast and orchestra.

At the end of 1988, we agreed terms, and I was appointed music supervisor and remained for fourteen glorious years.

Scene 2: Audition Advice

Hal Prince was the revered Broadway and film director/producer who had directed *Phantom* in London, subsequently Broadway, followed by territories all over the rest of the world. The show was such a success that he had various assistants who would go in advance and do the main body of casting and rehearsing before he came in and put his magic on the production.

Ruth Mitchel was one of his long-time assistants and had a very strong personality. She also liked her small glasses of red wine. As a result, lunches would sometimes overrun and nearly always involve red wine. One audition afternoon, after an excellent lunch, Ruthie and I were sitting next to each other at about 3pm in the auditorium of a Shaftesbury Avenue theatre discussing the various auditionees we had seen, when, in mid-conversation between the two of us, and whilst I was uttering my pearls of wisdom to her in reply of hers to me, her head, still facing me, gently fell forwards and she fell fast asleep. Her pen, with which she was writing down my wise words, gradually drew a crooked line down the page as she did so. The rest of the team were in hysterics and have forever reminded me how boring I can be, pointing to this episode as proof!

Auditioning is a necessary by-product of running a West End show and is the way we cast new people into the production. It can be a nerve-wracking experience for the auditionee, however much an attempt is made by the producers to make it informal.

Once a year, we had a refresh of the show, recasting those who wanted to leave and those we wanted to leave. We would let a cast member go for a number of reasons. Maybe they had become too complacent and were no longer performing at their best; perhaps they needed to go and find other work so their experience and acting ability would broaden; sometimes their voices had changed, and the vocal range was no longer suitable for the role. It goes back to what I was saying earlier.

Despite their boredom, people can elect to stay in a (re)creative position because it's paying the mortgage or rent. Occasionally, they needed a gentle push to go out there and find themselves. If talented, they would get something else and grow. Sometimes, those performers would return with renewed vigour and energy and maybe in a different role. Many of our main Phantoms, Christines and Raouls have come from within the production, either having left and grown or grown from within. We also had those in the production who were as good on day one as they were at the end.

At this point, special mention must be made of Philip Griffiths who is now in *The Guinness Book of Records* as the longest-serving cast member in the same West End production. By the time the show closed due to the pandemic on Monday, 16 March 2020, he had been there seven months shy of thirty years! However, he was not the most long-lived employee of the production! At the end, I had arrived in January 1987 and Lynne Jezzard, who became the resident choreographer, had been at the first day of rehearsals in July 1986. We also had six musicians in the orchestra who were in the pit at Her Majesty's Theatre on the opening night and remained to the end. They were: Mike Stanley (keys 1), Gordon Buchan (violin), Francis Walker (violin), Keith Marshall (oboe), Dave Rose (double bass) and Bob Norris (second cello). Bob was famous for hardly ever taking a show off. In over twelve thousand performances of the show, it is estimated that Bob only ever missed about fifty performances in total, maybe less. If you've seen *Phantom* in London, Bob was almost certainly playing cello in the performance you watched.

We would start auditioning late March or early April, and the auditionees would be asked to bring a couple of contrasting pieces, a ballad and an up-tempo number. Quite a lot would bring popular opera, thinking that would be what we wanted. Puccini was common, especially with Christines and Piangis (sopranos and tenors), as was Gilbert and Sullivan and the modern West

End repertoire. We didn't care as long as they could show us what they had.

Only occasionally would we get high opera. On one occasion, someone brought along an aria from Tchaikovsky's *Queen of Spades*, written with six flats and fiendishly difficult, expecting our accompanist to be able to sight-read it. Fortunately, that day we had a man by the name of Paul Bateman who could. Not only had he been music director of the show, but he was also a phenomenal pianist. I did take the lady aside afterwards and say she was lucky with Paul, advising her to bring her own accompanist if she was going to take that aria to a West End rather than opera audition again.

Then there was the occasion we had been offered some choices of music, one of which included some Wagner. When the options were given by the auditionee, our pianist Leigh Thompson, who is one of the best all-round audition pianists I know, but would be the first to admit he was more West End rep than high opera, drew his finger across his throat at the name of Wagner with a pleading sign for me not to choose that; the aria was obviously difficult. I'm afraid that, as we already knew the person singing was through the first part of the audition process and I love Wagner, I turned towards Leigh and, with an evil grin, chose the Wagner. It was impossible to sight-read, though he made a very gallant effort and, despite the interesting music from the piano, the singer excelled themselves and was through. It does just show, if you choose a difficult piece, bring your own pianist.

One of the best pieces of advice I give to any aspiring performer is, when going to an audition and you cannot afford to take your own pianist, bring a well-written-out, logical piece of music in the right key. We all hate music that says: at this sign you repeat back to here, but the second time, you cut from here to here, then take the coda which is bar 134 and repeat round the phrase until I give a sign and oh, by the way, it's all in the wrong key and should be up a third!

The auditionee will not be heard to their best advantage! Either the pianist will struggle, which will put off the singer, or we will look at the pianist and admire their skills more than the auditionee!

Having passed the first round of auditions, the successful candidate would be invited back for another audition, and this time they would be sent some excerpts from the show to see what they could do with it. They would then be given some coaching through the part. Anyone through that round is then invited back for the final round when, with Andrew and Cameron, we saw all the principals together, maybe bringing people in from the current cast to sing with them.

Rehearsals for the new cast started around the end of July. The existing company was brought in towards the end of August, and we dress rehearsed with piano, then with orchestra, before the opening night which was normally the second Monday in September.

In the early days of *Phantom*, you could only work in the West End if you had full Equity membership. Equity is the actor's union, and to protect the interests of their members, of which there are always a lot, only those who habitually worked at their trade and had full Equity membership would have the privilege of working in the place everyone wanted to work: London.

To become a full member of Equity, you first had to join the union by becoming a provisional member working outside London. This was easier said than done. To protect the provincial theatre from too many aspiring actors, producers were only allowed to offer a certain number of provisional Equity cards per production. It must be added, in the 1980s, there were plenty of opportunities for performers, as most seaside towns and cities put on a pantomime and summer season. Many repertory theatres around the country were also in existence, all of them having lengthy seasons. Only after forty-two weeks of working with a provisional Equity card did you become a full member, providing you had worked those forty-two weeks within the space of two years! Then you could work in the West End. The theory was, if you had worked a lot in the provincial theatres, you must be good enough to come into London.

There were good and bad points to this. It was quite difficult to obtain work outside London, as the established production companies tended to stick with people they knew and employed the same performers year on year. This of course stifled the new blood and made it difficult for people straight out of drama schools to obtain work. Those that did maybe did a twelve-week panto then a twelve-week summer season. You could then pick up other work here and there which would increase your weekly credit. Do that for two years and you would have full membership. The good point was we only saw experienced performers.

However, *Phantom* was a new genre; a sung-through semi-operatic drama, we did not do front cloth numbers and, after a while, we had seen all the full Equity members who were suitable for our show; we just ran out of people. Just in time, the rule was relaxed and, of course, the parliamentary act of 1990 ending the closed shop in the UK, finally ended the rule of full Equity membership in London completely.

Accordingly, in the early 1990s, we threw the *Phantom* auditions open to everyone and thousands came! For a couple of years, we saw queues snaking around Her Majesty's Theatre as everyone and anyone came and sang to us, believing they had voices good enough to sing in *Phantom of the Opera*. In order to hear them all, and some came vast distances, I'm afraid we would only hear a minute, maybe two, before 99.9% of the time saying, "Next!"

Sometimes, auditions did not go according to plan. Sitting early one morning in the auditorium, stage management alerted us to an incident. They told us there was a lady rather the worse for drink, who they had put in the downstairs stalls bar on a settee to sleep it off. In the afternoon, she arrived onstage, still obviously affected. She stood centre stage swaying, shielding her eyes from the glare of the lights, and I asked her what she wanted to sing. This caused her paroxysms of confusion. She clasped her hands to her forehead and agonisingly said, "Oh, what is the name of the piece? I've forgotten it! Don't tell me; I do know; it's on the tip of my tongue. It's… it's…" then, with great delight, she turned towards us and, with enormous glee, announced, "it's 'Memory'!" It did not bode well, and indeed it didn't.

A piece of guidance I pass to anyone who asks me for the one best piece of advice I can give is never to turn anything down. You never know who, what or where it will lead. This stems back to an incident that happened to me at the Royal College of Music.

I was assistant conductor to Edwin Roxburgh, who was better known as a composer but on this occasion was conducting the first orchestra in Stravinsky's *Rite of Spring*. As well as performing it in the Concert Hall of the college, the orchestra were also going to perform it in The Maltings in Snape near Aldeburgh. The town was famous for being the home of the British composer Benjamin Britten; indeed, he founded the famous Aldeburgh Festival which still continues. I was asked whether I would like to go. My girlfriend at the time wanted to do something else in London that weekend, and I did not really want to sit on a coach for fifteen hours, or however long it took on the roads to Suffolk in those days. So, I said no.

Edwin's car journey was delayed by several hours, and they had no one to conduct the rehearsal! I gather the director of the college, who at the time was Sir David Willcocks, gave the down beat to start the piece, then left the orchestra to their own devices as he did not know it. The orchestra did not get too far through the piece! With Ben Britten still alive and attending the rehearsal, who knows whether my life would have been different and where it would have subsequently taken me?

However, I may not have met my gorgeous wife and had my equally gorgeous children!

Scene 3: Performing Advice

I always saw the job of Music Supervisor at *Phantom* as being in overall charge of the musical side of the show. To help me, there was also a Music Director who oversaw the day to day running of the show, and he had two assistants and a rehearsal pianist. As much as possible, I wanted the audience to see the show as close as it was to the opening night, within the parameters of time, casting and modernisation. I saw my job as quality control and have been known to liken it to McDonald's! You can go into any chain of McDonald's anywhere in the world and have the same thing cooked in the same way. There will be slight regional variations to cater for local tastes. Similarly with *Phantom*. Go to any production around the world and it will basically be the same as it was in London on the opening night all those years ago, but with slight regional variations.

I was someone who was not there on a daily basis, and could come in with fresh eyes and see where tiny fractures were beginning to occur in the production. These could then be put right immediately. There is no doubt that over the course of a number of performances, tiny adjustments would be made by performers. This is quite natural. One night speaking a word rather than singing it (which was the most common mistake) felt right, which would make whoever had uttered it start to speak adjacent words. Over time this would build up until sometimes I would go in and hear more of a play being performed than a musical. On one occasion when I had not been in for a while, Andrew watched the show and berated me with the question "Why aren't they singing the notes I wrote?" A good question, and one to which I had no adequate response.

The same is true with tempos. Tempo is quite naturally a perceived opinion based on one's own tiredness or alertness, and in order to make a piece of music more 'exciting', it is possible to create excitement by adding a very small increase in tempo. This has two effects: one it makes the performer more alert as something different is happening, and two, that alertness by a sort of osmosis, communicates itself to the audience. Of course, the performer wants to maintain that connectedness between themselves and audience the next night, so the music stays the same. Over time, this can see further incremental increases in tempo as the excitement generated by the first increase wears off and further increases are made. Before long a marked difference in tempo goes unnoticed by the performers, who have got used to them. My job with fresh eyes was to say, hang on, this has become so far from the composer's original intention it needs to go back to square one; we know square one works!

The solution is to generate excitement through your performance by perfectly natural means and not artificially create it by the simple method of Tempo. I too am guilty of this, so can talk about it with conductors and performers from a sense of experience. It is often resisted by artists who do not believe their tempo has changed! Then, I quote them a true story!

During the run of *The Two Ronnies*, occasionally a dancer would complain to me about the tempo: "It was really fast tonight," or another would say, "it was really slow tonight." I would then remind them that that was impossible as both they and I were performing to a click track recorded some months previously.

A click-track is a means whereby you record a basic rhythm section, just piano, drums and a metronomic click. Then, at a separate recording session, the dancers sing live in the studio to that rhythm track through a set of headphones so they are the only ones to hear the piano, drums and click. Simply, this creates two tracks and means when we get to the theatre, the dancers' recorded track is played over the front-of-house speakers, while the conductor, in headphones, gets the piano, drums and click-track as used by the dancers in the studio and conducts to that.

The synchronised live orchestra and recorded voices play over the front-of-house speakers as if both are live. It can never alter, otherwise the voices would be slightly sharp (or flat) as the tape would be running quicker (or slower) in relation to the live orchestra playing in tune.

Besides, all West End conductors can quote occasions when actors have come up to them and given diametrically opposite opinions about the same performance: it was so fast/it was so slow.

At *Phantom*, I would always try and take part in the rehearsal period as much as possible. To any new actor to the show, I told them it is like moving into a Grade 1 listed building: the four walls of the building are there and cannot be altered. You make the building your own home by the furniture you install, the pictures you hang on the wall, the curtains, carpets and blinds you put up. So it is with *Phantom*. It is how you move from A to B that makes it your performance, how you sing the music, the inflections and colour you put on the words that creates the individual performances, and for *Phantom* to survive, that had to remain the case. You must not try to imitate other performers, but at the same time, 'don't try and fix something that ain't broke'!

I also wanted the audience to work as much as the performers. I did not want the audience relaxing into the back of their comfortable seats, eating their snacks, drinking their wine and letting the performance come to them. A very good example of what I mean is the opening of the show.

It starts with an auction on the stage of a theatre which has seen much better days and has whisps of decaying dust lying in the air. Some people, clearly no longer in the first flush of youth, are scattered at the front amidst the debris of a broken set and a shattered chandelier, covered by a muslin cloth. They are bidding on items from an old production called *Hannibal* by the composer Chalumeau: a poster, a pair of duelling pistols, a monkey musical box which still works. The auctioneer takes the bids, and an old man in a wheelchair starts to sing, reminiscing about the music box and an occasion that happened a long time ago, though how long we are not aware.

At this point, I want the audience, who have only just settled into their seats, to lean forward, straining to listen carefully (and quietly) to every word while the old man recalls, almost to himself, memories of the music box and a love remembered, now obviously lost. There is a moment of uncomfortable silence, before the auctioneer continues. That is what I mean about an audience working as much as the performers. Once you have them leaning slightly forward in their seats, listening from the start, you have them for the evening.

Whilst I am here and on the subject of the audience settling back in their seats with snacks and drinks, I think the theatre lost so much when food and drink were allowed to be taken into the auditorium. I know the reason of course: it is to increase the bar takings. That's just not good enough for me! It makes the audience believe even more that they are sitting in front of their personal entertainment system and can behave as they would at home. They can get up from their seats, which may well be in the middle of a row, to visit the rest rooms they forgot to visit before the show started; they can talk to their neighbour, look at social media on their phones and generally behave as if they are sitting with their family and friends in their own front room. The art of attending the theatre is being lost, gradually eroded by some people's selfishness.

At the moment, the majority still know how to behave and are as outraged as I am. But, at every single performance in the West End, I have seen behaviour that makes me cringe and feel sorry for those patrons who just want to enter the magical world of make-believe.

As for those who start filming on their mobile phones! They

will never capture those moments of performing gold through a two-dimensional camera lens. Much better to fully immerse yourself in a shared musical three-dimensional experience and commit it to memory. That is what makes us human, not some false image probably never looked at again but which, meanwhile, has ruined the concentration of yourself and the people around you by the brightly lit screen.

We have had some wonderful Phantoms, some not-so-wonderful Phantoms and some odd Phantoms. Odd in the sense they wished to inhabit the part rather more than was good for them.

Michael Crawford, while inhabiting the part and making it the benchmark by which all others were judged, was unique. Michael used to sit in the make-up chair in his dressing room for hours having all that latex and make-up applied, never taking the mask off so we could see him close to. If he went to visit other performers around the building, he would keep the mask on, maintaining the mystery of what was under the mask to everyone in the building. So professional and different from some who followed, taking their masks off, even if they made a speech at the end of the show, thereby shattering the illusion. I always thought that such a shame – keep the mystery of theatre until everybody has gone.

On the odd occasion in subsequent years that a Phantom or Christine had to be substituted mid-performance, the change could be done very quickly and within the time frame of the interval. I am afraid I have had to request/instruct it on more than one occasion, generally for loss of voice after curtain-up. None of the people who went off mid-performance liked it; most were understanding when they came back a few days later. My raison d'être being, the audience expected the best musical performance, and through no fault of the performer's (apart from the fact, maybe, they should not have gone on in the first place), they were not getting it.

Some Phantoms who were to play the part were thought a bit

strange. One would put his hands in the dressing-room fridge just prior to his first entrance as he thought the character would have cold hands. There was another who asked us during rehearsals whether we thought the Phantom had been breast-fed as a baby. Apparently, this would inform his portrayal of the role. However, in all the years of the West End show, I don't think we ever had a terrible Phantom.

Scene 4: My Wilderness Years and Triumphant Return!

After fourteen years, all good things come to an end, and after one particularly awful opening night in 2002 with a new cast, at which both Sir Cameron and Lord Lloyd Webber were in attendance, the resident director and I were summoned to Cameron Mackintosh Ltd offices the next day and dismissed. To be honest, it hadn't come as a very big surprise. By now, so busy, I had attended very few of the rehearsals and not looked after the job. I was less outraged than the resident director who had, some weeks previously, announced his retirement.

"You can't fire me; I've already retired," was heard reverberating round the offices. They paid the resident director off and offered me a continuing contract but not as supervisor. They were going to create another new position for me, music consultant. I said no; I wanted to leave. They were kind enough to persist, and through my agent Sue James, they uttered those words that everyone who is ever employed wants to hear, "What are your terms?" Sue said there were three: one, that I was to continue with a weekly salary and pension; two, I would never have to set foot over the threshold of Her Majesty's Theatre ever again; and three, the contract was to run for the length of the show. There was a slight pause and then… "OK!"

I think the belief was that I would be at the end of a phone so that the new music supervisor could ring the old supervisor (me) should he have any problems and ask for solutions. I knew the last person the new music supervisor would ring was the old one, and I was right; I was never consulted about anything!

During this time, I went back only twice. Once to compile a report on the show and the second time to conduct it during the sound upgrade.

For five blissful years I was wont to call 'my wilderness years' or, as Trevor Jackson called them, 'my interregnum', I received a salary from *Phantom of the Opera*, at the same time, travelling the world conducting great orchestras without having much of an idea as to what was going on at Her Majesty's Theatre! I felt no guilt. I had looked after the show for the previous sixteen years pretty well!

Trevor Jackson, aside from being a wonderful friend of mine, is the man who rose from the stage doorkeeper at the Palace Theatre to be executive producer and casting director of Cameron Mackintosh Ltd. A lesson for us all: start small; end big!

In 2007, I was in Hong Kong when I received a phone call from Trevor inviting me back to Her Majesty's in my old job of music supervisor. Knowing they wanted to change things around a little, the phone call was not a surprise. However, I was very happy with my current job and no responsibilities at *Phantom*, so declined and put the phone down.

Arriving back in England, there was another phone call and, once again, there was that wonderful question uttered, "What are your terms?" Sue, with my full agreement, then said there was really only one, and whilst the music consultant job was not to be touched, there would be another job as music supervisor with the salary and terms of that position. There was an even longer pause this time but then, once again, those immortal words, "OK!"

The reason for our demand of course was that if I had taken early retirement, or either party wanted to end the supervisor relationship, there would still be the consultant job which was to remain for the length of the show. Of course, Covid-19 would have a hand in that, but that was all in the future, and for now, there was no pandemic and a seemingly never-ending musical to be enjoyed.

For the remaining run of *Phantom of the Opera* prior to shut down, I had two jobs and two salaries: music supervisor and music consultant. It took the accounts department of CML a number of months to sort out why they were paying out two bank transfers every week. In the end, after repeated phone calls reminding them there was one or other salary still to be paid, it got sorted.

Everyone in the business wanted just one of my jobs!

As a little postscript to this story, about six months after going back, I decided to have some fun with my friend Trevor and rang him with my serious voice. "The music consultant and I have had a little conversation, and we have decided that I should have a salary rise."

There was a puzzled pause and then he asked, "Who is the music consultant?"

"I am," I retorted, which was immediately followed by a click as he replaced his receiver!

Scene 5: Phantom25

People often ask me, what the highlights of my career are, and they will be listed later. While talking about *Phantom*, it would be remiss of me if, at this point, I did not mention the twenty-fifth anniversary of *Phantom of the Opera* as being one of them. Cameron had this idea of celebrating his long-running shows with an extravaganza; a performance that would rock the musical theatre world. He'd done it with *Les Misérables* and now wanted to do it with *Phantom*. I think I would have killed him if he hadn't asked me to conduct and musically supervise it.

There was an issue with timing which needed resolving before agreeing terms. I was scheduled to conduct the Adelaide Symphony Orchestra in Adelaide, Australia on Sunday, 18 September 2011, and with rehearsals for *Phantom25* starting in London on Monday, 19 September 2011 at Ealing Studios, there was no way I would be able to do the first two days of rehearsal. Flying back on the Monday and arriving Tuesday lunchtime made that impossible. In the end, I used the advantage of the arrivals club for a wash and brush up and went straight from long-haul via Heathrow Airport to Ealing Studios, the home of the Ealing Comedies, where I began rehearsing what was to become one of the greatest musical experiences of my life.

We cast mostly from existing and ex-cast members for the very good reason we had less than two weeks to rehearse and no time for anyone to learn it. Two weeks on from the first day of rehearsal, it would all be over!

There was no need to worry of course as it was a super cast! Ramin Karimloo (who I knew) as the Phantom, Sierra Boggess (who I did not) as Christine and Hadley Fraser (who I also did not know) as Raoul. He was the only member of the three principals who had never been in it. Cameron and I only cast him just before I left for Australia, and he was a very late addition to the team. He had about three weeks to learn the show but is a brilliant performer and professional actor and was off the book by the time we started. Rehearsals continued excitingly for ten days, though I had a small battle with the director.

Laurence Connor had been involved with *Phantom* in a residency capacity before the twenty-fifth, when he had stepped into the great Hal Prince's shoes as associate director at Her Majesty's.

Hal's theatrical credits and awards are extraordinary and a lasting testament to one of the nicest directors I have ever worked with. I adored the man and was devastated at his death in 2019 on a flight between Europe and the US. It was a huge pleasure to call the man a friend, and I have a signed photo with a personal message on my office wall. In the early 2000s, he was getting of an age where he wanted to step back just a little, so he approved the appointment of Laurence at Her Majesty's Theatre.

Whilst I was away in my capacity as music consultant, Laurence and the producers wanted to update the production, and Laurence quickly brought in a steelier approach, generating 'heat onstage' as he called it; little pause for reflection, keep it going.

An example of the differences between the two directors was in 'Past the Point' that I discussed earlier. Moments before the first verse, out of view, the Phantom kills Piangi, who is singing the role of Don Juan in the opera within the show, and dons his cloak and hood over his head to disguise himself as Piangi.

In Hal's version, Christine thinks she is singing to Piangi and does not know she is singing to the Phantom. Some, when they were disguised as Piangi, even went so far as to sing with an Italian accent, furthering the illusion. She only realises who he really is when, in the passion of the opera, she accidently brushes against his mask under the hood, pulling it back a short time later to reveal him; an utterly compelling moment.

In Laurence's version, she knows very quickly when alone onstage with the disguised Phantom/Piangi, and he starts to sing. This means, because it is not a surprise, the reveal of the Phantom has to have momentum. Different ways of playing the scene, and I preferred Hal's!

During those five years I was away, I went back to conduct the show for two weeks so the sound could be updated as both Andrew and Cameron were to be in attendance a lot. The production team wanted someone conducting the show both the good lord and the noble knight knew and trusted.

When I watched the show from a seat in the auditorium prior to conducting it, I was saddened by what I saw. For me, there was little love. There should be moments when a look says it all or a pause, even more! It was all so fast and breathless! So, before conducting my second first night, the resident team, knowing my fondness for romance, asked to meet up with me so they could explain their concept of the show to me.

First off, I refused, then thought maybe I should, so rather than they explain their concept to me, I could explain mine to them. We met in the company office at Her Majesty's Theatre; they were on one side of the desk, I the other. One of them started explaining the change in the show since I had conducted. Interrupting, I said in a very calm, measured voice, "Before you say anything, let me just say one thing. There is only one way I know how to conduct this show, and that is my way! I'm sorry if you don't like it, but there it is, and that's the way it will be. Now, having heard me say that, if you don't want me to conduct these two weeks, that's absolutely fine. There will be no hard feelings, I shall quite understand, pack my bags and leave the theatre, never to darken its doors again!"

There was a bit of bluster, before one of them said, "I guess there's nothing more to be said then." There wasn't really! I got up from my seat and went home before, a few days later, conducting the show for the first time in about three years, once more without a rehearsal.

I must say, putting all modesty aside again (oh sod it, I'll fling that to the wind!), it was a triumph and, rather like my opening night eighteen years earlier – this time without the first inversion Il Muto error – it went really well. Dan Bowling, who had taken over from me as music supervisor, and had sat in the box for the whole performance, came up to me afterwards and was extremely complimentary, adding I had the music in my soul. I agreed with him – I do! And 'Past the Point' was performed Hal's way!

That story is by way of explaining where Laurence and I were as *Phantom25* began. I liked the man; I just didn't see eye to eye with everything he did or wanted at *Phantom* and of course vice versa. We had a bit of an artistic difference during the twenty-fifth, but once again, I held all the cards – it was me conducting the performances. Plus, I had as an ally one of the principal members of the cast. I rehearsed it how I was going to conduct it, and we spent a wonderful week at Ealing Studios, before transferring for a few days to 3 Mills Studios where we could pre-build the basic set prior to setting foot in the Royal Albert Hall.

The Albert Hall set was incredible. For those who don't know the hall, a brief description may be necessary. The building is round on the outside as well as the inside, with a stage squaring off the Prince Consort Road end. Boxes on three levels extend all the way round from one side of the stage, choir seats and massive organ, to the other with a huge circle above the topmost row of boxes and stalls below the bottom row of boxes. An arena where the seats can be taken out and people can stand fills the floor area in front of the stage.

For the set of *Phantom*, Matt Kinley, who took up the reins of the show after the original designer Maria Bjornson's sad early death, continued the boxes round over the choir seats. We put the chorus in these boxes in costume, so they looked for all the world as if they were members of the audience, commenting on the action. It was a very neat way of adding to the overall sound and making sure we had lots of voices in the ensemble, and not just from the stage.

Laurence and Matt cleverly used back projection to convey the stage of the Opera Populaire of Paris. Curtains would fall; candles would rise but from back projection. The only thing we couldn't do, and we were criticised quite heavily for it, was make the chandelier fall at the end of Act 1. Instead, lots of fireworks and bangs came from it. But there's no dispute, it stayed resolutely immobile! It was of course completely impossible to do anything else without re-engineering the Royal Albert Hall, a complete non-starter for a protected building!

I wanted the orchestra in front of the stage as in an opera house. I was promptly overruled by Cameron who, presumably with an eye to ticket sales and not removing seats, put us high up at the back, above and behind the stage, in front of the organ. This I knew would make co-ordination between stage and me extremely difficult, as I could not physically see the cast. I had a monitor, but it was from a camera far away and only gave me an overall view of the stage; I was not able to see their eyes. On the other hand, the cast had a monitor close-up view of me everywhere. They were all across the front of the stage, backstage, even in my dressing room where the Phantom sang his offstage moments. There had to be a lot of trust between the cast and me. I couldn't really see them, but they could me, so we agreed very early on, they would have to follow me. In the end, it worked well.

I don't know whether money was no object, however I do know there were thousands of people backstage (well, quite a few anyway), onstage and an orchestra of fifty-four, which was very much bigger than the orchestra of twenty-seven at Her Majesty's and twenty-eight at the Majestic on Broadway. Broadway had an extra percussionist, which was always intended to be there in London. We just did not physically have the room.

There were all-nighters; there were tears; there was exhaustion, as we struggled to overcome the technical difficulties of putting on this show in such a short space of time, and I nearly died at *Phantom*… again!

There was a trap door immediately behind me, from where the Phantom would appear as if on the roof of the Opera Populaire. One rehearsal, it hadn't been locked off, and I stepped on it, only for it to slide from under my feet. I grabbed the podium rail that was there and prevented myself from falling about forty feet to the ground. I was extremely angry! When my lengthy tirade had been exhausted, there was silence. No one said anything. So, I stomped off to my dressing room to recover my composure.

A few days later, I was to hear what happened after my exit. Trevor Jackson, sitting with Matt Eastaugh who worked in Cameron's office, was sitting in the auditorium listening to this outburst. When I had finished and had stomped off the concert platform, one of them turned to the other and, with a direct quote from Monsieur André to Carlotta in *Hannibal*, the opera performed at the beginning of *Phantom*, said rather prissily with a thick French accent, "These things do 'appen!"

To which the other retorted, "Better luck next time!"

I forgive them both!

After one of the most intensive periods of rehearsing, we were still not ready for the opening night. Saturday, 1 October 2011 dawned, and I knew we were in trouble. Opening night was that night, and we only had one scheduled dress rehearsal in the Albert Hall. Sure enough, as I knew would happen, we only got through the first act before 5pm. The performance was in two and a half hours, and we had not run the second act.

When 7.30pm came round, adrenalin was flowing everywhere. Tickets had sold out for all three performances within twenty minutes of going on sale, so it had to be good, first time. We knew Act 1 would be OK, but Act 2? We had not run it, let alone dress rehearsed it, and that act was technically extremely complicated! We put ourselves in the hands of the acting and musical gods.

At 7.30pm, Earl Carpenter, who had been a London Phantom but was the auctioneer at the Royal Albert Hall, brought the gavel down on a wood block and said, "Sold." We were off!

Hadley Fraser, who was old-man Raoul in the bath chair, sang about memories, and Earl thrillingly brought his voice up to fever pitch ,"...perhaps we may frighten the ghosts of so many years ago, with a little illumination, gentlemen." My cue, and I brought the baton down to start the large orchestra with that famous overture.

I am told that in the hall, the effect was electrifying. Even as I write this, the hairs on the back of my neck are rising up. The gods smiled down on us and nothing could go wrong that night. A lot of very talented people both backstage and on, the incredible score and the brilliant staging, ensured we got all the way through by flying high. That night was the best performance of *Phantom of the Opera* I have ever conducted. It was extraordinary. Nothing could go wrong, and everybody did what they were supposed to do. We gave three performances of the show that weekend. If you can, buy the DVD; it is compelling and something of which I am very proud.

At the end of the last performance, Laurence and I were in my dressing room, and we collapsed into each other's arms, possibly with relief. It had been the most strenuous of times. He then looked at me and said, "I need to be reminded that *Phantom* can work like this." He was about to take the show out on a UK and US tour in a completely new production, with a new choreographer, new music supervisor, new set, new everything. I was of the opinion that if it wasn't broke, why fix it, so had not volunteered to be involved. To be fair, they hadn't asked me either! From that previous meeting in Her Majesty's Theatre's company office, Laurence knew I would not alter what I knew to work and do a production that was alien to my way of thinking. Therefore, when he said he needed reminding of the legitimacy of my overall musical shape of the show, I took it as quite a compliment. I returned it by saying I had really enjoyed our collaboration on this show but was glad I wasn't doing the tour as I think we might have killed each other.

As a little postscript, I went and saw Laurence's new version on tour and enjoyed a lot of it. I had to suspend my love of the brilliant original and look with fresh eyes and ears, but there was a great deal to like in his production.

Scene 6: The Advance of Technology in Orchestras

Andrew Lloyd Webber is one of the most mercurial men I have ever met. Uncomfortable in social circles of which he is not an active member, difficult to read, impossible to argue with, he is without doubt, a genius. He has written some of the greatest tunes known to humankind and, in my opinion, written the greatest work of musical theatre, though perhaps I should qualify that and say that, although I think *Phantom* is his greatest creation, maybe *Sunset Boulevard* contains some of his greatest songs. He finds it incredibly difficult to accept criticism, however well-meaning, and is at heart a rock and roller needing to include a rhythmic beat somewhere within his musicals. He and I have had our moments, and even after all these years, I am not entirely certain he knows who I am. He very rarely calls me by name and then only after someone else has!

However, he most certainly knew who I was after our last little disagreement! He believes that synthesisers are now so good, some sounds are indistinguishable from the real thing, and he has a point: to some, they really are that good.

Andrew had decided at *Phantom* on Broadway to bring the two synths forward from the back of the orchestra (or in our case in the box over the pit) to be grouped around the conductor, so the seven violins, two violas and two cellos could mimic the articulation of the keyboard players and be more integrated into the overall sound. He wanted to do the same in London and summoned us down to Her Majesty's Theatre for a meeting with him, where he announced this bombshell to me, the rest of the music staff and the production team of Cameron Mackintosh Ltd.

I did not like this idea one little bit, especially for the symphonic score of *Phantom of the Opera*. I argued against it, telling him that, as a conductor, I liked the sound of finger on wood, bow on string and the immediate contact of musicians around me to whom I could convey my intentions by a look or a flick of the baton. I liked seeing the whites of the musicians' eyes as they played their instrument to the best of their ability; I liked the human touch. Andrew was having none of this and argued against me. He stated that he would bring in another synth and cut the orchestra in half, which in the end was rather prescient! I replied he couldn't do that to one of the greatest scores and orchestrations of the twentieth century. It all began to get quite heated, everyone else keeping well out of it! He finished the argument by playing his ace card: he turned to me and, I'll never forget his exact words, said, "I wrote the music; I own the theatre; this is what I want!"

As a way to win the argument, it's a good one! I can't fault the accuracy of the statement: he did write the music, and he does own Her Majesty's Theatre! There was of course no further point in arguing my case, so Trevor Jackson gently put his hand on my shoulder and eased me backwards! Then, we all adjourned to our respective corners to cool down.

Two weeks later, it was all resolved by health and safety. The pit at Her Majesty's Theatre was so incredibly small that some twenty-six years after it had opened, there was no way we could alter the layout of the pit without severe penalties in the form of space, thereby limiting the number of musicians we could put within that space. The time was not yet right for a reduced orchestra, and we had to put twenty-five musicians back into the same space! Who would have thought H&S would come to my rescue?

Andrew's belief in the ability of synths is, in a way, a valid one. On the 2020 *Phantom* tour, where I had been engaged as music consultant, and with an orchestra cut in half and an extra synth player brought in, the reduced orchestra of fourteen sounded pretty good. Sitting in the auditorium of the Curve Theatre in Leicester prior to its cancellation, I was amazed at the sampled sound of a harp and assorted percussion instruments. Also, when you contemplate what it does for real musicians, not a little scary. Why have separate people playing a number of different instruments when one player can do them all? Theoretically, with the rapid pace of synthesised sounds, the days of live music with real strings and wind players are numbered. My only consolation is who wants to go and see a Beethoven symphony with only three or four keyboard players onstage? There is nothing as exciting as a stage full of the perfections, and yes, occasional imperfections, of live musicians striving to play their very best for a silent and absorbed audience. Mark you, you could argue it is the ultimate musical co-operative: four musicians and no conductor playing symphonies!

In Leicester, I was aghast to see the beautiful harp arpeggio under the heartbreaking violin solo in the mausoleum scene, being played as a patch by the synth player fingering an ascending chromatic scale. A chromatic scale as an arpeggio? How does that work? When a musician plays an arpeggio, there is a natural inclination to make a crescendo as you go towards the top and then an equally natural diminuendo as you come down; you lean as you go up, you fall as you come down. It is imperceptible. Write it and it's too much, but nevertheless it is there, and very natural for a musician. In a chromatic scale the natural lean up and fall down is absent. "How," I said to the remarkably talented programmer Stuart Andrews, "is that replicated in a chromatic scale?" He replied that as part of the training synth players now have to undertake, they must listen to what they play and, if necessary, understand the subliminal musicality of playing a phrase, even if it's not what they are actually playing. I thought a bit, then added that I wasn't sure on a wet Wednesday afternoon in Cleethorpes, any player would be bothered to try and play something that was so unnatural.

As you can see, I remain to be convinced. I was astonished by the sound at the beginning of a high-profile show in Leicester, when everyone was concentrating and giving of their best: it did sound big; it did sound full, but to my ears, it also sounded false.

Sadly, I can't raise an argument against the financial realities of having a pit with a smaller orchestra in it, against not having a show at all. The cost of mounting a musical is enormous, the risks so high, that it is very difficult to insist on an orchestra the size of which can be the difference between profit and loss. Why risk it when the majority of people who matter, the audience, won't notice?

At the moment, we are on the cusp of yet more change, though it can be argued that orchestras in musical theatre have always evolved. From the days of a large pit orchestra without sound enhancement, through the period when sound amplification came in and orchestra numbers reduced as each advancement in sound equipment improved, to now, when musicians playing original instruments can be replicated without any discernible difference to an audience.

We are experiencing the gradual diminution of pit orchestras, as the long-running shows that used to have the large ones – *Miss Saigon* (over thirty at the Drury Lane Theatre), *Les Misérables* (twenty-three at the Palace Theatre) and *Phantom* (twenty-seven at Her Majesty's Theatre) – are all having to scale down drastically to survive. No new show these days has a decent-sized band. Synthesisers now fill the gap of missing instruments. I will not go down without fighting! Always, in my opinion, a bigger orchestra, with musicians playing original instruments live, will sound richer and be more musical than a small orchestra with musicians playing electronically or, as I like to call it, artificially!

The new 2021 production returned to Her Majesty's Theatre and the orchestra playing that wonderful score now is the same that played in Leicester. It has half the musicians of the original and one musician less than we had playing the 1982 *Two Ronnies* stage show, when there were no strings. However, I do not believe the smaller orchestra at *Phantom* is entirely the fault of either Cameron or Andrew; there is an additional reason.

When the show closed in 2020, there were pit screens everywhere. Some musicians had wrap-around seats as well. One had both baffle board and wrap-around seat and wore a set of headphones as ear defenders. The welfare of musicians, and especially their hearing, must take priority. In 1986, it had not seemed to matter so much. If you could cram twenty-five musicians in a tight area and they had room to extend their arms, that was all that mattered.

During the hiatus of the pandemic and enforced closure of *Phantom of the Opera*, the pit of Her Majesty's Theatre was converted back to its original setting, which meant the rails joined the stage rather than the boxes. This considerably reduced the size of the pit. We have already seen that the twenty-five musicians would never have been allowed in the old pit, so there was no chance they would have been allowed in the new, smaller one, even if the producers had wanted to!

In a way, you could say that *Phantom* is in the perfect theatre for the show but the wrong theatre for the orchestra.

Now, it is a much smaller orchestra, yet will sound just as full to the people who matter the most: the paying audience. Acoustic sound will have been banished, which of course was the brilliance of the original orchestra: it was the natural sound, enhanced. The trend today is for the sound desk to control everything, from the loudness to the crescendos and diminuendos via the faders. To do that, as much acoustic sound as possible is taken away, so the musicians and conductor really are in the hands of the person on the control desk. Some will notice the artificiality of it all and not like what they hear. In the main, they will be people like me, the older generation and those who care about their music being live.

Andrew's brother Julian, though, is someone with whom I have always got on very well. I should do, we were Royal College of Music students together though he, being slightly older than me, was ahead of me in terms of arrival. Since then, we have often performed together: Tchaikovsky's *Rococo Variations* in Belfast, his brother's *Variations* in Budapest and an Elgar *Cello Concerto* in the Royal Albert Hall remain vivid in my memory. Julian and I meet up and have a thoroughly entertaining time, rehearsing well, performing magnificently and playing hard afterwards! I was sad when he retired from performing live due to a neck injury.

I also knew their mother, Jean. I was once tasked with performing her husband's composition *Aurora* at an open-air Kenwood concert with the RPO. She asked me round to her South Kensington flat and begged me not to perform it the same way as Lorin Maazel had recorded it with the London Philharmonic. According to her, it was a last-minute decision to put it on the Variations CD Julian and the LPO had recorded, and was only there because of time left over in the sessions. There was, however, not a lot of time to record *Aurora*, so the recording was rushed, and Maazel had not obeyed a tempo change marking. She asked me to make sure I did. I have performed this wonderful tone poem many times since and have always done as she asked.

Afterwards, towards the end of her life, there began some communication and a few coffees between us. Just before she died, she asked whether I would like some string pieces composed by William Lloyd Webber she was about to throw away. I do not think they held happy memories for her. In any case, I took them and later gave them to Julian who was grateful I had rescued them as he had been searching for them. Not so grateful, he remembered my request to conduct them should they ever be recorded!

Before leaving *Phantom*, I should mention the first tour we did in 1991 with the full twenty-seven-piece orchestra. There were many incidents, one of which included stopping off at a Chinese takeaway in Manchester on the way home. Suddenly, from the kitchen, we heard a great deal of shouting and screaming followed by a man running extremely quickly through the door that divided the back from the front. He was closely followed by the chef who had in his hands a meat cleaver raised above his head. The winner was clearly going to be the man in front as he was younger and visibly fitter. The chef, who obviously enjoyed his own cooking, had his size as a hindrance but nonetheless possessed a remarkable turn of speed. The last we saw of the two of them were both disappearing through the front door into the night. Thinking our order would now take a while, and being quite frankly terrified, we too followed them through the door and to our car.

Preparing for that first UK tour, members of the resident creative team travelled around the country, trying to give people who couldn't afford the trip to London a chance to audition for the show. On any production there will be tensions where creative people are concerned. Perhaps one member of the team sees something in an actor others may not and wishes to persuade the rest of the team of their qualities. Even my greatest friends say I can be a bit annoying by extolling the merits of an artist and hoping to persuade others of their merit.

Come the lunch break one audition day, Trevor Jackson and I were left alone together in the audition space, obviously too good an opportunity for me not to continue my praise of this particular auditionee, so I continued with my championing! After a while, Trevor exploded, picked up a chair and hurled it in my general direction with a great deal of force. It went some way but, I'm happy to say, missed. With that, he turned on his heels and walked out. It left both of us a bit shocked, and I sat down thinking, *well, that was unexpected*; I had not seen that one coming!

About three minutes later, he came back into the room, looked at me and burst out laughing. He confessed he knew the thought process of why he had done what he had but not why he had actually carried it out. No sooner had he gone out of the room, than he realised how ridiculous he must have looked and, having thrown the chair and walked out, didn't know where he was going. He had to negate the whole effect by coming back in! We still laugh about it now.

Scene 7: Do Not Read If Easily Offended!

Having been (almost) continually employed by Cameron Mackintosh since 1978, I must be one of the longest serving of his employees, and he is someone for whom I have a great deal of time and respect. Like Andrew, he passionately loves the theatre and pours his heart and money into saving them and securing them for the future. His portfolio of beautiful theatres in the form of Delfont Mackintosh Theatres numbers eight and contains some of the most beautiful buildings in the country. His last acquisition was the Victoria Palace, and he has refurbished it to a stunning standard.

Again, like Andrew, he doesn't just sink his own money into the bricks, mortar and fabric of the theatres and the productions within but also into the next generation of performers. He is extremely generous in his scholarships, bursaries and foundation, all of which go towards improving the ability of anyone from any background to become an actor. His productions have numbered some of the greatest in theatrical history and include: *Phantom*, *Cats*, *Les Misérables* and *Miss Saigon*. However, there is another gentleman, who is an equally long-serving stalwart of Cameron Mackintosh Ltd, who should have a mention.

His name is Nick Allott, and Cameron had spotted him while he was front-of-house manager when *Cats* was at the New London Theatre, now the Gillian Lynne Theatre. Cameron very quickly employed him as his right-hand man. Apart from the fact he is a very nice man, great company and very good at smoothing troubled waters, he is also naturally amusing.

At this point I should warn you the following story contains a word I never use. No one is comfortable using it, and it is the last taboo of bad language! Try as I might, I can think of no substitute that has the same effect, and it is the reason I have never told this story in public. So, if you're sensitive to the C word, please skip the rest of this and go to Act 6.

In May 1994, I conducted the Israel Philharmonic Orchestra. They are a great orchestra and play with total passion and commitment, their hearts truly on their sleeves. They also look after you extremely well, putting their guest artists up in a private house rather than yet another anonymous hotel. I was elated at being surrounded by music-making of the highest order. Wherever one turned, there was a famous artist practising, rehearsing or performing with this world-famous orchestra. I had an intoxicating time.

Shortly after my week with them and back in the UK, still on a natural high, I met up with Nick for a coffee. As only Nick can, he began teasing me. Finally, after taking it for some time, I had had enough. Dragging myself up to my full pompous height, I said, "Nick! Nick! That's enough. I have just come back from conducting the Israel Philharmonic, one of the world's greatest orchestras, and they have spent the entire week calling me maestro!"

Quick as a flash, he retorted, "Yes, Anthony, maybe that's true, but what you don't know is that *maestro* is the Hebrew word for cunt!"

Act 6

Scene 1: Life Outside the West End

Throughout my early West End career, I always harboured a desire to get back to my classical routes: conducting symphony orchestras. So, in 1983, I had got myself a classical agent called Basil Douglas. It went reasonably well, and for four years, I conducted either the BBC Concert or BBC Radio orchestras.

I began to get corporate jobs as well. These are shows which range in size from quite small to huge extravaganzas for a multinational company, requiring an enormous orchestra and chorus. Recommended by Chick Norton and Alan Franks, who were orchestral fixers and had looked after *Irene*, *My Fair Lady* and *Phantom*, I landed the job of providing the music for Crown Paints at the Cunard Hotel in Hammersmith. Then, when Allied Dunbar wanted some music, I had the bright idea of using the orchestra they sponsored, the great Philharmonia Orchestra, and we took eighty musicians to Wembley, providing incidental music at their annual conference.

After Basil retired, I changed agents a couple of times, before, in the end, completely dispensing with the services of an agent. I realised that, in the main, most of them did not obtain work for you. You are only as good as your last job, and you create your own work. The only thing classical agents did for me was clear the cheques, then take their 15–20%! There are of course a few agents who are different. Incredibly powerful, they can definitely make and break an artist. They are the ones with whom the orchestras, opera houses and other organisations have a very cosy relationship, some say too cosy.

Arts organisations can ring up one of these few powerful agents and ask them to supply one of their artists for a concert, or even a position, and it is done. Easy! Perhaps I am too outspoken, or just not good enough, but I never reached those heights. Money was never a really important factor for me. I just wanted to be able to live comfortably, provide for my family and conduct orchestras; the better they were, the happier I was. Sue will always be there for my commercial work, as that is different from the classical one and sometimes requires a buffer between management and artist.

In the 1980s and in pursuance of an orchestral career, I took orchestras performing at corporate events to the ballroom of the Dorchester Hotel, the Grosvenor House Hotel, the Royal Albert Hall, the Royal Festival Hall, the Royal Garden Hotel, Hall 8 at the NEC, for companies such as Travel Trade Gazette, British Insurance, Crown Paints, Huawei and Motor Transport Awards, with presenters such as Jeremy Clarkson, Dara O'Brien and Joanna Lumley.

Further abroad, Qudos (the production company I did a lot of work for) hired an orchestra in Sorrento to launch the Fiat Tempra. We used an orchestra from Naples Opera, and all I really remember about Italian orchestras was that sections loved to talk to other sections during the rehearsal, and the further apart they were, the better! First violins talking to trombones was bedlam!

We also went to the extraordinary Palais 12 by the Atomium in Brussels, the equivalent of the NEC in Birmingham, and launched a lot of tractors for Case International Harvester.

By a large margin, the most expensive show I ever did was the Volvo show in Gothenburg, which was a multi-million-dollar extravaganza, the like of which has not been seen since. It was amazing as we utilised every aspect of this incredible place, from the house orchestra and chorus plus dancers, to the backstage workshop and their incredible in-house craftsmen. It was choreographed by the great Kenn Oldfield, a sadly underused man who was given free rein to his brilliant imagination for pieces such as the *Humming Chorus, Nessun Dorma, An American in Paris* and Vangelis' *1492*, to which we actually revealed the S80. It was an extraordinary show, as vast as it was imaginative, having the added bonus of cast and crew spending a few summer months in the beautiful country of Sweden. A flat was rented for me and the whole family, plus my mother came out. It was an idyllic summer, in an idyllic country.

The most extraordinary private event I ever did was a wedding at Wroughton House in North London, with a cast list almost as long as the guests! The daughter of the man who had built one of the residential wharfs along the Thames was marrying her fiancé, and the father of the bride wanted to give his daughter a wedding she would remember for the rest of her life. For a start, as entertainment, he had a full symphony orchestra (the National Symphony), The Royal Ballet, José Carreras, The Black Eyed Peas, and for the choir, he booked a local one but also wanted something more. As you do, we flew to Prague for the day by private jet from Luton Airport and auditioned the Bambini Choir.

Now I have done a lot of commercial flying in all classes, plus a lot of light aircraft flying, and of all the ways to travel, private jet travel is right up there as the only way to go! For a start, I travelled out on my own, the father of the bride meeting me out there. I was to fly back the same day by commercial airline; he would travel back on the private jet the following day.

Upon arriving at the offices of the jet company at a private area of Luton airport, I was greeted very warmly and given a cup of coffee. It was such good coffee, I asked for another cup, and it arrived just as the pilot came in and asked if I was ready to go. I replied that I had just got another cup of coffee.

"No problem," he said. "When you've finished and you're ready, we'll go." With that, he went out to his seat; I sat at mine and finished my coffee. At the end of the coffee, I said I was ready, taken to the aircraft, strapped in; the door was closed; and off we went. So simple, so wonderful, so expensive!

After the event, and just to be certain everybody in my family understood, I stated very quickly that when my own daughter got married, she need not expect the same!

All this BBC and commercial work brought me to the attention of various orchestra managements, and I began to get some conducting work from them. My first effort was with the Philharmonia Orchestra in April 1987 in Hemel Hempstead, when I had the great pleasure of conducting the Mendelssohn *Italian Symphony* and Grieg *Piano Concerto*. This in turn brought me to the attention of Victor Hochhauser, a well-known concert promoter who started asking me to conduct some of his concerts. My first engagement with his 'house' orchestra, the National Symphony (NSO), was on 30 April 1988 at the Barbican and also included the Grieg *Piano Concerto*. Almost immediately, I started working for Raymond Gubbay, an alternative concert promoter to Victor Hochhauser and between whom a perceived rivalry had opened up. Raymond, for a very brief period, had worked for Victor, who remained resentful towards him for the rest of his life.

There is no doubting that my main income was from Raymond and Victor, and for a while I managed to juggle the two and work for them both, until getting the call from Raymond telling me to choose!

I had been booked by Victor to do a concert with Igor Oistrakh, the son of the great violinist David, and really wanted to do it. However, Raymond said if I wanted to continue working for him, I had to pull out. This was a hell of a dilemma, as I never like letting people down. But I had this feeling Raymond was the one to work for. He was thrusting, dynamic and had real artistic flair as well as great ideas. A demanding but very fair employer giving opportunities I might not otherwise have received. I chose Raymond and have never regretted it.

It was an awkward conversation with Victor, who screamed at me about loyalty and honour, with which no one could disagree. Then he rather turned me against him by archly shrieking at me, "Who is this grubby man anyway?" Maybe that was an occasion where an agent would have been of benefit!

I extracted myself from the Oistrakh concert and never worked for Victor again. However, a new chapter was opening with an employer who would take me all over the world and give me memories that would last as long as I.

Some of those were either at the St. George's Day or BT concerts at the Royal Albert Hall. The BT concert in particular was a wonderful opening celebratory Christmas festive concert promoted by Raymond Gubbay with sponsorship and support from British Telecom. Always very diverse programmes with the London Concert Orchestra, Royal Choral Society, soloists, the RAF Sqadronaires and the BT Melodium Steel Drums, we would sing, play and put on Santa hats. A number of 'personalities' presented; amongst the most notable were: Fiona Bruce, Brian Blessed, John Sergeant, Leslie Phillips and John Humphreys.

I think I might have got some revenge on behalf of all politicians with John Humphreys! He was a BBC presenter on the early morning Radio 4 news programme *Today* and famous for a number of things; mercilessly grilling politicians and not being terribly good at relaying the correct time to the listeners were two of them. At the concert he was presenting, I got him to conduct the orchestra in the hornpipe, which involved counting the orchestra in for the first beat by saying the numbers one and two. He completely messed it up by saying the numbers far too fast; as a result, the orchestra could not start playing. I was able to tell him that it was really very simple and just involved saying the numbers one and two in the time of the music but added, almost as an afterthought, I realised he had a problem with time! It got a good laugh, and John could only reply that he wished he had me the other side of a BBC studio microphone!

Brian Blessed's voice is truly as magnificent as it sounds and filled the Royal Albert Hall without the aid of a microphone. Leslie Phillips was as gentle a gentleman as he seems. We had a lot of fun together, as he appeared not to be able to read a script and just carried on speaking, ignoring all music cues. I kept having to interrupt him to say I thought, as I had an enormous orchestra in front of me, we ought to play some music, especially as it said so in the script!

I was asked to do my first commercial recording in 1991, though it is a medium with which I am not totally comfortable. Not in the sense of finding the environment difficult but more I believe music should be a live, shared experience and not listened to in the privacy of your front room through a set of headphones or earbuds, able to press play and then, more irritatingly, pause. My children do this constantly and it annoys the hell out of me. They'll listen to half a pop song and then move on to something else, sometimes without even pressing pause! I mean, the keys don't even match!

I dislike the way recordings are broken up for mistakes in either the recording technique, extraneous noises in the studio, wrong notes or just because someone either in the control room or on the studio floor doesn't like what they are hearing. This, to my mind, makes them artificial and manufactured.

Recordings can be made up of many different takes, so how can that be a performance? We don't stop in a concert hall and say, excuse me, would you mind if we do that bit again? Do purchasers of recordings expect perfection? I think they do and, to a certain extent, can understand that. Who wants to hear the same mistake repeated every time you listen to a particular passage? You start waiting for it! The only way I can see for a recording to be made is to record it from a live performance. Maybe a few edits if there are really obvious mistakes, but a living event makes them much more real and, for any blemish, more understandable.

On studio recordings, very often I can hear where edits are made. Maybe the two sections stitched together are not quite the same tempo; maybe the sound levels do not quite match up; the edit is fractionally out; maybe the 'feel' of the piece just sags between the two sections recorded at different times, perhaps even different days. Whatever it is, I can hear it and, for me, that is just as bad as the odd occasional blemish.

You may be surprised to learn I have no music on my mobile phone or iPod and seldom listen to it at home. I put old radio programmes on my iPod, and the older the better: *Round the Horne* (is there anything funnier than Julian and Sandy?), *The Navy Lark* (the old 'left hand down a bit'), *Men from the Ministry*, *Hancock's Half Hour* and leave my phone for calls and emails. There is no music on either because I am lucky – there is so much in my head I can hear at any time. I like the performances too! That is the reason I have the radio tuned at night to a talk programme, either live or as a podcast; it takes the music away, and I can sleep without all those marvellous tunes buzzing around my head!

Having said that, I have of course recorded; it is a necessary by-product of what we all do. The first recording was with Vanessa Mae, who was a twelve-year-old prodigy playing some Mozart and Sarasate with the London Mozart Players. I then went on to many other recordings with the Royal Philharmonic, Philharmonia, London Philharmonic, Warsaw Philharmonic, Israel Philharmonic, Slovak Philharmonic orchestras, Santa Cecilia Orchestra Rome, Bournemouth Symphony, Cracow Radio Symphony, Hong Kong Sinfonietta, Prague Sinfonia,

Netherlands Radio Symphony and London Symphony orchestras (LSO).

I was rather pleased with the LSO one as I had commissioned *Phantom Fantasia* from Andrew Lloyd Webber, and it had been orchestrated by Laurence Roman, a wonderful orchestrator surpassing the colourful music of Szymanowski or Korngold! A friend of mine once took one of his compositions to Lawrence for help and advice and was just told to spray a little perfume around it! I wanted to call the piece *Phantom Phantasia*, but it was rejected by someone at RUG. Years later, Julian recorded a *Phantasia* based on *Phantom* with Sarah Chang; the idea cannot have been that bad!

Our recording was nominated for a Grammy, the holy grail of recording awards. We didn't win, but I was proud to have been nominated, paying my first visit to the Plaza Hotel in New York in order to attend the award ceremony held at Radio City Music Hall.

Scene 2: Classical Spectacular and Other Stories

In 1990, Mike Reed (him again?) had recently conducted the first of a series of concerts at the Royal Albert Hall that ran until 2021. Raymond had the idea of doing a show of favourite classical music, accompanying the orchestra with lights and finishing with the *1812* using the orchestra, two military bands, a choir and the Moscow Militia. In reality, the Moscow Militia were a bunch of British people who liked to dress up in civil war outfits and fire muskets. He called it *Classical Spectacular*! It was hugely successful and, after Mike's first year, Bramwell Tovey did a year, and then in 1992, I was invited to take over.

Before actually committing to me, they had to see whether I was capable of taking this show on and decided to try me out on the first *Class Spec* (as we called it) overseas trip. We went to Ireland, and it was a bit of a disaster from the word go. Arriving at Stansted Airport for our Ryanair flight, I saw Raymond and his new right-hand man Anthony Findlay approaching the departure gate and waved at them. Raymond did not recognise me and looked behind him to see who I was waving at. I have never failed to remind Raymond that he did not recognise one of his own conductors!

Then, in Ireland, we had an orchestra of the old school; you could not strike a match anywhere near them as the fumes alone would have spontaneously combusted the whole stage. We were performing Ravel's *Bolero* and there is a very difficult trombone solo in the middle of it. It is notorious and well known, needing nerves of steel when playing, as it reaches, and some say surpasses, the heights of the instrument's range; it is also very exposed. Just strings, a few woodwind instruments and snare drum quietly accompany the trombone who has the tune.

I knew from rehearsals the solo was going to be interesting in performance, and with some trepidation, I started the piece as the final item of the first half. Well, if the trombonist had played half as well as at the rehearsal, I would have heaved a sigh of relief. This was far worse. Every top note was splashed all over the auditorium; carnage abounded. At the end, I left the platform of the arena and overheard the player say as he walked off, "Oh Jeez, I fooked it again!" He certainly had.

However, I think even that fades into insignificance when I remember back to a certain performance that I conducted of the same piece given by a well-known British orchestra in Vienna, one of the biggest musical capitals of Europe. Throughout *Bolero*, the snare drum plays an incessant, hypnotic two-bar rhythm that gradually gets louder and louder until, fifteen minutes, later it comes to a crashing and shattering conclusion.

On this occasion, I can only assume the snare drum player

had got his bars mixed up and spent more time in the wrong one, as no two musical ones sounded the same. Literally none, as his control of the sticks splattered far and wide. It was one of the most embarrassing musical moments of my life.

Another famous anecdote of performing this difficult piece was when I conducted it at the Royal Festival Hall with the National Symphony. Generally speaking, we would programme *Bolero* to finish the concert as the piece ends with a huge crashing chord and is difficult to follow. There are those occasions we will perform *Bolero* in the same programme with a piece of music that has an even bigger ending, such as the *1812*. Difficult to follow a composition that ends with canons and bells! In that instance, we put *Bolero* at the end of the first half.

At this performance, the saxes, and there were two of them, had assumed *Bolero* was in its traditional position, closing the concert. After the rehearsal, as they weren't in anything else, they went to the pub and stayed there.

When we came to the piece at the end of the first half in the evening's concert, I did not notice the lack of saxes until, very shortly after giving the down beat to start the piece, Perry Montague-Mason, the concert master of the orchestra, leant across to me and whispered, "Anthony, the saxes are not here!"

Of all the messages you don't want to hear just after you start a piece of music that contains two saxophones, each of whom has an important solo, that sentence is pretty high up the list. I looked over and indeed quickly saw there were two empty chairs where the saxes were supposed to be sitting. Apart from their own solos, one of them was also playing Eb clarinet, and that instrument also has a solo, so that made three solos. Sadly, both sax solos follow each other and, unless I could think of something quickly, this meant there was likely to be thirty-eight bars of no tune, just basic strings and snare drum playing the rhythm! In actual fact, it needed quicker thinking than that, as the Eb solo came earlier!

There are two basic tunes in *Bolero*, let's call them A and B. Reasoning that if I could persuade a different player playing the same version of the tune as the saxes, which was tune B, to play their solo more than once, we would be saved. There was not a lot of choice as only the bassoon, Eb clarinet, saxes and trombone have tune B as a solo, and out of the four players with the correct tune, two were missing. As we have already heard, the trombone solo was difficult enough to play once, so knew I could not choose that. That just left the bassoon, another notoriously difficult and well-known solo passage amongst the bassooning fraternity! His actual bassoon solo followed the flute and clarinet and was third up. He was followed, fourth up, by the Eb clarinet.

At the end of the bassoonist's own solo, which he played very well, I indicated to him with hand gestures to play it again. This he graciously did. A little later in the piece, we came to the first of the saxes, and I indicated to him, again please. He looked at me, sighed and played it. Then, following that, it was the turn of the second missing sax solo. Asking him again, he looked at me and just shook his head! I had a refusal!

My options were now very limited. I had two bars to think of a solution and was running out of time. In fact, with less than six beats to conjure up something, I had now run out of options! With the two-bar intro finishing, I just closed my eyes and resigned myself to the fact that at the UK's premier concert hall, in front of a full house, we were going to have sixteen bars of *Bolero* rhythm and no tune at all; still, that was better than the thirty-eight originally conjectured!

I brought the baton down for the third bar and, glory of glories, as if from afar, came the sound of the oboe d'amore playing tune B. What I had failed to take into account was that, although the oboe d'amore only plays tune A as a solo, later in the piece, when everyone is playing both tunes, tune B was written down for her and, with enormous presence of mind, she had played it. Saved by an oboe d'amore, which of course, in literal translation, means oboe of love, and I certainly did!

It also taught me a lesson: look around and make sure everyone you need is on the platform prior to starting a piece of music. If you ever come to one of my concerts, you will notice that is precisely what I do now... every time!

Talking of not noticing missing instrumentalists, a similar occurrence happened to Sir Thomas Beecham once but only at a rehearsal. He was conducting away, head in the score of a piece of music he did not know particularly well, when he shouted out, "Horns! Horns! You're playing far too loudly."

At this, just as Perry had done to me, the concert master leaned over to him and said, "Sir Thomas, the horns have not yet arrived!"

Not stopping, arms flailing about everywhere and without looking up, he said, "Well, tell them when they do get here, they are playing too loudly!"

I obviously passed my Irish *Class Spec* audition and, in November 1992, first conducted the Royal Albert Hall season of *Classical Spectacular*. When I started, we did four performances once a year; there was little lighting, no amplification and no introductions. When I left, fifteen years later, I presented and conducted two seasons of six performances each at the RAH, plus a number of overseas tours with a lighting and sound rig that would be the envy of most pop supergroups!

The amplification and lighting came about because Anthony Findlay took hold of the show and, having come from the offices of Harvey Goldsmith, a great promoter of mainly pop events, decided to ramp it up a notch or fifteen.

The presenting came about because when we had taken the show to an arena in Belgium, there had been a power outage mid-performance, and everything ground to a halt in the darkness as the orchestra lost their stand lights. The technicians managed to get some sort of emergency generator rigged and, during the hiatus while Anthony Findlay and others were crawling around the legs of the musicians trying to discover the source of the problem, which turned out to be a musician who had accidentally kicked one of the plugs out of the mains ring, I told one of my stories – in English! Not only that, but it was *The Two Ronnies* story, a story about two people most Belgians did not know, in a language not everyone spoke. This went well, so well that it was decided I would start talking to the audiences at the Royal Albert Hall, the home of *Classical Spectacular*. It became an integral part of the show for the rest of its life by the conductors who followed me.

I enjoyed *Class Spec* until, some fifteen years later, I had to leave. It didn't hit me all of a sudden; it was a slow realisation that for this show to be taken further, somebody else needed to do it. I had done as much as I could and was now repeating myself. I found the repetition of the music too restrictive. It was always *Nessun Dorma* and the *1812*, always a popular overture, aria, duet and instrumental composition. I kept having to come up with new ways of introducing the same pieces, and there's only so much you can say about the *1812* or *Nessun Dorma*. The audiences hearing it obviously loved it, and when they came back, they would hear something they had not heard for a while, but I had! It was beginning to become a little like repetition in the West End.

As with constantly conducting a show, you know when it's time to leave, and that was when I was beginning to enjoy more the 'stand-up' I was doing in-between the music, than the actual music. I love the sound of laughter, and when I am firing on all twelve cylinders and the audience is coming along with me, there's little better, apart from great music-making!

In the early days, some of the musicians were not always completely comfortable with the show either. It was loud and a very difficult arena in which to perform at your best. The public, on the other hand, flocked to it. If you are not a devotee of the purest form of classical music, it is an excellent way of listening to some great classics, performed well and in a modern and contemporary way.

There came a tipping point in 2006, when I was conducting the City of Birmingham Symphony at the National Indoor Arena in Birmingham. The sound amplification was so enormous that what had up until then been a difficult environment onstage, became impossible.

One of the main things an orchestra has to do is listen, listen to each other and listen to themselves. It is absolutely vital, as only then can an orchestra become a homogeneous whole, rather than a lot of individual musicians playing together. On that stage in 2006, it became impossible. The sound was like a wall of indeterminate noise, and I had to stand there and frantically wave my hands around, trying to keep the whole thing together rather like a traffic policeman. Making music went out of the window; it was an exhausting exercise in staying together. I blamed myself when the two sides of the stage played apart.

I went up to Anthony Findlay in the interval and said he had to turn it down, as we were in serious danger of falling apart; we were unable to hear each other, let alone the two sides of the stage. His reply is etched in my memory, "Maybe, but it's sounding ruddy marvellous out front!" He was, of course, as all promoters should do, prioritising the desires of the audience who were, to give him his due, loving it! At that point, I knew I had to leave and hand it on to others who were better at coping with the situation than me. John Rigby provided wonderful continuance of that great show until someone at the Royal Albert Hall, in their infinite wisdom, decided to end its residency.

For me, *Class Spec* had been fifteen years of fun, laughter, great music and making new and lasting friendships, especially with the man who provides the bangs.

Lincoln Parkhouse is his name, and he would not mind me

describing him as a large gentleman with as big a personality to match. He has been responsible for all the pyrotechnics in *Class Spec* from the very beginning. His company Just FX is the doyen of companies involved in the 'banging' industry, though suspect I might have to explain the word 'doyen' to him! If you want an effect with a bang, then Lincoln is the go-to guy. He is also very amusing and not above making you look a fool!

I was about to conduct 'Thunderbirds' in a concert at the Royal Albert Hall and got very muddled with the name of the man who created the wonderful miniature models in *Thunderbirds*, *Goldeneye* and *Superman*, amongst many others. Both Lincoln and I felt enormous admiration for this incredible genius called Derek Meddings, whose name could so easily be spoonerised!

In trying to mention my admiration for him to the audience, I got my tongue completely twisted. After uttering names like Meyrick Deddings, Derek Beddings, Meadow Geddings and getting hopelessly confused, I recalled our mutual admiration and shouted in some desperation up to the gallery of the hall, where I knew Lincoln would be getting ready to fire his rockets, and asked him to remind me of the elusive name. I am not entirely certain at this point what I expected, after all, I was on the concert platform, and he was several miles away at the top of the Royal Albert Hall. There was an expectant silence from the audience, obviously anticipating someone to come quickly to the rescue of this dithering idiot on the podium. After a slight pause, and with perfect timing, in a clear, ringing voice which echoed everybody's thoughts, there came from on high not the answer I was seeking but the exasperated roar from Lincoln of, "Get on with it!" Even now, if conducting a concert and I realise I am wittering on, I can hear his voice and obey!

Lincoln's character is as large as his form, and I will always remember him telling us the story of taking pyrotechnics abroad for the first time. This happened to be that first *Classical*

Spectacular I had done in Ireland. Although at the beginning of the '90s, the 'troubles', as they were called, were approaching the end, his carnet declaration to the custom officials of explosives, wiring and canons, resulted in an interesting conversation with those officers to say the least!

Taking *Class Spec* to a Scandinavian country was another 'event'. Our technical team had enquired from the local team whether they complied with their laws, and everything was exactly as it should be. We were assured it was. You can imagine my surprise at the end of the *1812* when, about to give the cue to the choir for their entry, I saw the ladies and gentlemen all starting to scatter and flee the platform, closely followed by the orchestra. Our pyrotechnics had set fire to the backcloth which, despite those assurances, did not comply with the local laws, was not flame-proof and now well alight. I must say I also did not linger long on the concert platform. However, there are no crews as good as the British ones, and with the standby fire extinguishers they always placed nearby, they soon had the situation under control, and back we went to finish the performance!

We went to Germany and played in some of the main arenas there. These included Cologne, Hamburg and Berlin. However, the most moving and oddly uplifting venues were in Nuremburg and Frankfurt. Part of the programme the Royal Philharmonic Orchestra and I were performing were the pieces at the end of a Last Night of the Proms programme: 'Rule Britannia', 'Land of Hope and Glory', you know, the ones William Glock hated so much! There, in the Festhalle Messe in Frankfurt, a hall that, having sent mass transports to the Nazi concentration camps, has a terribly dark history in the Second World War, we were playing pieces of music indelibly associated with Great Britain. Yet the Germans were loving it, joining in and waving their flags just as the British do. This just proves great music is great music wherever and however it is played and can be a powerful force for good. I just hope the madman responsible for so many deaths was looking up from the depths of hell and reflecting on the errors of his ways.

The show at the Royal Albert Hall also provided my father, who you may remember in my childhood had got me out of bed by playing 'God Save the Queen' in F major without a Bb, with an enjoyable diversion as well. He was hugely proud of my achievements on the concert platform but had not necessarily enjoyed them for the right reasons. He once insisted on watching the test match in my dressing room backstage, instead of taking his seat in the auditorium while I conducted one of the world's great orchestras, the Royal Philharmonic, in one of the world's great symphonies, Beethoven's *No. 6*. He may have been right and chosen the better performance!

At *Class Spec*, after listening to one piece of music, however short it was, he thought he had listened to them all and found a diverting way of amusing himself. The show has an enormous number of performers on the stage but not always at the same time. For instance, if we are performing the *William Tell Overture* at the very beginning, the number of musicians required to perform that piece is very much smaller than say, those required for *Bolero*. Some musicians might come on after *William Tell* if they are required in the next piece, yet crucially, some musicians might go off. Maybe the cor anglais, required in *Tell*, is not required in the next few pieces, so off the player would go whilst I chatted to the audience.

Dad's one task he set himself while watching was to count the total number of performers in the orchestra, choir and military band who appeared onstage. However, and this was crucial, to his delight, not everyone appeared at the same time! Was the organist the same person who played the piano and celeste on the stage? There was quite a walk between the two instruments which inevitably involved a backstage route. Did the same person do the walk, or were there two? Percussionists were always a good one for Dad. We had six in total at *Class Spec*, seldom onstage at the same time. Perhaps two were required for the first piece but none in the next, so off they would go. Then, a little later, a piece of music might require three, but they may not have been the two in the first piece and were perhaps brand-new musicians. Or maybe one was the same and two were new! He would spend the entire performance trying to remember faces, always recognising those who were on, those who had not yet come on but, crucially, always remembering those who had come on but gone off, before coming on again! That was bliss for Dad!

For a while after leaving the show, I was persona non grata at Raymond Gubbay Ltd. However, all was soon forgiven, and I even went back and conducted the twenty-fifth anniversary performances of *Classical Spectacular* at the Royal Albert Hall. All sound issues had been solved by the upgrading and modernisation of the system and everyone, including the musicians, loved it. Hell, even I loved the music-making and intros of well-loved pieces of music!

I still shudder when remembering the base bins placed under the stage in the early days of the amplified show. They would make the stage floor vibrate until you felt sick!

As of summer 2020, I have conducted in the hall 251 times, causing a former chief executive to once say, he thought no one had appeared as a featured artist more often in the hall than I had.

Scene 3: The Scandal of Musicians' Pay

The first professional orchestra I ever conducted was the BBC Concert Orchestra in a studio recording for the BBC R2 programme introduced by David Jacobs called *Melodies for You* in the Queen Elizabeth Hall on the Southbank on 21 July 1983, subsequently alternating between the BBC's concert and radio orchestras.

When, in 1991, the BBC, in their infinite wisdom, decided to scrap the BBC Radio Orchestra, I argued with anyone who would listen, that if they had to disband any of their London orchestras, and only if they had to, the radio orchestra was not the one to go. They had such a different identity from the other two BBC orchestras in London: the BBC Concert and BBC Symphony. With smaller groups from within their ranks, such as the Big Band and the Radio Showband, the radio orchestra were able to form many different ensembles. If any orchestra should disband, I reasoned, it was the Concert Orchestra, as they had an almost identical line-up to the Symphony Orchestra and very often crossed repertoire. I once argued this at the top table of the Classical Brits to a lot of important BBC bosses. No one listened, and the BBC, not for the first or indeed last time, retired one of their jewels!

What is not widely known is that, whilst BBC and regional orchestras are salaried, the members of the Philharmonia Orchestra, London Philharmonic, London Symphony and Royal Philharmonic are not. This means they are freelance and independent which, whilst giving them a lot of benefits, such as creating their own working environment and the ability to appoint a board from within the orchestra itself, also brings some downsides. The main one being, they only get paid when they work, work gained for them by the management of the orchestra, who themselves are salaried and employed by the members of the orchestra. Basically, when the orchestra works, they get paid, and when it doesn't, they don't. The fee paid to the orchestra by promoters has to pay for the musicians and also the management team. The Arts Council also gives a grant to each orchestra, and each gets a differing amount so they can promote their own concerts. Hopefully, sponsorship makes up the shortfall. The City of London looks after the LSO, and the RPO gets the smallest slice of the cake.

Work is sometimes extremely hard to find. Four independent, world-renowned orchestras fighting for the same limited market. Every orchestra at some point suffers from a dearth of employment, and it has not been uncommon for the fabulous musicians in these famous orchestras to paint and decorate or mini-cab to earn a living. A scandalous state of affairs, made all the more ridiculous when star-name conductors and soloists can command fees of £50,000 or more for one concert, and the people actually making the glorious sound for them are paid so poorly. There are one or two employers for whom I have not increased my salary in fifteen years. I am already getting a decent amount and to charge more would, for me, be immoral.

Let's take the average pay of a day in the life of a rank-and-file violinist in one of those orchestras. In London, they have to attend a three-hour rehearsal, then perform in the two-and-a-half-hour concert; they have had to pay to travel to the concert venue – if they have gone by car, they have had to pay to park the car as, let us face it, public transport late at night is not great – they have had to purchase the expensive instrument they will play on; they have had to buy their meal or take it with them to eat between the rehearsal and concert; they have had to provide the clothes they will perform in, in the case of men a choice of either tails or white tuxedo and black trousers, or black dinner jacket, white dress shirts, bow ties, maybe black shirts; in the case of women, long or short black or coloured dresses or an assortment of tops and skirts. All this after they have reached the standard necessary to perform at the highest level with years, and I mean years, of dedicated practice and tuition. The reward for this endeavour? The princely sum (in 2021) of approximately £120 – for the whole day! Travelling outside London, it is slightly different as they will receive allowances for travel and, if necessary, overnight stays or late returns, the idea being that covers their expenses for the journey. No wonder some musicians are disillusioned, living for the performances that are on a different level, that transport them to places and feelings that are unimagined, for when that happens, the experience is priceless.

Meanwhile, I found a niche as a conductor who, thanks to *The Two Ronnies*, was at ease communicating with an audience. I found I could talk to an audience and make them laugh and yes, occasionally cry. There is nothing better than the dialogue between an audience and me. Gauging what mood they are in and whether they are going to be easy or hard work. Sometimes I forget what I'm going to say as there is no script and occasionally can be completely thrown.

For instance, one performance at the Royal Albert Hall, I went into the audience, as I often did, trying to see if anyone wanted a one-to-one chat with me, to maybe bring them up onstage to conduct the orchestra. I could see a very excited man, probably about thirty years of age, waving at me; he seemed like fun! Approaching him closer, I could see this might be a mistake. He was full of energy and bouncing around all over the place. Anyway, I thought, too late now, what could possibly go wrong? As it happened, quite a lot! I said to him, "Hello. What's your name?"

"Cecil," he replied in a very camp voice.

"Have you come far?" I asked him.

"No, just around the corner." Now some people think, especially when it goes well, that the people I talk to in the audience are plants, that is people I know and put in the audience. This is always untrue, so I will generally say to the person, "We've not met before, have we?"

Instead of the usual expected answer, the excitable young man said, "No, at least not since last night!" I looked at him and he added in a very coy manner, "Don't you remember last night?"

"No, I most certainly don't," I replied extremely quickly. Meanwhile, I could see the Royal Philharmonic who, accustomed to my wanderings, did not usually pay too much attention to my act with members of the audience, now paying full attention to the drama unfolding in the auditorium of the Royal Albert Hall.

I tentatively asked him up onstage with the immortal words, "Follow me," before realising what I had said, hastily adding, "Not too close though!" What followed had the audience and orchestra in fits of laughter. I love it when unforeseen episodes occur and the sound of uncontrolled laughter is filling whatever venue you happen to be performing. I also like the sound of silence, when the music of Beethoven or Mozart fades into nothing, or you reach the climax of some wonderful piece of music, and you are left shattered. No words are then necessary.

Scene 4: Divorce, Music-Style

By 1990, I was earning a living at conducting orchestras but still not enough to enable me to marry, buy a house and have a family; my parents taught me never to rely too much on the state.

There have been times, particularly in the corporate world, when I have known I can charge more than my usual fee, but more importantly, so can the orchestra. It's an odd thing, in the business world – the more you charge, the better they think you are at your job. If you charge too little, businesses think you can't be any good! This of course makes no sense at all to us musicians, as we can all name people who are earning a fortune yet are terrible at their jobs! On those occasions when I have thought there's money, I have said to orchestral managements, you can charge a higher fee and distribute it to the players.

At high-profile corporate events, an entire orchestra will cost half as much as a top guest star and for a few glorious years we were extremely fashionable, as bosses filled the stage with eighty musicians, as opposed to one guest star. Especially as that one guest star would come out, do twenty minutes of stand-up, which may or may not go down well, distribute a few awards and go off pocketing £30,000 or more! Eighty musicians looked much better value than one star, and we were probably half the cost!

There have only been three orchestras with whom I have had major disagreements, walking out on all three! I like to think I am a very mild-mannered guy – I like people; I like orchestras – but one thing to really get under my skin is a lack of effort!

The first orchestra I walked out on was a British one, the occasion, a concert at Crystal Palace. It was outdoors; the weather was not good; and the orchestra was a contract one. However, that was no excuse for what was about to happen.

There had been a bit of horseplay, larking around and a general lack of goodwill and discipline in the first part of the rehearsal. It was taking far longer to rehearse than it should have done as the orchestra was so restless. Then we came to the *William Tell Overture*. As I always do when performing this piece, because the opening is for five cellos, two double basses and timpani, I rehearse these eight musicians on their own immediately prior to the break, letting the rest of the orchestra go for an early break. We played the opening through and the principal cellist at the end said, and I've never forgotten his exact words, "Yes, very nice, Anthony, very nice, but I think you'll find our way the best way!"

That was the spark! I had had enough and flung down my baton, saying, "Do it any bloody way you like – you'll have to do it without me," and walked out!

Eventually, just as I was considering my options, after all I had a contract, the cellist came and found me and tried to patch things up. Reluctantly, I went back and tried to continue the rehearsal. When it came to the concert, they played terribly, just awful. Subsequently, I found out the horn section was having a competition with the trumpet section to see who could play the loudest, with the obvious split note results. More was to come.

In the middle of the *Blue Danube Waltz*, there is a two-bar phrase that sometimes has a ritardando (slowing down), and sometimes does not. I had specifically rehearsed this passage and told them, no slowing down, it's not in the score so let's keep going! During the concert, and you're ahead of me, despite me conducting it in time, they slowed down and then looked at me as if to say, what are you going to do about that? So, I told them! I shouted at them they were the worst bloody orchestra I had ever conducted! They looked shocked, as indeed was I.

I've only been back to them once in thirty years, and there was an uneasy truce between us. I still didn't like them, even though the main culprits had gone. I know I have lost work as a result of the orchestra and me having an unspoken agreement not to work with each other. They have not asked me, and I have not asked them to do either my commercial or concert work, occasionally having to tell managements to choose between them or me. So far, it has always been me!

Interestingly, when the principal cellist left this orchestra, he was booked into the National Symphony. At the beginning of the rehearsal, he came up to me and said, "This must be your worst nightmare."

I took great pleasure in informing him that no, it was his! After that concert, I never saw him again.

The second orchestra was in Holland and is now defunct. We were doing a piece of music based on a new musical and there had been too many copying errors in the parts that we were recording. Silly things like a bottom F for the violins. As the lowest string on the violin is tuned to a G, the F was a tone lower and couldn't physically be played. I guess, unknown to me, the orchestra knew the writing was on the wall for them and were not a happy band. Things went from bad to worse as we tried to sort out the many errors in the parts. In the end, their attitude got to me. When we got to the two-day pause in the sessions, pre-planned as I had a concert with the Philharmonia Orchestra back in the UK, my intolerance once again got the better of me and I shouted at them that I was off to conduct a real orchestra!

However, they did give me the experience of appearing in one of the great concert halls of the world, the Concertgebouw in Amsterdam. It was decided that, as an awful lot of money had been spent on this recording, we would do a full performance with the piece as the second half of a public concert. We had to find something else to fill the first. They chose a dazzling orchestral tone poem by the Dutch national composer Wagenaar, called *Cyrano*. His tone poem is similar in style to *Don Juan* by Richard Strauss and *Aurora* by Britain's William Lloyd Webber. I then also programmed *The Firebird Suite* by Igor Stravinsky.

I have to say it was a fabulous concert, especially in the Concertgebouw. For me, it was difficult to top the beginning!

I was in my dressing room prior to the concert and, not knowing the hall terribly well, wasn't exactly sure where it was. A couple of people came to fetch me before the start of the concert and, after walking for a short while, they stopped outside two huge double doors. Although I could hear the orchestra tuning up, I couldn't see through the usual narrow gap between the doors leading onto the stage. Standing to one side of these massive double doors, one of the men said, "No, Maestro, please stand here!" I moved to the other side. "No, here!" I was forced to stand in the middle. They then got clearance and, with one broad sweep, opened both doors at the same time.

I couldn't believe it. I was not at the usual side of the stage but framed and spotlit in the opening of these doors at the top of the tiered platform of the stage. There was a red carpet leading down from these double doors, through the choir seats filled by the audience, through the orchestra, all the way to the podium.

I walked down this carpet; the orchestra stood; the audience clapped; I reached the podium and took a deep bow. However good the concert was, the music was always going to be a slight anticlimax after that!

The third orchestra was in China. I have been to China a number of times and never had a problem, until the last visit. I won't name the orchestra, but it was huge. I believe there were well over two hundred and fifty musicians of varying standard in the orchestra, and that was the problem. I required an orchestra of fewer musicians than normal, and they elected to give me the least capable, leaving the top players at home with their families and their Sunday evening meal. At the first rehearsal, I gave the down beat for the first piece of music, which was the overture to *Ruslan and Ludmilla* by Glinka, and what came out was unrecognisable... literally! I tried to rehearse it, eventually coming to the conclusion that it would be forever beyond their abilities. Having reached that inevitable conclusion, for the first and only time in my life, I fired the entire orchestra, which I admit is quite a claim! As there was an audience coming to the first concert, which was outdoors and a free taster for the main concert still to come, I played the piano and talked, yes, in English, to a bemused Chinese audience! However, the main concerts were still to come!

The recriminations began immediately. This is where I discovered that when you booked a Chinese orchestra, you paid for the whole two hundred and fifty plus musicians, and the orchestra management then decide who to send! As the wages are not high in China commensurate to the West, no one hiring an orchestra outside the country would know this. I became incensed at the least capable musicians being sent, taking it as a personal insult. After much discussion, which did not involve me as it was held in Chinese, the management agreed to provide a better orchestra for the remaining concerts in a couple of days. We were to meet at a rehearsal the next day. Meanwhile, I was quietly seething. Of course, I should have moved on and forgotten it. I hadn't, and it only needed a spark. One was provided!

The different and better musicians who came to the first rehearsal of the new orchestra were now equally as resentful as me. They had, after all, been given a few days off when their less talented colleagues had been booked. Thanks to my tantrum, they had now been told to play instead. They let me know their irritation in no uncertain manner. Truculent, piqued, lazy, all words to describe the attitude of some of them. In the end, I saw one of the first violins looking so bored and slouched in his chair, hardly moving his bow, that I'm afraid I singled him out.

One thing I do know is that the Chinese never like losing face in front of people. They are just as likely to agree or say yes, even when they don't, rather than admit they do not know something. I stopped the rehearsal and shouted at him, "You! Either sit up and play properly or go home. There is no room for you in an orchestra if you don't pull your weight. You're letting me down; you're letting your colleagues down; and you're letting yourself down!"

There was a deathly silence, so I called a break in the rehearsal. I'm not sure how accurate the translation had been, but when we came back from the break, he'd gone home. For me that was fine; for him it was humiliation.

Later, I apologised to the concert master of the orchestra for the way I had spoken to the musician, and he gave me to understand that it was fine and pretty much to be expected. However, I knew I had overstepped the mark and it is another of those occasions remembered with some shame.

So, my last visit to China really was my last visit to China! I know this as a British orchestra, intending to tour that country, had asked me to conduct. Negotiations proceeded along nicely until the Chinese heard who was going to conduct. All they said was, "Anthony Inglis? No!"

Ah well, I don't think it's too bad to have had issues with just three orchestras out of the eighty-nine I have conducted. Working with an orchestra is very much like a marriage. You have to get on, to appreciate each other and admire each other's abilities. Plus, yes, to overlook their faults (up to a certain point!); we all have them. Otherwise, you musically divorce your orchestra, and I have been musically divorced exactly three times.

Scene 5: Great Conductors of the past and My Personal Favourite

Conductors once thought they were second only to God, though I'm sure some thought it was the other way around! They would come on the stage, nose in the air, ignoring everybody and everything, close their eyes and make sure they looked wonderful. At a rehearsal of *L'Après-midi d'un Faune*, I once saw Stokowski destroy David Gray, the wonderful principal horn of the LSO. Stokowski's bullying manner meant that each time David Gray was made to play the difficult solo over and over again, it just got worse and worse; awful to watch.

There were of course many fabulous exceptions, and at this point I should mention my favourite conductor of all time, the one who, to me, personified musicianship combined with great artistry and humility yet had the gift of persuading every single musician he was conducting solely for them, encouraging them to surpass their already great ability.

In the early 1970s, each of the four main London orchestras had their own chief conductor, and you notice I discount the BBC Symphony; I have already mentioned Pierre Boulez and William Glock were busy ruining them at the time! The London Symphony had André Previn, the London Philharmonic had Bernard Haitink, the Philharmonia had Lorin Maazel and Riccardo Muti, but the Royal Philharmonic Orchestra had the greatest of them all: Rudolf Kempe. He is 'the one' I've been keeping. Other conductors would go to his concerts, and I remember once seeing the eminent British conductor Sir Charles Groves in the audience. No wonder! I went to all Kempe's concerts and the RPO played for him like no other. Every single one was an event not to be missed.

I am a conductor, and it is like magicians when they see someone else perform a trick, they generally know how it's done. I can see how a conductor is working and how he's either succeeding with the orchestra or not as the case may be. With Kempe, I couldn't. How did he get that sound that no other conductor could? How was the orchestra playing so together when there was a minimum of beating? How did they play so musically when there appeared no overt emoting?

I started conducting the orchestra while there were still a number of musicians in it who had played for him and asked them what it was that made them play like that. People like Jim Warburton who played fourth horn, Erich Gruenberg who led the orchestra and with whom I did some concertos, the co-leader Pan Hon Lee, whom I appointed to the *Phantom* orchestra, and Anne Collis, percussionist and first female player into the orchestra. The answers were varied and fascinating, the overriding one being they adored him and wanted to do their utmost for him; they wanted to play better for him than even they thought they could. Some said it was his eyes. He could look at the entire orchestra, yet all thought he was looking directly at them, urging them to give of their best, and they did so because they wanted to. Whatever the reason, he was the greatest conductor I ever saw or am likely to in the future.

The ending of the relationship was sad, as the story I was told was that there was some dispute between him and the management of the RPO. They had engaged an American conductor by the name of Henry Lewis to conduct in the Royal Festival Hall, and the music Mr. Lewis elected to conduct was… the tone poems of Richard Strauss. Now if there was one section of repertoire at which even Kempe surpassed himself, it was Richard Strauss. Kempe then took the recording of the Strauss tone poems he was scheduled to conduct with the RPO to the Dresden State Orchestra. I can do no better than recommend those recordings. In my opinion, no finer recording of anything exists! Just listen to the *Dance of the Seven Veils*. The energy, the fire, the passion. Surely that was in one take?

I went to one of Mr. Lewis's concerts, and one only; I did not buy any of his recordings!

Of course, it might have been the other way around and Kempe chose to record with the Dresden orchestra over the RPO and in riposte, the RPO invited Mr. Lewis to conduct the same repertoire. In my view, whatever the truth of the situation, the management of the time should have done everything in their power to avoid losing the greatest conductor who ever lived!

Kempe resigned shortly after, accepting the position of chief conductor at the BBC Symphony, before dying months later at the early age of sixty-five. Some members of the RPO were heard to mischievously suggest Kempe went in, conducted the BBC orchestra and gave up the will to live!

Talking of which, there is a story of a Philharmonia Orchestra recording session in the 1950s with Herbert von Karajan. Karajan was famous for closing his eyes at the beginning of a piece of music, only opening them when he reached the end! This was rumoured to be because he did not know who was playing what or when, so by closing his eyes he didn't need to cue or look at anyone. A very different technique to Kempe!

At one recording session, and because he knew what people were saying about him, he stopped the orchestra, and with his eyes still closed, he went down the score naming the actual note each and every instrument was playing. Some feat of memory, unless of course he had pre-planned the whole episode!

Karajan, whose membership of the Nazi party during the Second World War was controversial, casting a cloud over his career to the end of his life, was notoriously cantankerous and dictatorial. Towards the end of his immediate post-war era with the Philharmonia, the relationship between him and the orchestra broke down completely. He was in the middle of one of his tirades in 1960, when the orchestra violinist and Second World War RAF fighter pilot Peter Gibb stood up and quietly told him that during the war he had shot better Germans than him. Karajan immediately walked out, followed by the orchestral management who tried to persuade him to return. They said they would ask Mr. Gibb to apologise. Karajan replied he would only come back if the entire orchestra apologised! The orchestra refused and Karajan never conducted a British orchestra again.

This reminds me of another wonderful story involving a conducting competition, where students had to rehearse and conduct a short piece of music. One of the judges thought he would be clever and get the horn player in the orchestra to deliberately play a wrong note and see if the student noticed it. The first student came on and duly conducted the passage containing the deliberate wrong note but did not stop and correct it. The judge, halting the orchestra, asked the student why he hadn't spotted the wrong note played by the horn. To which the horn player stood up and said, he was terribly sorry, he'd forgotten to play it!

Over the years, I have had my share of bad behaviour in orchestras. There was a brilliant principal flute player in a British orchestra who appeared to enjoy baiting conductors.

On first visiting this orchestra, the player would try and intimidate me. Better people have tried and failed, and I think that's my West End training. In fact, the management rather admired the fact that I could not get wound up. In the player's favour was brilliance, and I forgive a lot if there's brilliance! I was told later by the orchestra manager that their music director, almost in tears in the middle of a rehearsal, said to her that he couldn't go back out there and face them.

Conducting the *Nutcracker Suite* with this orchestra, we came to the *Dance of the Mirlitons*, a pretty little movement for three flutes, made even more famous by Frank Muir extolling the virtues of a fruit and nutcase chocolate bar to the tune! In rehearsal, each time we played a ritardando at the end of a phrase, the player would deliberately mess it up, put the flute down across his knees and stare at me with a quizzical expression, as if to say, "There, what are you going to do about that then?"

I rehearsed it three times, each time with a small explanation yet the same result. After the third, I asked, "Are you enjoying yourself?" There was a slight smile and nod of the head, to which I said, "Neither the orchestra nor I have time for this," and moved on. It was perfect in the concert.

I have also had my share of poor orchestras. Nevertheless, I have still got on with them because they were trying hard, and that is all you can really ask. There is one I conduct in Europe, and I like the musicians; they do their best. However, their standard never gets beyond a certain level because they do not possess the ability to do so. Audiences seem to enjoy them, and I guess whatever your own personal feelings, that is the main thing.

One rehearsal that sums it up was when I decided to hold a string sectional on a difficult piece of music. It was probably a mistake, as nothing was ever going to alter the fact they could not play the music. At least with the whole orchestra playing, the strings were masked by the sound of the woodwind, brass and percussion. All sectional rehearsing achieved was to highlight their own inadequacies. I came off the platform at the end of that rehearsal, where the music the strings had played was frankly unrecognisable, and saw the promoter of the orchestra standing on the side. Having listened to the playing, I looked at him; he looked at me; I raised an eyebrow; he raised one of his; I raised the other; he raised both of his; I made as if to say something, but before I could, he shrugged his shoulders and said, "Such is life!" And you know what? He was absolutely right!

Scene 6: Wedding Bells and Start of Family (Not Necessarily in That Order!)

By 1993, I was earning good money and thought a family could be started. Jan became pregnant and I decided, after thirteen years of dating, to propose to her. She accepted, and some five months after Eleanor had been born at Queen Charlotte's Hospital in Hammersmith, we were married on 9 October 1994 at Kingston Parish Church, coincidently where Jan's parents had also been married.

It was some occasion, with people flying in from all over the world. Alison even flew over on Concorde as she now lived in Los Angeles and work commitments only allowed a very brief visit. Someone said of the day, it was like stepping back in time and seeing friends one hadn't seen for years. I liked that!

The wedding was a mini-production and included an orchestra made up of all the best players from the London orchestras, the church choir (who were and still are brilliant), plus Fiona O'Neill, a soprano I knew. We had two of my adored Victorian/Edwardian anthems sung by the choir: *The Evening Hymn* by Balfour Gardiner and *Expectans Expectavi* by Charles Wood. I had grown up with these anthems at Marlborough College and indeed had played the organ for them and sung the alto and bass lines at different times.

There is a marvellous organ introduction to the *Evening Hymn*, and I programmed it years later for a performance at one of the Cunard concerts in Liverpool Cathedral. Upon hearing the Cathedral Choir rehearse it, the organist Dr Ian Tracy said to me afterwards, "Don't worry, Anthony, I'll make the organ growl a bit more for the performance." A marvellous description of what the instrument is capable of doing and needs at the beginning of that piece.

We also had *Morgan* performed during the signing of the register. Written by Richard Strauss as a present for his wife and based on a love poem by John Henry Mackay, it is a beautiful song. When performed during the service by Fiona and Chris Warren-Green on the violin solo, it was a moment of utter romance.

The wedding was also remembered for the fact that, whilst I was signing the register, Jan turned round to the audience, oh alright congregation, and after thirteen years of being together, mouthed the words, "Got him!"

During the wedding, and much to the annoyance of Leo Andrew, Jan's friend who was giving her away as substitute for her late father, the vicar told the story of the dress rehearsal. When it came to me repeating the phrase, 'with this ring I thee wed, with my body I thee worship and with all my worldly goods I thee endow', I paused after saying it, adding the line, 'except the Porsche', the car I was driving at the time! Leo said at his reception speech he nearly killed the vicar as that story was due to be featured prominently in his own speech!

We walked out of the church to the most beautiful performance of the Bach *Double Violin Concerto* played by Chris and Rolf Wilson, two of the highest regarded violinists by their peers in the country. We slightly defied the vicar who had not wanted Eleanor to be a part of the service. She was now such an integral part of our lives, I insisted I pick up this little love bundle of joy from the nanny as we walked out of the church. My parents had walked out of the church under raised swords; we went under a parade of raised batons!

The reception was held on Raven's Ait, an island in the middle of the Thames at Kingston, and it was rather wonderful watching everyone trying to get across on this rickety launch. It cost me a lot of money as, sadly, both Jan's parents, the people by tradition supposed to pay for the wedding, were both no longer alive. This explains why, when the children suggested a few years ago we renew our marriage vows on board a Cunard ship, I said, to much indignation, "Good heavens no – it was bad enough the first time!" I still maintain I was talking about the expense, not the occasion!

My father, meanwhile, quaffed as much champagne as he could with the line, "If my son is paying for this, I'm going to drink as much as I can," and he did!

To make amends for the renewal of our marriage vows misunderstanding, twenty-five years later, almost to the day, on 5 October 2019, Jan and I held our silver wedding anniversary and went back to Raven's Ait. Too many people from our wedding reception were unable to be there as they were no longer with us. However, all our brothers and sisters bar one, all our children, most of our nephews and nieces and nearly all our first and second cousins were present. With as many people as possible from the wedding reception and the friends we had subsequently made, it was a perfect BBQ on a very special island with very special people.

It would be invidious of me to mention any single person by name who was there, but I must mention one as the story about him got a good laugh! That man is Anthony Findlay. He has been at most of the Superman strips onstage I have done. I must confess, the actual strip when I reveal a costume underneath my concert clothes does make me feel very much like the Man of Steel himself, as I certainly need the nerves!

The first time I did it was in Melbourne, and he and I literally collapsed laughing with relief into each other's arms in the dressing room afterwards as we realised the gag had worked. For all the discussions and planning, you never know if anything is going to get a good reaction until you actually put it in front of an audience. We were so relieved it had, that Huw Humphries on the management of the MSO, said our reaction in the dressing room afterwards, as Anthony helped me out of the suit, was almost funnier than the moment onstage.

Getting into the costume is a two-person affair and trial and error has ensured a routine that makes sure the costume is tucked in and hidden from the closest of observers. There is a particular annoying join in the crutch of the trousers that has to be folded and velcroed correctly otherwise the trousers can come apart. He has a routine that involves prodding a pencil up and seeing if it disappears! This enabled me to slightly bend the truth and say that I was thrilled Anthony Findlay was there as, 'he has had a finger up my backside more times than my proctologist'!

In September 1995, I was confronted, really for the first time, by close death. My father had had a colostomy for the family disease of colon cancer quite early in his life but never any follow-ups to see if there had been a resurgence of colon cancer. When one occurred, we were all very angry about this, none more so of course than my father. If there had been, he might have had a much longer life. Who knows, he might even have seen his grandson join the service of which he was most proud. As it is, he had a lingering death, where the cancer slowly spread through his body, eating away at him from the inside. Shortly before he died, I went down to see him but found it incredibly difficult to acknowledge his time was up so did not stay. He was a shadow of the man he had been, needing help for the most basic and menial of tasks. I have always regretted not having the courage to stay that night and confront his death. We had never been close; boarding school had seen to that. However, I made sure I told him I loved him, and he understood what I was saying. I watched as his eyes filled with tears. He died the next day.

Scene 7: Family Pride

Our first child Eleanor, born in 1994, was quickly followed by Dominic in '96 and Alexander in '98.

About an hour before Jan gave birth to Eleanor, I had arranged a meeting with some Japanese producers for a recording I was about to do and, as they were flying back that evening, they insisted they would come to the hospital on the way to Heathrow! They asked if they could see the mother-to-be, and instead of saying, no, absolutely not, on no account, no, I went and checked with Jan. She is one in a million and, thinking this was important to me, said that would be fine. So, rather stupidly, I took them up to the maternity ward of Queen Charlotte Hospital in Hammersmith. She actually got up and managed to stagger to the door of her room, peer round it, smile weakly at this group of what looked like Japanese tourists (without their cameras I'm happy to say), wave weakly once or twice, before heading back to bed to give birth. Game girl!

Eleanor was the only one I actually saw being born. I thought I should, though after my medical experiences, I desperately wanted to be the typical old-fashioned father pacing the corridor outside. Therefore, I did see this grey little thing being born. She was a meconium birth, which is some medical term for 'panic everyone'. Doctors and nurses rushed this silent baby out of the delivery room, before bringing her back in, happily screaming sometime later.

I was much more sanguine about the next two that came along, even packing my wife off in a taxi for the third when contractions announced it was time. I must confess to not being entirely certain the taxi driver would agree to the fare! Sadly, both my wife's parents and my father were at that time no longer with us, and my mother was elsewhere. I still maintain my excuse for the taxi was that someone had to stay home and look after the other two, even the nappy changing. Though my wife maintains to this day that they were even brought into the hospital for that!

Eleanor followed her mother into acting and appeared in films like *Beauty and the Beast*, *Star Wars* and *Suffragette*. Of course, with a mother who spent a season or two with the Royal Shakespeare Company at Stratford and London, one of them was bound to follow. She has appeared so often in major Hollywood movies that I think we've become slightly blasé! Actually, some of the smaller films like *Hollow Crown* she made for the BBC were more interesting, as the parts she got were bigger and better. She ended up winning best actress at the 2019 Movievalley Bazzacinema Awards for her role as Angie in the film *Chopper*. She now has a successful career with a new company in the food industry.

Dominic is at the beginning of his flying career with the Royal Air Force and has elected to go rotary. He trained at Shawbury and is now flying Chinooks. He also got his fixed-wing Private Pilot's License and, as a Christmas present in 2016, gave us a surprise flying trip from RAF Scampton to Duxford, from where my uncle flew and fought the Battle of Britain.

He had not told us that, between courses, and in addition to his RAF pilot's fixed-wing training at Cranwell, he had done what was necessary to gain his PPL. He asked us up to Cranwell for a day on base, keeping the secret of his PPL success. Changing the base from Cranwell to Scampton on the morning of our arrival had us wondering what was going on. I guessed a back seat in a Red Arrow (home to the squadron in 2016) and Jan had guessed a flight in a Chinook. We both thought he had more influence in the RAF than he does!

The true reason for our visit to RAF Scampton was kept secret until we were checking for FOD (Foreign Object Debris) on the Scampton outer perimeter road, and he told us about his PPL and that we were off down south to Duxford for lunch. He took us to the RAF's PA28 and did his pre-flight checks.

It was odd seeing our son negotiating the tricky route between Scampton and Duxford, avoiding the congested air corridors around East Midlands Airport, whilst at the same time, realising my uncle was not much older when he flew spitfires in 1940 to and from the same airfield we were heading to, all the while being shot at!

The PA28 was an elderly plane without many of the navigational aids in most modern aircraft. All Dominic had was a good old-fashioned map, telling me at one stage to look out for the sugar factory as he had to turn left over it to avoid some restricted airspace. I must confess to a certain nervousness as I wondered what would happen if I missed it and we didn't turn left, and anyway, what the hell does a sugar factory look like from five thousand feet!

Fortuitously, we found it shortly before circling the control towerless Duxford (flight manoeuvres being controlled by a man with a walkie-talkie walking around the field), landing safely, just as my uncle had done nearly eighty years previously whilst avoiding enemy fighters.

As my young-looking twenty-year-old son got out of the left-hand seat, I did tell the Duxford marshaller who guided us to our parking spot on the apron and was staring with surprise, that his great-uncle had flown Spitfires out of Duxford in 19 Squadron during the Battle of Britain.

The only issue was the landing gear collapsed as we landed! No, not really, but the oil in the dampers did something and caused the oleo strut within the right telescopic undercarriage arm to collapse in on itself. All he had to do was get under the wing and, with his back, lift it, which caused the oleo strut to reposition itself. Not a particularly encouraging moment for the flight back!

Alexander worked hard at his music and showed a gift for it which, even after getting grade eight with distinction on the cello, he has decided not to pursue. He is now hunting various opportunities, until finding the right one.

They have all given me moments where I thought my heart was going to burst with pride. Eleanor, when she performed the role of Maria in *West Side Story* at the Leatherhead Theatre. Her final scene was unbelievable, both heart-wrenching and powerful, my whole body wracked with tears.

Dominic, when he passed out on Graduation Day at RAF Cranwell, winning the Bertram Dickson Trophy for best all-round performance in the air and on the ground and Bryan Memorial Trophy for best performance in ground school! Then again, a couple of years later when his family and godparents watched him on Wings Day at RAF Shawbury, passing out as a rotary pilot and winning three trophies in the process: the Captain Albert Ball VC Trophy awarded to an RAF pilot for best overall performance and the Scarf Trophy, also awarded to the RAF pilot obtaining the highest marks within the tactical phase. Plus the biggest one for the course, available to pilots from all three of the services, the NAS Shark Shield for best pilot.

Alexander's moment came when he led the cello section of Thames Youth Orchestra in a superb performance of Mahler's *Symphony No. 2* at the Barbican Hall on 29 March 2015. I spent the entire performance silently crying; this time it wasn't my schooldays and was good silent crying. I was watching my second son playing heaven-sent music and taking such an important role within that performance. At that point, I had conducted ninety-six times at the Barbican Hall, but no performance of mine had ever equalled the joy I felt than with that one.

They've also given many other moments of sheer unadulterated pleasure. Both the boys have sung at the Royal Opera House many times. We were lucky to have Tiffin School locally, and through their inspirational head of music, Simon Toyne, the boys were often invited to sing at Covent Garden, supplying children's choruses for *La Bohème* and *Hansel and Gretel* amongst others.

Dominic was also in the production of *Hansel* with Diana Damrau and Angelika Kirchschlager, conducted by Sir Colin Davis, that was broadcast on Christmas Day 2008. Alexander played and sang the boy treble solo in Puccini's one-act opera *Gianni Schicchi* with Sir Tom Allen, conducted by their music director, Antonio Pappano. I've been able to repay those moments of pride and joy Simon has given me by hiring the Tiffin boys' choir for a concert I was doing with the Philharmonia Orchestra at the Royal Festival Hall, then asking him to conduct his choir in their solo performance with orchestra. I think he enjoyed conducting this marvellous orchestra.

Not to be outdone, Eleanor was in the English National Opera production of Bellini's opera *Norma* at the London Coliseum. She did not have a singing role but was the actress in the opera.

It could be said that all my children have achieved more in the world of opera in their short lives than I have in my long career!

I don't think I was the greatest of fathers in terms of pulling my weight around the house and looking after the children. My only excuse is that by now I was working extremely hard, travelling to many overseas countries, even on one occasion travelling twice to Australia within the space of three weeks: first week Melbourne, second UK and two concerts, one of which was in the Channel Islands, and third week Perth. I did what I could but agree did not do much below the waist. I once saw my daughter projectile poo over my mother and thought, *I am never going to put myself in that line of fire!* Employing some nannies helped, but Jan was a very hands-on mother, and with me away so much, she was very much on her own.

Whilst Jan was bringing up three small children, I was being paid to travel the world, and one of the great joys of travelling and working at something you love so much is that it occasionally affords you free time. If I could, and even if on my own, I would visit local places of interest or notoriety, one such being the Auschwitz/Birkenau Concentration Camp.

While working with the Cracow Radio Symphony Orchestra in the south of Poland, I took a taxi further south to visit this scene of death.

It is true what they say: there is an awful, eerie silence about the place. Birds do not sing, and people walk around in silence. There is an air of oppression that pervades the atmosphere; the stillness is overwhelming. The most awful aspect of the visit is that visitors can see the rooms where there are thousands of spectacles, pairs of shoes (some very small), suitcases with initials denoting a family and other artefacts of human existence piled high from floor to ceiling. Each shoe, each suitcase, each pair of spectacles, each strand of human hair representing someone who was either exterminated in an instance or by a long, slow, painful death.

Then, there is Doctor Mengele's headquarters: the building where pain, misery and death were inflicted upon twins and children in the so-called name of science. Difficult for modern humans to comprehend.

My visit there made watching Stephen Spielberg's film *Schindler's List* in a small cinema in Tel Aviv a few years later grim. But, it does give much more poignancy when I conduct John Williams' emotional music in the concert hall.

Act 7

Scene 1: Katherine Jenkins; Favourite American City; Embarrassing Stories

On 26 June 2004, I conducted the Royal Philharmonic Concert Orchestra at Althorp House with a new upcoming mezzo-soprano by the name of Katherine Jenkins. Little did I know how important she was to become to me in my life, both on a professional and personal basis.

She had had an amazing first recording release titled *Premiere* and was riding high in the classical charts. Despite the age difference, or perhaps because of it – I was about to be fifty-two, she in her very early twenties – we quickly struck up a good rapport. One concert followed another and very soon I was flying around the world with her.

Success followed success for Katherine, and it could not happen to a nicer person. Like all great artists, she expects those she employs and those around her, even if she is not directly employing them, to know their job, and woe betide you if you don't. This is what all successful people at the top demand, and quite right too, otherwise how long would they stay there if those who were responsible for helping to keep them there did not know what they were doing? Great artists have to have their own talent to maintain their position at the pinnacle of their profession, and Katherine has it in buckets. I adore accompanying her and think it shows in the fun she and I so obviously have onstage.

There are tears too, such as the time we went to Whitehaven shortly after the Derrick Bird/Cumbrian massacre and she sang 'In the Arms of an Angel'. I don't know how she got through it. I certainly didn't as she sang to those most affected by the killing rampage. We were both in tears at the end.

I am very poor when it comes to keeping my emotions in check. I remember conducting the BBC Philharmonic in Manchester's Bridgewater Hall, shortly after the local taxi driver Alan Henning's beheading by ISIL, and dedicating the Barber *Adagio* to his memory. My voice cracked with emotion as I announced it, tears rolling down my cheeks as we played at the thought of the senseless ending of someone's life who was only trying to help those less fortunate than themselves.

Then there are the once-in-a-lifetime opportunities Katherine has given me. These days, I can no longer play the piano as osteoarthritis in the form of Heberden's nodes have struck the joints at the ends of fingers. Some have rather impolitely said I never could! I think it was Cameron who, after I had accompanied someone in a *Phantom* audition, said that my playing sounded like Mrs. Mills on speed. But before they became too painful, I used to accompany Katherine and she was invited, along with my father's idol Dame Vera Lynn CH DBE, to officially attend the Chelsea Flower Show. It was agreed they would sing together, and I would play the piano.

The piece Dame Vera and Katherine chose to sing at the Chelsea Flower Show was the iconic, 'We'll Meet Again'. My father would very definitely have thought that playing the piano for Dame Vera was the pinnacle of my career. Sadly, he had died some ten years previously but would certainly not have counted anything if he had witnessed that! He adored Vera and often said that is why he fought the war: for Vera and girls like her. I am sure she had heard it before, but that day I was able to tell her on behalf of my father.

Katherine gives her time freely to many worthwhile causes, and I help where I can. For instance, one Christmas special she did at the Royal Albert Hall, she invited Colin Thackery, the Chelsea pensioner who had won *Britain's Got Talent*, to perform with her on the stage. However, he had no music. All he had were the backing tracks of 'You Raise Me Up', his winning song from the show. I don't like combining live music with a recorded backing track in a concert; it creates different sound spectrums, and both suffer as a result. Therefore, I asked him for some music in order that the orchestra could accompany him. His management company searched for an arranger to convert the track to musical notes and were quoted £1000–£1500 which he would have to pay. I thought this was grossly unfair; Colin had served his country and fought in Korea; the least we could do was pay some of that back. It did not take me too long to do an arrangement and print the parts, giving it to him as a present in case he ever needed it again. At the performance, the whole hall stood and applauded this courageous man.

Katherine and I have been to many overseas territories together – Japan, Argentina, Australia, all over Europe, USA, South Korea, Taiwan, Thailand, China, Dubai, South Africa, Hong Kong, Brazil, so many – and all have been a wonderful experience. We always try and visit local sites, some touristy, some not so much. We went to a private safari park and climbed Table Mountain in South Africa, visited Buddhist temples and the largest reclining Buddha in Thailand. We have performed in the incredible opera house in Buenos Aires and journeyed on the bullet train in Japan and the boats of the Bangkok waterways. We have ascended to the top of the Burj Al Arab and ridden the gondolas in the extraordinary Jumeirah Al Qasr Hotel in Dubai. All have been incredible experiences, and I'm very lucky to have done this, while doing a job I love, with a person I adore.

But there are two visits with Katherine, which, for completely different reasons, will always hold a very special place in my heart.

At the beginning of 2011, my mother rang me one morning and informed me her eyes had turned yellow. She had made an appointment with her local GP and would ring again after her visit. I immediately drove down from Kingston and was at her house in Warsash when she got back from her appointment. She told me he had done some tests and she was to go back in a few days for the results, would I go with her? It was very strange. My mother, who had had her difficulties with medical issues, including having to walk with a stick for a large part of her life, looked as well as she normally did, apart from those yellow eyes. We went back together to hear the results of the tests and, as we suspected, it was not good news. She most probably had cancer and needed further tests to discover exactly whereabouts.

Through the course of the spring and into the summer, there were many visits to the hospital as they tried to cut out the pancreatic cancer but to no avail, and by the time of her eightieth birthday celebrations, it was becoming obvious the end was near.

Confined to a wheelchair, she had a huge celebration on 19 June when old friends, new friends and relatives came from far and wide to the Warsash Sailing Club. It was a wonderful day. My mother made an emotional speech where she stated quite clearly, she was not afraid of what was about to happen to her; I made a speech which was interrupted by a distant bar bell and me shouting mid-sentence, "Last orders, run!"

The highlight at the party for my mother was definitely when I accompanied her grandchildren singing her favourite song. When a child at school, some were given the opportunity of choosing the hymn to be sung at morning assembly, and when it came to her turn, she chose the same one every time. Apart from the fact she adored the hymn, she remembered nothing of it except the lyrics were the famous speech 'This Sceptred Isle' spoken by John

O'Gaunt from William Shakespeare's history play *Richard II*. The music and composer remained a complete mystery. However, she wished to hear the piece one more time.

I needed to find this and rang an old school friend of hers called Caroline Pratt. By a process of internet investigation and elimination of song titles amongst her school contemporaries, I discovered it was an anthem called 'England' composed by Sir Hubert Parry. I downloaded a rare copy and sent the music to all the grandchildren prior to the celebration. Amidst much emotion, we performed it at her eightieth.

Shortly after the party, I was due to set off on tour for a week to South America with Katherine but was obviously worried about going. We had twenty-four-hour care in place with a wonderful lady from South Africa living in the house who had experience of guiding people at the end. My sister was also there. I spoke with the doctor who told me I should go; there was nothing I could do. In any case, in his opinion, nothing would happen for a while and certainly not until after my due return.

Therefore, on 13 July 2011, just three short weeks after the party, I left for Brazil. Almost immediately, my mother's condition took a downwards turn, and she became confined to bed with some morphine in place. My brother flew over from France; I was in Buenos Aires, unable to leave my friends and colleagues and get back home. This is where Skype came to my rescue. My brother and sister set up a camera in her bedroom so I could be with them, and the night before flying back, we were all with her around her bed when she died.

I was so pleased that before she went, we were able to grant her last wish and perform 'England' for her. She had it performed at the beginning of her life and heard it again at the end. She also got it from the grandchildren at her funeral. I just wish it had not taken her passing for me to find the piece, and I had been able to take her to the Royal Albert Hall on 22 April 2012. For then she would have heard her favourite hymn performed by the Royal Choral Society and Royal Philharmonic Concert Orchestra in an arrangement I had done. I think she would have been very happy.

The other visit, and definitely my favourite place to visit with Katherine, has to be an airport in America. In March 2013, Katherine and I, plus her touring party (manager, tour manager, personnel assistant and sound engineer), did a mini-tour of America with local orchestras, Florida and California being the main beneficiaries of our expertise! It was at an airport, where we were catching a connecting flight, that the incident occurred that has made this my favourite place.

At Fresno Yosemite Airport whilst waiting for a connecting flight, one of our group went up to a bar and ordered a round of drinks. When they were brought back, we all sat in the bar's lounge consuming them. As I was about to take my first refreshing mouthful of beer, a waitress from the bar came up to me and asked to see my ID! Enquiring as to the reason, she told me that in Fresno they have a law whereby you are unable to consume alcohol in a public place under the age of twenty-five. She then added she merely wished to confirm I was over twenty-five and consequently allowed to consume alcohol on their premises! At this point in my life, I was sixty, very nearly sixty-one years of age!

Of course, I immediately thought this was a prank being played on me by someone in the touring party so refused. However, they swore blind it wasn't and, in the end, I had to show my passport to prove my legal ability to consume alcohol in Fresno.

To this day, no one from that tour party has ever come out and said it was a prank, and we still talk about it. Therefore, I like to believe that in 2013, at the age of sixty, the bar staff at Fresno Airport really did think I was under the age of twenty-five! I love Fresno!

Katherine and I have done many UK concerts, tours and overseas concerts. One that will be in my memory more than most is the time I was asked to conduct the Diamond Jubilee Concert at Buckingham Palace that celebrated Her Majesty the Queen's sixty years of reign. Many artists were asked to perform that evening, and I was the conductor for them all. One of them was Katherine, and she sang, and we danced together as the amazing National Youth Orchestra of Great Britain, a group of musicians who were all still at school, yet have the most amazing ability and enthusiasm for playing music, accompanied us. Also appearing that evening were Russell Watson, English National Ballet, New Adventures, Louise Alder, Kiri Te Kanawa, Laura Wright and Scarlett Strallen, amongst many others. It was quite an eclectic group.

For our Buck P dressing rooms, we were each given a private cubicle, curtained off for privacy, in a tiny corner of one of the large state drawing rooms overlooking the gardens. My cubicle contained a chair, a mirror and a small table all to myself, plus for company, a fabulous Reubens painting hanging on the wall. I was not to remain alone for long. Russell Watson was singing 'Bring Him Home', and the composer of the musical *Les Misérables*, Claude-Michel Schönberg, was going to play the piano from within the orchestra. I had known him since commissioning both him and Alain Boubil (the French lyricist) to write a symphonic suite based on *Les Misérables* and *Miss Saigon*, which I had recorded with the Bournemouth Symphony Orchestra and Chorus some years previously. For some reason, he had not been allocated a space, so I immediately invited him to share mine. The three of us, Claude-Michel, Reubens and I squashed into this tiny space. From that moment on, we had a steady stream of visitors who all wanted to pay homage to the great man.

We spent a happy few hours chatting about musicals, Buckingham Palace and family life. Incredibly, he lived next door to Sir Jeremy and Lady Belinda Morse in South Kensington and had done for a number of years, so they were firm friends. Belinda was an old school friend of my mother's, and they had kept in close touch until the death of my mother parted them. Sir Jeremy was the man after whom his great friend Colin Dexter had named his famous detective. Detective Chief Inspector Endeavour Morse was a fictional character who, in addition to the surname, bore more than a striking resemblance to Sir Jeremy with their shared love of cryptic crosswords and classical music. Sir Jeremy had nothing to do with the police though, as he became chairman of Lloyds Bank.

After the concert, I was able to renew my acquaintance with His Royal Highness Prince Edward, who famously had been, what the UK tabloid press loved to call, the tea boy for Andrew's RUG, though in reality he was not that at all. He was a much-valued member of the production team for *Phantom of the Opera*.

To be honest, I was surprised he spoke to me after the concert at Buck P, as I could not help but remember back to the occasion we were all sitting in an office at Her Majesty's Theatre having a meeting, and he said something that was of little relevance to the *Phantom* team. Forgetting who he was, or indeed where we were, I said in a very camp voice, "Ooooh, hark at her, dear!"

There was a ghastly moment of silence as everyone's cup of tea froze mid-air. Prince Edward was heard to say in an outraged voice, "Her? Her? What else do you call me behind my back?" Of course, in the theatre world, everyone is either of an indeterminate sex, a darling or a dear, and it was nothing personal, Your Royal Highness!

Anyway, as already discovered, if it was not for primogeniture, I might have outranked him!

Scene 2: Australia Revisited; Social Media

In June 2006, after an absence of seventeen years, I went back to Australia for the first time since *The Two Ronnies* and, once again, loved the country. We took *Classical Spectacular* there, first performing it with the Melbourne Symphony Orchestra in the Rod Laver Arena in Melbourne, before performing it with the Sydney Symphony Orchestra and taking it north to the Queensland Symphony Orchestra in Brisbane. The Australians had never seen anything like it: the noise, the music played at rock concert levels, the spectacle.

In fact, Anthony Findlay often tells the story of how, at the beginning, he found it almost impossible to make the local sound engineer amplify the orchestra at the rock-stadium level he required. A gentle technician, the man was used to raising an orchestra level to a normal place, where listeners could sit back and quietly contemplate life! That was not *Classical Spectacular*! Finally, in the Rod Laver Arena with the Melbourne Symphony Orchestra and Chorus, he got it and, announcing to no one in particular, said, "Forgive me for what I am about to do," reached over and, with one sweeping movement, pushed all the faders up as far as they would go!

It was in Brisbane on that tour I came out with one of my riskier jokes. Could I do it now? I'm not sure. Judge for yourselves.

At the Entertainment Centre Concert with the Queensland Orchestra, we had a soprano and tenor soloist, and the tenor, who was first on looking incredibly smart in his white dinner suit and bow tie, had sung an aria, holding a top note for what seemed ages. As he went off to ringing applause, I said to the audience, "Rosario in brilliant form, and for those interested, the note at the end was a top C." Then the soprano swept onstage in a stunning evening gown that made the audience gasp in admiration. Low-cut décolletage and a shimmering sheen to her beautiful green dress, she looked amazing. She had a voice to match and sang her aria with another huge top note at the end, this time a tone higher than Rosario. As she went off to even more ringing applause, I turned to the audience and said, "Not to be outdone, that was

Amelia singing a top double D," before hurriedly correcting myself, "Err... top D!"

There was a moment's stunned silence, before the laughter started. It came in waves, starting at the back, rolling down to the front (no pun intended!). The leader of the orchestra was shocked and, in the interval, came up to me demanding to know if she had been told what I was going to say. I assured him, as I do you now, that she had. If one is going to make a public personal comment about an individual, you have to ask that individual for permission. I had approached her before the concert and asked if she would mind me making this joke, making sure she understood I had absolutely no problem should she object. With no hesitation whatsoever, she said she didn't mind at all and thought it very funny.

I think the sad comment on this is that to some, I now have to explain and justify a joke. If it's funny and no one at whom the comment/joke is aimed is hurt, then it works. I thought it polite to ask her; she told me to go ahead; the audience were in hysterics! *Est factum*, or fait accompli, or even bish, bash, bosh, as my children would say.

There was a viola player in one of the British orchestras, who took me to task on social media for some of my comments.

During one of my 'stand-up moments', I mention the fact that I believe men are intelligent creatures: "We can multitask too, you know!" I announce. "I can drink a beer *and* watch England beating Wales at Twickenham." This normally gets quite a reaction, especially when saying it in Cardiff! Not sure how that time I escaped from the building! By now, in full flow, "I can even read a map and tell my wife how to drive the car at the same time!" Most find that innocuous and funny, but not this violist in this orchestra! When he remonstrated with me on social media for being sexist, others told him to get a life! Even my wife responded by saying, although she was not there on this occasion, she had heard it many times, found it funny and was not at all upset!

That somebody thinks it is worthy of criticism is a sad reflection on the times in which we are currently existing. I mean, honestly, if people really believe England always beat Wales at Twickenham and I really do tell my wife how to drive the car while reading a map are true facts, then we are living through incredibly humourless times. It seems only one person needs to find something unfunny for them to desperately search for a reason for their lack of humour. We need to ignore them and leave them to live in their sad, tiny little worlds.

Scene 3: Cunard

In 2003, Alison, living in Los Angeles, rang me and said she had heard that Carnival Corporation was building a huge, brand-new, ocean-going transatlantic liner to be called the *Queen Mary 2*, which was to have a naming ceremony at Southampton. Surely, they'd want some music, and shouldn't I get in touch? Cunard had been struggling with their one acknowledged great liner, the aging *QE2*, and other smaller ships in their fleet and desperately needed this new liner to survive and become as popular as the *QE2*.

Cunard had been bought by Micky Arison who owned Carnival Corporation in 1998 and, having bought out many shipping companies, was the largest fleet operator of cruise ships in the world. Now, as the parent company of Cunard, he wanted to resurrect the great Cunard name and bring it back to its glory days. The company had been founded by the Canadian Sir Samuel Cunard and had an incredible history, never more so than on the transatlantic run. By building the *QM2* as a liner and not a cruise ship, he put his faith in that service, a route most people thought long dead and buried.

One of the differences between a liner and cruise ship is the shape of the hull and the way it travels through water. Liners have a narrower, V-shaped, deeper hull, able to slice through and displace the water at speed, especially in the North Atlantic where the weather can sometimes be inclement! Whereas speed is not required for cruise ships which tend to have fatter, shallower hulls and sit on the water.

After Alison's phone call, I immediately wrote to the Cunard head offices in Southampton, attaching my biography and eulogising about watching those great ocean liners of the '60s with my brother while living in Cowes during my childhood. The story of the foghorns was mentioned!

My letter was answered by a man called Neil King and something of my passion for them must have communicated itself to him, as he invited me down to a meeting at the Cunard offices in Southampton. He met with me but was singularly unqualified to make any judgement on my musical ability so passed me to another Cunard employee, the head of PR and a man by the name of Eric Flounders. He, with his deputy and sidekick Michael Gallagher, were also singularly unqualified to judge my talents. However, they were in charge of the ceremony, and in my favour was the fact that the ceremony was only three months away, and they had been unable to locate the previous musical incumbent of the Cunard ship naming ceremonies; the still vacant position needed filling!

Eric, Michael and I got along well from the start and, as they had nobody else, Eric offered me the job of music director. He never fails to remind me that I was only passed to him as I was persistently bothering Neil King for the job, and Neil wanted rid of me.

Our first production meeting concerned a visit to a production company in North London, who were vying for the job of staging the naming ceremony for the *Queen Mary 2*. We met up with a youth with long hair, torn jeans, open-neck white shirt who was impossibly cool. This did not impress Eric, the man from

Yorkshire, who did not like to waste either his own time or anyone else's. Not long after arriving, Eric could see the meeting was going nowhere and said, very bluntly, he wanted to talk to the organ grinder, not the monkey! The company were very quickly out of the final running for the job! Another was soon found, and after much work, we proceeded to give the cruise industry a naming ceremony that was pioneering and still talked about to this day.

The president of Cunard, at that time a lady by the name of Pamela Conover, gave me a very short brief: she wanted the music for the event to be contemporary, sexy and magical! The only musical item they had in place was Heather Small singing her own song 'Proud', to which they would reveal 150,000 tons of steel. The other musical choices were up to me. Contemporary? That was 'Proud'. Sexy? That became 'Amazing Grace' in a special arrangement I did with a bagpipe playing the first verse on the bow of the ship, with the Royal Philharmonic in the auditorium. That way, we were able to bring the ship into the performance. Magical? That was obvious: *Harry Potter* was all the rage and John Williams' 'Hedwig's Theme' from the first film became the magic.

The reveal itself was extraordinary. How on earth do you reveal 150,000 tons of steel that, by its nature, had to be floating on water; it's quite difficult to hide! We were quite clever and took the guests, who had been wined and dined on board, by a blacked out circuitous route onto the shore. We put them into a tent and, though realistically they probably knew they were on the shore, they weren't really aware whereabouts on the shore they were. Just before Her Majesty the Queen named the ship, we performed 'Proud'. At the climax of the song, we did a Kabuki Drop, which required the dropping of a piece of lightweight cloth behind the performers at the back of the stage. Even though the Royal Philharmonic Orchestra, Royal Choral Society, Heather Small and I were giving our all, I could still hear the gasp as the magnificent *Queen Mary 2* was revealed in front of the audience and behind the performers.

We ended the ceremony with a stunning firework display from barges moored in Southampton Water to the finale of Beethoven's *Symphony No. 9*. An extraordinary event, which meant when the next ship came along, we had to repeat the formula in a different way.

Slightly more than three years later, on 10 December 2007, the next new ship in the fleet, that of the *Queen Victoria*, was to be named by HRH the Duchess of Cornwall, accompanied by her husband, HRH Prince Charles. As the ship had the first purpose-built proper theatre with theatre boxes on board, it was decided to recreate the feeling of the theatre on shore by the side of the ship; we even built an orchestra pit, into which we put the London Philharmonic Orchestra. The story we told at the ceremony was of a character akin to Phileas Fogg and played by Sir Derek Jacobi as he travels through time narrating the history of Cunard, bringing it up to date with their new ship the *Queen Victoria*.

Katherine Jenkins was to be the star musical attraction, and the choice of music to reveal the ship caused much conflict between members of the creative team. I was the sole voice behind the choice of 'Dance Bohème' from Bizet's opera *Carmen*, while everyone else wanted 'I Could Have Danced All Night'. They all thought the title was very apt and suited the occasion: everyone dances the night away on a Cunard ship. Yes, of course they do, but for me, and this was the big problem, however suitable the title, it did not have that obvious moment (a key change or an increase of tempo) that suited pulling the curtain across at the back of the stage, revealing the ship to a fanfare of fireworks. They all said to me, "'Dance Bohème' is a tune all about gypsies dancing in an opera – of what relevance is that to the *Queen Victoria?*"

My reply was that they had specifically wanted 'In Paradisum' from the Fauré *Requiem*, which is traditionally sung during the

Mass for the dead as the body is taken out of the church. "Of what relevance was that to the ship?" This went back and forth for some time until the day came, and we had to present the concept of the show to the bosses for sign-off. The two main ones were Peter Shanks and Carol Marlow. We were presenting in the afternoon following a meeting where we were to finalise our choices.

I will admit that at that morning meeting, in the interests of unity, I agreed to toe the party line and say that 'I Could Have Danced All Night' was the best piece to which to reveal the *Queen Victoria*. We presented the show to the bosses, and it went well. They loved everything, but the final reveal piece was queried by Peter Shanks. Was that the right piece? Were we all agreed? There was a general murmur of agreement. Peter, sensing something, went round the table asking everyone individually if they really meant it. There were about twelve people there, and I was last! Everyone extolled the virtues of the relevance of 'I Could Have Danced All Night', except me. I broke ranks and said what I really believed, that 'Dance Bohème' had that bullet point moment, when the emotion would be lifted as the curtains drew back to reveal the ship. There was a pause, and the big boss, Peter Shanks, said, "I agree," and that is how we came to reveal the ship to *Carmen* and not *My Fair Lady* and the reason why no one from the creative team would talk to me after that. I sort of understood their anger. They had weaved the plot around the title 'I Could Have Danced All Night'. Instead, they now had a rewrite with 'Dance Bohème' as the reveal music. Not sure there was too much rewriting though; after all, it's still a dance!

Looking at the video now, I know we were right, and Peter and I still talk about it over the lunches we continue to have together. I honestly believe the writers and production team were so wrapped up with the title of the song in the story we were telling, they did not see that we needed a lift in the music.

Other performers included: Alfie Boe, Garðar Cortes, Jon

Christos (our own three tenors) and the choir of Winchester Cathedral. Again, another stunning naming ceremony, especially when the choir processed through the audience, holding candles, onto the stage while singing Fauré's 'In Paradisum'.

10 October 2010 saw the third magnificent ship, the *Queen Elizabeth*, join the fleet, with a naming ceremony held, as with the other two, on the dockside of Southampton Cruise Terminal. How could we follow those two naming ceremonies and not make it formulaic for the third? Simple, hold it outside and increase the number of performers!

It was undoubtedly a risk. The October date chosen was a time of the year when the weather could so easily have gone against us, as there was to be little wind and rain protection for the audience. There was a rectangular arena, with one short end for the royal box where Her Majesty the Queen and her retinue with assorted VIPs would be sat. The other short end was for the performers, which included the huge Bournemouth Symphony Orchestra and Chorus. One elongated side for the guests; the other was the quay and ship. In the middle was another performing arena, and in that we would put the massed bands of the Welsh, Scottish and Irish Guards who would march up and down. Only the three sides would be covered. In all there must have been getting on for three hundred performers, all controlled by one man: yours truly! Actually, there was help. The massed bands were conducted by the director of music, Lieutenant-Colonel Graham Jones, who were playing behind my back.

As soloists, we had Lesley Garrett singing the song that has become synonymous with Cunard and been sung at most of their concerts: 'Amazing Grace'. With the QM2, I had already had the idea of putting the bagpiper on the bow of the ship, connecting the outside with the inside, but it was too good an effect not to repeat. Consequently, we did it again, this time putting two bagpipers on the mooring bridge at the bow of the ship. Again, it was a marvellous moment as all eyes turned to the other great Elizabethan star of the show, the cruise ship *Queen Elizabeth*!

In addition to my arrangement of 'Amazing Grace', I had done a new version of 'Jerusalem' which required a solo boy singer at the beginning. I chose for the performance a young lad, well-known to me (and my wife), who sang treble in Kingston Parish Church Choir. Of course, I'm referring to our son Alexander, thereby incontrovertibly proving the old adage, 'it's not what you know, but who'! I would like to add, he was paid out of my own pocket, which of course, in many ways, I had been doing before and since!

He had a wonderful pure treble voice, and I had had experience of Alexander singing solo, so knew he was special. He had been a chorister at St. George's Chapel Windsor and Kingston Parish Church and was now in the Tiffin Boys Choir, at the time the children's choir of choice by London orchestras and the Royal Opera. I asked them to perform two Christmas concerts with me at the Royal Albert Hall. The choir master chose Alexander for the solos. He sang the opening solo verse of Psalm 23, 'The Lord is My Shepherd', and also the first verse of 'Once in Royal David's City', when he had processed down the side of the stalls holding a candle to stand beside me at the front of the stage. I do not suppose many children can say they have sung solo at the Royal Albert Hall and for the Queen!

Cunard have given me the opportunity to meet some amazing people, all of who were at one point important to the company in one form or another. People such as Terry Waite, the man held hostage by the Lebanese as he was trying to negotiate the release of hostages; Murray Walker, the Formula One racing commentator who I also met as president of the RAF Ibsley Historical Group when we were battling to save the historic control tower from demolition; Jennie Bond, the royal commentator and travel writer; Squadron Leader John Peters, the RAF Tornado pilot shot down in the first Iraqi conflict and paraded battered and bruised on

TV screens around the world, and who I still see regularly; Roy Barraclough who, with Les Dawson, as Cissie and Ada, made me laugh so much – I even cracked a Les Dawson gag on board the *Queen Mary 2* while Roy was on board and then publicly thanked Les for the joke (I didn't remember any of Roy's!) – Mervyn King, the ex-governor of the Bank of England who sang in the on-board choir on the *Queen Mary 2* and got to conduct the orchestra. As he was singing tenor in the choir, I wanted to reward him with a tenner but only had a £20 note on me!

There was one occasion when an idea I had for Cunard did not work out. On the maiden voyage of the original *Queen Mary* in 1936, Cunard hired the celebrated band leader Henry Hall to play on board the ship every night as she sailed across the Atlantic from Southampton to New York. Further, that concert was broadcast live by the BBC back to the UK. I wanted to celebrate the eightieth anniversary of those extraordinary evenings when sailing with the NSO on our regular 2016 crossing. With the blessing of Cunard, who thought the idea brilliant, Sue James and I took the idea to the then head of BBC Radio 2, Lewis Carnie, who was excited, saying this was exactly the sort of thing the BBC should be doing. However, he had not reckoned with one of his producers, a man called Anthony Cherry. At a meeting in Broadcasting House between Cunard, the BBC, Sue and me, Mr. Cherry said he did not like the idea as the technical issues of broadcasting live back to the UK were difficult to overcome. We were all incredulous, and I think I summed up all our feelings when I said, with a fair amount of disbelief, I had not realised that broadcasting live in 2016 had got more difficult rather than less in the past eighty years! And it never happened.

Leaving that disappointment with the BBC aside, Cunard and I are still doing some wonderfully glamorous engagements together, such as the famous Liverpool Cathedral concerts. There was always an excuse to celebrate something with this great company and have an uplifting concert in the cathedral to which the passengers from a moored Cunard ship in the docks were invited at no cost to themselves. Whether it was the fortieth anniversary of their magnificent liner the *Queen Elizabeth 2*, saying goodbye to the ship itself, or the 175th anniversary of the founding of the company, all were given a concert in music and words overseen by that master of the English language, Eric Flounders. He really should have had a career in entertainment as he knew exactly how to extract the utmost emotion from an already emotional occasion.

It was a sad day for everyone when Eric retired. He is an extraordinary man; why use one word when a syllable will do and definitely nothing longer than a short sentence? He would make decisions without referring them 'upstairs', dealing with any possible fallout later when it was impossible to terminate contracts already agreed. There never was a fallout as he had an innate instinct of what would work and what would not. All the Cunard concerts were at his instigation, and all were extraordinary, still talked about to this day. As producers, Eric, Michael and I were a great triple act. We knew how to raise the emotions of the audience, bring them back down before raising them again for a shattering ending. The concerts were a real roller coaster of an event, rushing along on a great tide of emotion.

For instance, during the *QE2* Falklands story, I had the idea of marching The Band of the Welsh Guards in from the great west door of Liverpool Anglican Cathedral all the way up the nave while they played 'We Are Sailing'. Due to a flight of stone steps, there was a bit of discussion between the band and us as to whether this was feasible. In the end, they thought they could, and Eric brought in Simon Weston CBE, the ex-Welsh guardsman who had received 46% burns in the Falklands War, to introduce them. The whole cathedral, all two thousand of them, stood and applauded as they marched through.

For me, my favourite Cunard concert has to be the celebration of 175 years of Cunard; there were so many highlights in that concert: the parading of the Boston Cup, which is the cup denoting flagship status; the sounding of the cathedral bell when the names of the ships that had been sunk during the Crimean War were read out; the slow march of the Welsh Guards into the cathedral; and finishing the concert with 'Close of Day' and 'The Last Post' as the band marched out, bringing the concert to a solemn but uplifting close. Even while writing those words, the emotion stirs up as I remember the atmosphere, the cheering and the pride.

Not only did we give concerts in the cathedral whilst the ships were moored alongside the docks, but we also took the Royal Liverpool Philharmonic and Hallé orchestras on board both the *Queen Elizabeth* and *Victoria* to give concerts on board the actual ships. Jon Cristos sang Horatio Nicholls' hymn to the *Queen Mary*'s original maiden voyage *Queen of the Sea*. This time, I became the Phileas Fogg character and, in-between conducting the concert, narrated the story of Cunard as well. Seventeen years later, Eric lives in Wales and we're in frequent touch. He still makes me laugh!

Every year since 2009, apart from two when the world was brought to a grinding halt with the Covid-19 pandemic, the National Symphony Orchestra and I have boarded a *Queen Mary 2* transatlantic voyage, giving performances during the crossing. Peter Shanks, then boss of Cunard in the UK, loved my pitch to him of an orchestra on board the ship, performing two evenings of music as we gently crossed the ocean. The first concert is a salute to the United States of America and the second, to the British: a Last Night of the Cunard Proms. He particularly liked the idea of involving the guests in an on-board choir for this concert, so they could sing with the orchestra as we traversed the Atlantic making friends, eating gloriously and drinking fine wines.

The whole idea was made worthwhile on the very first crossing. A lady in her late eighties approached at the end of a rehearsal and thanked me for fulfilling her ambition. When she had been a little girl at school, she had been told by the music teacher that her singing voice was so appalling, she was to mime and never utter a sound at school concerts. She adored singing and had always wanted to join a choir but never been able to, as this one remark had given her a fear of singing in public. She had now experienced what it was like to sing with one hundred other like-minded people and absolutely loved it.

One occasion crossing the Atlantic with my family did cause much embarrassment. All five of us were going on the QM2 and we had two business and three economy-class tickets for the journey to New York, where we would board the ship for the return journey. How to share them out? As my wife and I could not leave the three young children alone in economy, we decided that our daughter Eleanor and I would start the flight in business with my wife and two boys in economy, then swap over halfway. Seemed fair, but we reckoned without the airline rule that seats were not allowed to be exchanged mid-flight, and we had to remain in our take-off seats for the entire journey! Despite my feelings of guilt, the champagne and excellent food helped me fall into a troubled sleep on my flat bed, wondering what was going on in the back of the plane and what the ramifications would be! I found out shortly after disembarking.

Apparently, on approach to JFK, our youngest son had become air sick, and as there were no air sickness bags in the backs of the surrounding seats, Jan had beckoned to the cabin crew for help. Because the seat belt signs were on, they were unable to come to her aid, so my wife reached for the nearest available receptacle, which happened to be his brother's backpack. Hurriedly emptying out as much as she could, she gave it to Alexander to use, which he did... prodigiously. This did not impress his older brother very much. Such was the very disgruntled scene that greeted a very relaxed Eleanor and I as we all met up just off the air bridges!

After a frosty walk through the airport and baggage reclaim, there were the usual queues at JFK immigration, not helped by the fact that our tour party smelt rather badly. After 9/11, there were no bins available for disposal of items, including ones that had been used for little boys to be sick into!

The queues to exit the airport were lengthy and the boys were bored, so they went off exploring by themselves around the immigration hall. Suddenly, maybe because the officers were fed up with two small children on the loose, or perhaps the source of the smell, which by now had permeated everywhere, had been traced, we were called to go through. Dominic came when called quite quickly, Alexander less so. However, this was soon sorted by Dominic shouting out across the huge hall as loudly as his high-pitched voice would carry, "Here, puke boy. We're going through!"

I have made friends with a number of the officers on board the Cunard ships, notably Captain Kevin Oprey. I always ask the captains whether they would like to conduct the orchestra during one of the on-board concerts, and they have all partaken with great glee. Kevin has given us a great many laughs on board the ship. This included the occasion that, having agreed to swap jackets so he could wear my white one to conduct the orchestra, he promptly had me 'arrested' for impersonating a senior officer. The ship's security officer cuffed me in a pair of pink fluffy handcuffs and led me offstage. Where on earth were those found on a ship halfway across the Atlantic? Kevin then proceeded to conduct *Top Gun*, which, unknown to me, he and the orchestra had rehearsed, though he did scare them with his announcement to the audience they were going to perform *Superman*.

I had my revenge, making him sit at the keyboard while I asked some singers from the ship to sing the Gilbert and Sullivan song, 'I am the Captain of the Pinafore' with *Queen Mary 2* substituting for Pinafore. At appropriate points, I would stop the song and make him play a note on the keyboard which sounded like a foghorn.

I should have had better revenge when, later, I got him in uniform onto the stage of the Royal Albert Hall to conduct the Royal Philharmonic Orchestra. However, no one knew either him or our history, so we played it for real, and he conducted well. He should have done; he'd had enough practice! We still stay in touch in his retirement on the Isle of Wight.

The captain who took over when Kevin retired was Captain Aseem Hashmi, and we have had no less fun. He is married to Marina, a concert pianist, who had taught him to play 'Twinkle, Twinkle Little Star' with one finger on the piano. Shades of my father, though Aseem plays it in C major which does not need any sharps or flats!

This gave me an idea. Dohnanyi wrote a wonderful piece of music called *Variations on a Nursery Rhyme*, and it begins with a huge introduction, finishing with a crashing chord. Everyone turns expectantly to the pianist who plays the opening verse of 'Twinkle, Twinkle Little Star' before continuing with the difficult variations.

I decided to do the same (without the variations!). Giving a big vocal intro as to how fortunate we were to have a great concert pianist in our midst, who could not only steer the *Queen Mary 2* (true), get us safely to our destination (true) and fly a Boeing 767 (true), but could also play a piano concerto (untrue). "This," I announced to the ship's audience in the Royal Court Theatre, "is too good an opportunity to miss. So please welcome the captain to the stage." We played a huge musical introduction as he made a great show of sitting at the piano, wiping his brow, putting the music stand down, demonstrating he was going to perform from memory. At the end of the intro, all eyes turned to Aseem, and he started to play with one finger a verse of the 'Twinkle, Twinkle' nursery rhyme tune. As he continued, I tried to look like an outraged André Previn on *The Morecambe & Wise Show*, before the orchestra finished with a tag ending, bringing the proceedings to an end.

The crossings started well and have now grown bigger. We have even added an afternoon where the strings of the orchestra combine with the string quartet of the ship and play music by Tchaikovsky, Elgar and Dvorak, amongst others. It is a much sought-after engagement by the musicians and a heavily subscribed crossing by those guests of Cunard travelling on board.

It is important that the orchestra members realise they are brand ambassadors, not just for the orchestra but the ship as well. To that extent there is a little meeting with the orchestra the morning after we get on board. It is the first full day at sea and is a day of rest before starting rehearsals. At this meeting, I reiterate the importance of exemplary behaviour at all times, especially whilst amongst the passengers. One of the unwritten rules is they will not form relationships with any of the guests, however desirable or brief. We cannot risk a couple having a row, resulting in a dalliance and an upset paying customer. On the first occasion I gave this speech, literally 11am the morning after getting on, I had just finished that statement when Rocky, one of the brass players, said, "Oh dear, I wish you'd told us that earlier!"

It is appropriate there should be this relationship between Cunard and me, as one of my distant ancestors was responsible for putting his engines into Sam Cunard's first Britannia-class steamships. The engineer Robert Napier is a first cousin five times removed, so not a close relative by any means, but it does give me a feeling of close kinship with this great shipping line.

If you go further back in the history of the Napier family, there is one John Napier who died in 1617, and I hope he would forgive me if I say three years too late. In 1614, he had invented logarithms, the bane of my mathematical childhood. This was something to be kept very quiet about at school while I, along with my fellow sufferers, was struggling to understand the principal behind the theory. I never did! Can you imagine the ribbing I would have received if it came out that my wretched ancestor had invented them?

Because I am proud of my ancestry, mention must also be made of David Napier, who is my great-great-great-great-great-uncle. He founded the famous engineering family D. Napier & Sons, who subsequently went on to build the engine of the Napier-Railton motorcar, holder of many speed records and on display at Brooklands Museum, and the equally important Lion aero engine of the Edwardian age. I was also told by a number of elderly relatives that General Sir Charles Napier, whose statue is in the bottom left-hand corner of Trafalgar Square, is also a relative, but I haven't been able to find out how or where. I am proud to say that I have given the name Napier as the middle name for one of our sons!

With all the Cunard events, Eric and Michael gave me many moments of pleasure, but one non-musical one in particular I shall treasure. They co-wrote a book on the history of Cunard, which is a fascinating tale on the history of the shipping line. At the launch in the City of London, they had a number of important guests attend, one of whom was John Prescott, now Lord Prescott, previously deputy prime minister. Before becoming a politician, he had famously been a steward in the late '50s on board the Cunard ships, and as a matter of course, was invited to several Cunard events. His and my politics are of different persuasions, but on the *Queen Victoria* in Liverpool Harbour, we had the most fascinating conversation over breakfast. Such a calm, reasoned discussion, and he listened politely to what I said. So different from the firebrand we sometimes saw in public throwing punches at people who hurled eggs at him.

At this book-launch party, I was chatting with the well-known TV pundit and editor of a right-wing national newspaper, when he spied John Prescott sipping the champagne and tackling the canapés with a good deal of gusto. As quick as a flash, he said to me in a conspiratorial voice, "Shouldn't he be serving the food and drink, rather than consuming it?"

For a few years, we played concerts for Warner Leisure in some of their hotels, which also entailed me giving a short talk the next day all about myself! These talks have now become quite an integral part of my life and have grown exponentially. It started on the Cunard transatlantic crossings when passengers on board began asking me about my career. So many enquired that the ship thought there would be a demand for me to give a presentation in-between all the other fantastic lecturers they had on board. They were right – there was!

I have now grown my presentations to talks from just about myself and career (when I can drone on for hours!), to one about my family and incredible RAF history; one about the history of conducting; and another about the history of music on board the Cunard ships. There is even one now about Great-Great-Great-Great-Granny Elizabeth Fry. What stories! They are all PowerPoint presentations, most with movies and pictures, and I really enjoy giving them.

On one of the early ones I did, when I took a presentation to other ships in the Cunard fleet, I remember standing in the lecture theatre on board the *Queen Elizabeth 2*, with a shiver of pleasure, realising that my father had stood on exactly the same spot, doing exactly the same thing twenty-five years previously.

Scene 4: National Symphony Orchestra; Films

No one can remember the start date, but for a very long time, I was music director of the National Symphony Orchestra. They were an orchestra with which I had a great rapport, and we performed many fabulous concerts together, all run by the much-loved lady I have mentioned before, Anne Collis. She had been the first female musician into the Royal Philharmonic in the 1970s, then taken over the management of the NSO when it was the house orchestra for Victor Hochhauser.

The orchestra had been founded in the 1940s and had David McCallum as their very respected leader. He was the father of the actor of the same name, who was best known for playing the role of Illya Kuryakin in *The Man from U.N.C.L.E.* TV series. The orchestra also had an illustrious history, having recorded the soundtrack to a large number of British films of that era, including *Vertigo*, *Genevieve* and most notably *Brief Encounter*. This is a wonderful soundtrack to a great film. The orchestra had accompanied Eileen Joyce playing the first movement of Rachmaninoff's *Piano Concerto No. 2* under Muir Mathieson, a conductor with whom they had a long association. I had played for him a couple of years before he died when playing orchestral piano at one of Mike Reed's film music concerts in Imperial College's concert hall. He came along to show us all how these great scores should be performed.

I had also met the piano soloist in *Brief Encounter*, Eileen Joyce, as she was great friends with Great-Aunt Nesta Inglis, sister of my grandfather, who had lived at Meadowgate in Brasted. Nesta was a formidable yet rather wonderful lady who owned and ran one of the oldest girls boarding schools in the UK called Tudor Hall. She had rescued it from obscurity in 1935, nurturing it through the war at Burnt Norton near Chipping Campden, before eventually outgrowing the space they were in and settling in Wykham Park, where it is still a thriving girls' school. She was a keen amateur cellist and formed an excellent trio with Eileen Joyce on piano and Marie Wilson, who had been a leader of the BBC Symphony Orchestra during the war years, then a first violinist in the LPO.

The NSO and I have appeared in some recent major

Hollywood films such as *Cole, Sherlock Holmes: A Game of Shadows* and the Netflix drama *The Crown*, but do not blink when watching these films as you will miss me. As so often happens, most of what is filmed ends up on the cutting room floor. Even if you do not blink, you may still miss me! Sue James is such a great agent, she negotiated a very good deal for *Sherlock Holmes*, making sure my name was in the end title credits. When we watched a preview, we sat in the theatre and felt rather guilty when my scrolling name in the credits at the end lasted almost as long as my filmed appearance!

In *Sherlock Holmes*, as we were not playing live for the Mozart *Don Giovanni* excerpt we were doing and miming in long shot, it is cheaper to utilise film extras instead of real musicians. We had musicians close around me, however, further back it was filled with extras, who of course had no idea how to hold musical instruments, let alone play them. Walking round the pretend orchestra even gave me pause for thought as I tried to remember which shoulder the trombone went over and which hand held the slide? Remember, I normally look at it from the front, not from the perspective of the player. The issue therefore was one of authenticity; visually, you had to have people actually holding the instruments correctly, even if they didn't know how to get a note out of it. Hopefully, long shot would not show up the deficiencies of the non-musician extras.

There was a particularly annoying extra, a man who obviously spent his life in the background of films, and he was delegated to playing the flute. He obviously valued himself as the comedian of the film-extra world and thought he was very funny but actually wasn't. He kept coming out with what he believed were witty one-liners, which one or two of his cohorts would laugh at. We tolerated this for a while. After I had instructed him how to hold his instrument, telling him in which direction to place the flute and which hand went in front of which, I'm afraid his comment to me, "You blow, I'll suck," was the final straw. Shortly after, he asked how he should address me. I brought myself up to my full height and replied, "You? You can call me Maestro!" To which he responded, very camply, "British Leyland? Oooooh, I think I'll call you Princess!" To understand why that's funny, you have to know British cars of the 1970s! Suffice to say, although he was driving us mad, we did all find that very funny. Reading it back, and with hindsight, I think you had to be there to appreciate it and understand that his previous comments were so poor, this was gold dust by comparison!

During her life, the driving force behind the orchestra, Anne Collis, had her comedic moments as well, and some were unintended. The orchestra and I were performing at an outdoor venue one summer and, like most outdoor concerts, it was one where you needed to keep your wits about you at all times: lots of different pieces in lots of different styles.

At this performance, I got ready to conduct Mozart's *Eine Kleine Nachtmusik*, which is a famous piece of music for strings only. I settled myself in for some gentle, beautiful Mozart and gave the down beat to start the piece. On reaching the bottom of the beat, there came from the percussion section the most enormous cymbal crash you have ever heard, completely drowning out the strings. It made everyone in the orchestra and the crowd jump. Startled, I looked over and saw Anne staring at the music with a very surprised expression on her face. She had of course not looked at the running order carefully enough and was playing the beginning of the Bizet 'March of the Toreadors' from the *Carmen Suite* which was scheduled to follow the Mozart. That piece does indeed require an enormous cymbal crash on the down beat. Her part was marked forte (loud) for the first note, and when Anne saw forte in her part, she gave it welly!

How we continued playing the piece that day, I have no idea. I can still see Nigel Shipway, who was the timpanist and a rather portly gentleman, sitting on his stool literally shaking with laughter, tears streaming down his face. This incident has now resulted in the National Symphony Orchestra being the only orchestra in the world to have a percussion part marked tacet (do not play) in their string parts to *Eine Kleine Nachtmusik*!

It may have been on this day that the role of a conductor was demonstrated most effectively and, I admit, to me, a conductor, most satisfyingly. There is sometimes some antipathy between a conductor and members of an orchestra, whereby musicians cannot for the life of them see why a conductor is needed, especially when they are overpaid and not very good. I was rehearsing a piece of music and wanted to hear what the sound was like from out front and asked them to carry on playing while I went to listen. I had no sooner reached the front than the orchestra ground to halt. There was a moment of shocked silence from the musicians, until Nigel Shipway said, "Oh bloody hell, we do need him!"

This was in contrast to another occasion I heard about, where the conductor again wanted to hear what the orchestra was sounding like in the hall and rashly asked them whether they could carry on without him. "We have so far," came the answer from the principal percussionist!

Anne Collis was hugely proud of her daughter Sally who, having left artist management, joined the navy, reaching command rank of the Lynx helicopter on board a frigate. She has now advanced still further.

In 2005, Anne therefore wrote a piece of music commemorating the two hundredth anniversary of the death of Admiral Lord Nelson called *Immortal Memory*, which I've since conducted. I went to its first performance in Southwark Cathedral performed by the New London Orchestra under its conductor Ronald Corp. The guest of honour was the Rt Hon Lady Margaret Thatcher. I had the pleasure of being introduced to her in the interval, though to be honest so did a lot of other people! By the time she got to me, she could not wait to get back to her seat and said to me, "I must go. I think they're restarting."

"Without you in your seat?" I said. "They wouldn't dare!"

At the beginning of October 2013, Anne sadly died, leaving us in the orchestra bereft at her passing, though I'm not sure she actually went when her huge heart gave its final earthly beat.

As she lay dying in her bed, I went to see her at her house in Devon and held her hand whilst we both listened to Classic FM. As we listened, they played one of my favourite overtures, Verdi's *Force of Destiny Overture*. By coincidence, I told her I was conducting it in a month's time at the Royal Albert Hall with her old orchestra, the Royal Philharmonic, where she had pioneered the advancement of women in orchestras. She was in and out of consciousness, so conversation was entirely one-sided, and I was not sure how much she had heard or taken in.

She died a couple of days after my visit and, for a while, we were all in a daze. At seventy, she was far too young to go; she had such a zest for life, and indeed was such a force in life, that we did not, could not, believe she had left us. Like her clothes and jewellery, which were always brightly coloured, she was so much larger than life itself.

Her funeral was held at the end of October and, as I had told her, a week later, and still in mourning, I conducted the first of those six concerts at the Royal Albert Hall, which were in fact the twenty-fifth anniversary series of *Classical Spectacular*.

We had just begun the first performance of the Verdi *Force of Destiny Overture*, the piece we had listened to together, when the largest, most beautiful iridescent butterfly you have ever seen came out of what appeared to be nowhere and started fluttering around me. I have no idea what kind of butterfly it was, but this gorgeous, multicoloured, glowing creature flew over my head and round my body, settling for a moment on the full score before resuming its flight around me, not seemingly fazed at all by the loud music played by eighty musicians or my arms moving about. Having flown around me for a while, it proceeded to land softly on my shoulder and sat there motionless, as if listening to the orchestra brilliantly playing the Verdi overture. The butterfly was so large and so bright that everyone in the Albert Hall could see it, as of course could the orchestra, who were mesmerised by this beautiful Lepidoptera. Roberto Sorrentino, the cellist I have known since he played in the Bournemouth Symphony Orchestra, stopped playing and, laying down his cello, came up to me whilst I was still conducting the Verdi. Gently cupping his hands around the butterfly, he took it carefully off my shoulder, left the concert platform and, walking to the stage door of the Royal Albert Hall, released it outside.

It was an extraordinary moment and one which, at the end of the concert, was the talk of the orchestra yet had not finished.

The next night in the second concert of the series, at exactly the same time and in exactly the same place of the Verdi overture, this beautiful iridescent butterfly was back, once again flying around before resting on my shoulder. This time, we let it stay there until the end of the *Force of Destiny Overture*, when it flew off of its own accord, never to be seen again.

Anne was an extraordinary character, and if anybody could come back and say goodbye to me and her old orchestra, it was her.

Scene 5: Goodbye NSO; Hello, London Concert Orchestra

As I've said before, all good things come to an end, and my twenty-five-year tenure at the NSO was one such. I decided a new challenge was needed, and it was time to move on. Besides which, a very interesting idea had arisen.

As mentioned, on 30 April 1988, I made my conducting debut with the National Symphony Orchestra in the Barbican Hall with, amongst other works, the Tchaikovsky *Piano Concerto No. 1*. This orchestra performed most of the Victor Hochhauser concerts and, though not owned by him, was his house orchestra. Exactly a week later, on 6 May also at the Barbican, I made my conducting debut with the London Concert Orchestra, this time conducting a programme containing Rachmaninoff's *Piano Concerto No. 2*. This orchestra had been formed by Raymond Gubbay in 1972 and, in addition to being the house orchestra, was also owned by him. Marcus Dods was its original music director, and with his death in 1984, the orchestra had been leaderless in the music department. In fact, both orchestras were an ad hoc group of musicians playing from venue to venue with a whole army of guest conductors.

I had a conversation in late 2017 with Anthony Findlay, by now CEO of Raymond Gubbay Ltd as Raymond had retired, and the events director in the organisation, James Rutherford. We agreed for the London Concert Orchestra to reach the next level and sustain even higher standards, it needed a music director. I was approached and agreed to the position, which meant leaving the NSO as it was still perceived to be a rival orchestra, chasing similar work.

I won't pretend leaving was not difficult. I have a lot of friends in the NSO, and the phone call I made to Anne's daughter Sally to tell her I was leaving was one of the most difficult I have ever had to make. However, it had to be done and, having done so, on 5 May 2018 in the Royal Festival Hall, almost thirty years to the day since making my debut with the London Concert Orchestra, I gave my first concert with them as their new music director, the only other music director since Marcus.

From the moment the orchestra and I began our new relationship, we made much wonderful music together, and the orchestra has gone from strength to strength in the concert halls of the UK, occasionally getting in guest principals from London orchestras to play with us. By taking our pick and inviting star players from other orchestras to play with us, it makes all of us raise our game and play even better; brilliance breeds brilliance!

We play in all the main London halls, including Royal Albert, Royal Festival and Barbican halls, plus Symphony Hall Birmingham, Royal Concert Hall Nottingham, St. David's Hall in Cardiff and many more. As a number of musicians have said to me, it has gone from being an orchestra that one played in to earn money, to being an orchestra everyone wants to play in. I love that. It has a great management team in place, and we have performed many thrilling concerts, none of which have been routine, with most receiving full standing ovations. I am enormously proud of the London Concert Orchestra and their ability to play extraordinarily difficult music on one three-hour rehearsal. I hope there are many more concerts with this fabulous orchestra.

Some people will say we do too much popular music, with Zimmer versus Williams film music being an example. However, John Williams and Hans Zimmer are so thrilling and of such high compositional quality, no one can ever say we don't do it properly, and we love playing it too. As a commercial organisation, the Raymond Gubbay company has to make money. No Arts Council grant for them as with other artistic companies. Therefore, if possible, everything has to finish with a plus and not a minus before the profit or loss figure. Zimmer vs Williams is popular and sells extremely well. I talk, and the orchestra will tell you for far too long, and there are some 'funnies', as we call them, during the concert.

These concerts also gives me a chance to support a charity very dear to my heart, the Great Ormond Street Hospital (GOSH). I was wondering what I could do that few others could, and a while ago I came upon the idea of buying a box for one of these child friendly concerts, stuffing it full of food and drink, and inviting three or four families from GOSH to watch. It is quite the best thing I do all year, and the expression on the children's faces as they walk onto the stage of the Royal Albert Hall at the end of the concert when everybody else has left, says it all!

One such 'funny', previously mentioned, requires the orchestra to play the opening fanfare of *Superman* while I do a full strip of my usual concert clothes held together by Velcro, revealing a *Superman* costume underneath. I will admit there is something faintly disturbing about an Old Age Pensioner, for that is what I am now, stripping on stages such as the Royal Albert Hall. It makes everyone whistle and shout and, of course, people are so far away, even in my Lycra, they cannot see too much of my stomach, or anything else for that matter! Writing it here probably strikes you as not very funny. I build up to it with patter and audience participation, which helps (a lot!). For me, everything I do has to have a reason; *The Two Ronnies* taught me that. Why do I strip? What is the point? Well, you'll have to come and see a live concert for yourself to find out!

I first did the full strip in Melbourne with the Melbourne Symphony in their beautiful home the Hamer Hall and experienced a wardrobe mishap.

As the strip comes with the encore at the end of the concert, I always change into my kit in the interval, rather than be layered up in costume for the first half as well. At that very first one in Melbourne, I left the battery pack for my lapel microphone in the usual place, which was my trouser pocket. However, the weight of the battery pack put too great a strain on the Velcro fastening of my trousers. So much so, that in the middle of Hedwig's theme from *Harry Potter* part way through the second half, the Velcro gave up the unequal struggle, and my trousers started to come apart. All that could be done if I did not want the *Superman* costume hidden underneath my splitting trousers to be revealed in the wrong piece, was to rush off the podium, leaving the orchestra playing live to their own devices!

As I hurtled through the violins for the platform exit, I realised I had not come across a closed door on that stage before. When walking on and off, doors are always already open. All the panels on the stage looked exactly the same, and I had to find out roughly where the door was before hammering on it, hoping someone would hear me. I must have looked a very strange sight to the audience, banging on the door with one hand and holding the back of my velcroed trousers together with the other, shouting to be let into the wings. It probably looked for all the world as though I had had an extremely hot curry before the concert and needed one of the littlest rooms in the building very quickly!

Fortunately, a startled stage manager opened the door and, sizing up the situation correctly, though I have no idea how as no one had been let into the secret of the strip, effected running repairs. I made it back onto the stage before the orchestra got to the held chord, when they would definitely have needed me, adding at the end some off-the-cuff comment about an invisibility cloak!

The full reveal later in that concert was greeted with gales of laughter. The orchestra management said they had never heard their brass players playing like that, as they were laughing so much while trying to play the *Superman* fanfare at the same time.

Ever since then, the battery pack has been placed in my inside jacket pocket!

Scene 6: Royal Air Force Pedigree

You will have gathered from this book, I am extremely proud of my family history and try to keep it alive, not just for my ancestors' achievements but for the next generation as well. My children, nephews and nieces should know from where they come.

I first went to the Battle of Britain commemoration service in Westminster Abbey on 15 September 1985 with my uncle and all those 'Few' pilots still living in the mid-1980s. I vividly recall him sobbing quietly when the Central Band of the RAF struck up the great Walford Davies *RAF March Past*, as he remembered all his friends and comrades who had not returned from serving their country. Sat next to him, I was helpless to comfort him apart from a slight squeeze on his arm, not daring to intrude too much on his private grief; an extraordinary privilege.

On 6 April 1990, I conducted the fortieth anniversary concert of the Battle of Britain with the Royal Philharmonic Orchestra at the Royal Festival Hall. The great and the good of the surviving members of the battle were there, including my uncle, and he was accompanied by my father with other junior and senior members of the RAF. HM the Queen and HRH the Duke of Edinburgh were also in attendance. The specially commissioned piece of music for the occasion from Malcolm Arnold called *Flourish for a Battle* was dreadful! Sir Malcolm did actually confide in me that he was not very happy with it and was sure no one was going to like it. He was right! Shortly afterwards, he withdrew it from publication.

We went to Westminster Abbey for the memorial service of the seventy-fifth anniversary of the Battle of Britain in 2015, broadcast live on BBC1. Our son Dominic followed the chief of the air staff and read the lesson from the Old Testament. In 2015, most of The Few had by now left us.

Held on the first Sunday of each July at the Battle of Britain Memorial site at Capel-le-Ferne, I attend all the annual Memorial Days I can as a continuing memory of the contribution my family have made to the Royal Air Force. The museum is on the south coast, and in 2012 when I first started, there were slightly more of The Few still with us. Sitting next to one of them, he looked at my surname and exclaimed loudly, "Peter!" His name was Ken

Wilkinson, and it transpired he had actually flown alongside my uncle in 19 Squadron out of Duxford during the battle and had immediately recognised the name.

Ken was an extraordinary man with many a tale to tell, and we became friendly. In fact, he lived just outside Birmingham, and I got him along as a VIP to one of my concerts in Symphony Hall and, for good measure, invited my son Dominic, who had just joined the RAF, to sit in uniform alongside him. Dominic remembers Ken flicking open the top button of his shirt and telling him, "Now, you're an RAF pilot!"

They sat in a box at the side of the stage and, just before performing William Walton's *Spitfire Prelude and Fugue* with the City of Birmingham Symphony Orchestra, I introduced them to the audience: the past, present and future, side by side. I must confess, I couldn't help it. Once again, my voice cracked as I announced them, the audience standing to clap and acknowledge their debt!

Scene 7: Reflections

As I get towards the end of the final act in this autobiography (and my life), it is time to reflect back on my career. I have met many artists and composers, and if someone asked me who the most famous were, I guess that, apart from Herbert Howells and Malcolm Arnold, the one most people would have heard of in the classical field was John McCabe. I conducted his *Concerto for Clarinet and Oboe* with Joy Farrell and Nicholas Daniel at Kenwood.

Kenwood was an outdoor music venue in the heart of Hampstead Heath, hotly objected to by locals, led by the actor Warren Mitchell, who disliked the fireworks and parking chaos that accompanied some concerts. Yet, it was loved by others who enjoyed picnicking in the park whilst listening to great classical music. Sometimes ten thousand people would head towards The Heath and try to park in the surrounding area in order to attend concerts promoted on behalf of English Heritage by an incredible man called Michael Webber. He was such an enlightened promoter, thinking nothing of putting on a John McCabe modern concerto and the Dvorak *New World Symphony* in the same concert or getting the Royal Opera House to perform a Puccini opera.

I must confess I did not really enjoy conducting the McCabe *Double Concerto*, not just because the original conductor had dropped out at twenty-four hours' notice but more because, once again, I became a traffic policeman. This time, it was not the volume of music. I would beat out some bars of music, pause while an instrumentalist from within the orchestra improvised for fifteen seconds before deciding that was enough and carrying on with some complicated time signatures. We all thought the credits of the programme should have read: *Concerto for Oboe and Clarinet* by John McCabe, plus other assorted instrumentalists from within the orchestra! When we came to the end, we felt a great sense of achievement from actually getting to the end after one rehearsal, rather than, from the listeners' point of view, experiencing great music.

With the lighter side of things, it was a great pleasure to have met Ron Goodwin, composer of so many famous film scores, at Crystal Palace. We were both there to publicise the upcoming summer concerts. He and I hit it off straight away.

The composer with whom I've had the most dealings, and, like me, has a foot in both camps of serious and lighter music, is Howard Blake. We first met when Michael Webber asked us to perform Howard's *Piano Concerto* for a performance with the Royal Philharmonic at Kenwood on 8 August 1992, with the composer playing the solo piano part. The piece was magical and the rehearsals at his house in Brighton a laugh. So began a long-lasting friendship, which has had its moments; a physical tussle in Hong Kong remains etched in my memory, the reasons for it, though, have long since disappeared in the mist of time.

I have conducted many of his compositions, which include his *Violin Concerto*, of course *The Snowman* and the world premiere performance with the Ulster Orchestra of *The Bear*, his follow-up to *The Snowman*. Personally, I think this contains even finer music than *The Snowman*. We remain friends and often have lunch or dinner together where we put the world of classical music to rights. Both of us have been hamstrung by the snobbishness of the BBC and other bosses within the classical music world. Both of us have been condemned as light music musicians and therefore not worthy of serious consideration. Both of us think they are wrong!

Occasionally, I am asked if I have ever composed a piece of music. The answer to that is yes, but I only write in the emotional throes of the breakdown in a relationship. I now have 645 symphonies, 1250 piano concertos, 2200… sorry, that is a gag I have used when I have conducted my one and only composition that has actually been performed.

On a few occasions, mainly with the Bournemouth Symphony, I have trotted out my *Romance for Violin and Orchestra*. It is a piece entirely reminiscent of the 'Méditation' from *Thaïs* by the composer Massenet, even down to the same key, time signature and harp intro. However, it has some small merit and appears to be enjoyed by performers. In reality, I leave the art of composition to those much better qualified and more inspirational than I.

I have done so many wonderful concerts that if anyone asked what my personal highlight was, I would be hard pushed to give an answer. As already mentioned, *Phantom25* was extraordinary, as was the Diamond Jubilee Concert at Buckingham Palace. So was the concert with the LSO at the Royal Albert Hall celebrating Mikhail Gorbachev's eightieth birthday. In terms of world leaders, the great and the good were all there to wish him a happy birthday, and the whole thing was introduced by Kevin Spacey and Sharon Stone. It stuck in the memory because it was so unexpectedly long.

I was only conducting the first half, with Valery Gergiev, principal conductor of the LSO, conducting the second. The orchestra had a rehearsal beforehand for what everybody assumed would be a normal-length concert, but nobody thought to time the speeches in-between the musical items, when the politicians would laud the birthday boy. Someone should have remembered that politicians love the sound of their own voice, especially to a captive audience.

The concert started at 7.30pm and was live on Russian TV. At 10.10pm, the normal finish of a lengthy concert, we came to the interval! I then overheard negotiations going on between the orchestra and the Russian production company about overtime and thought, *time to go!* I believe the concert did not end until after midnight.

The concert gave me a first: conducting a pop band. I had never heard of the German group the Scorpions, but apparently they were huge and became even bigger at the fall of the Berlin Wall. At this concert they were to perform their hit 'Wind of Change' and needed the LSO as their backing band. This involved conducting to a click, something I had done before, and then hanging on for the ride! I enjoyed it and got on with Klaus Meine the lead singer of the group, though he was surprised I was the only one to wear headphones and receive the click. Apparently, when they had performed it with the Berlin Philharmonic, the Orchestra had all worn headphones! I'm not sure why. I am a conductor and the orchestra play to my beat!

From pop to classical in a few minutes! Gergiev was delayed in Russia and couldn't make the final rehearsal, so I had to rehearse his repertoire. One of the pieces was the last movement of Rachmaninoff's *Piano Concerto No. 2*. This time, the soloist was to be Andrei Gavrilov, one of the world's greatest pianists.

Sadly, he did not much enjoy playing the Royal Albert Hall and its celebrated echo as, at the end of the run-through, he turned to me and the orchestra and said, "We will all go to heaven, as we have all just played in hell!"

However, Dmitri Hvorostovsky refused to rehearse, saying that if Gergiev was not at the rehearsal, nor would he be. So, we had to rehearse a difficult aria from Tchaikovsky's *Queen of Spades* without him. Covering as much of the piece as I could without the solo, it was no surprise in the concert when the whole thing nearly ground to a halt.

Another highlight was definitely doing *Carmen* in July 2016 with the orchestra of Welsh National Opera at the Llangollen International Musical Eisteddfod. I had always wanted to do opera and, having spent a lot of my musical career in the theatre, always thought myself a suitable candidate for opera. As previously discussed, the opera world is far too snobbish to allow someone in musical theatre into their rarefied world, and I was never asked.

I was only doing *Carmen* in Llangollen as Katherine Jenkins was originally going to perform the title role but had to drop out for personal reasons. For me, *Carmen* was a sensational evening as Kate Hudson and Noah Stewart, with some fantastic Welsh singers and a local chorus, gave their all. The orchestra were amazing. Yes, they could probably play *Carmen* without music, but to have an asset like that in Cardiff is a superb addition to the music scene in Wales.

In terms of the amount of people who have attended a concert, we once had fourteen thousand at the Milton Keynes National Bowl go to an outdoor *Classical Spectacular*, where I seem to remember horses charging across the arena as part of the battle scene in the *1812*.

At the O2 Arena, ten thousand people attended a Christmas concert introduced by Myleene Klass. I first met Myleene when she was a backing singer for a commercial gig. By the time of this concert, she was well known enough to be presenting. Funnily enough, the person who used to employ her as a backing vocalist provided the backing vocal group for this concert too. Her name is Annie Skates, and she is still very dominant in the recording/pop industry.

The O2 concert consisted of music, some of which I knew well (*Nutcracker Suite*) and some not so much ('Merry Christmas Everyone', 'All I Want for Christmas is You' and 'Rocking Robin'). Anthony Findlay at Raymond Gubbay got very agitated when I admitted I had no idea who Noddy Holder was!

For *Nutcracker*, I needed no help with the tempo, but for the more pop-orientated pieces, I needed lots and would get advice from the kit drummer as to the correct tempo before starting the piece. For some reason, probably because he did not see why he should set the tempo but not get the money, he ignored me for one number, so I set off at what sounded like a reasonable tempo. I must confess, as soon as it began, I knew something was wrong! I looked up at Annie trying to sing her heart out and mouthed to her, *is this the right tempo?* With some exasperation, she vigorously shook her head and mouthed back, *noooooo!* We ended up wishing it could be Christmas every day, but spending rather a long time doing it!

Which reminds me of a time the RPO and I were doing a corporate gig at the Royal Albert Hall. By raising the arena and stalls almost to the level of the organ just beneath the lower boxes, and putting large tables and chairs on the raised level, you can turn the hall into a very good supper and cabaret venue. At these shows, we often play music that would not normally be considered familiar repertoire to a classical orchestra, and on this occasion, we were playing the Queen song 'We Will Rock You'. At the time, I was not too sure who Queen were, let alone the song. Somebody told me to get the audience to do a rhythm. Unfortunately, I could not remember whether it was 'stomp stomp, clap' or 'clap clap, stomp'. Suffice to say, I chose the wrong one. I think I was the only one in the entire Royal Albert Hall not to be thoroughly confused.

One of the funniest corporate gigs I did at the Royal Albert Hall was with Jeremy Clarkson. I am not going to be able to relate any of the stories from that evening as context was everything! Suffice to say that, despite the production company warning the promoters before the event that Mr. Clarkson was well known for going off-script and improvising, they still insisted he was the compère. It was one of the funniest evenings of my life, and he had most of the audience in hysterics. The orchestra and I could hardly play as he talked about cars and the bosses of the transport industry to those very bosses of the transport industry!

One incident above all others, and there were many, was responsible for the end of the production company's involvement with this award ceremony.

There was a table full of car company executives, sitting very close to the stage, who kept heckling Jeremy Clarkson. Anyone who knows him or has seen his work, should understand he will always have the last word, and you keep a low profile with Mr. Clarkson. Halfway through, Clarkson had had enough of the barracking! He looked down at this table full of well-wined-and-dined car company executives and asked what kind of car they drove. They replied with a well-known German make. Instantly, Clarkson retorted with three words: "Nazi staff cars!" End of heckling; end of contract!

I have done many an outdoor concert which have included aeroplanes, more often than not with Carolyn Grace flying the Grace Spitfire. The one with the City of Birmingham Symphony Orchestra in 2004 when we went to Donnington Park, close by Castle Donnington, and celebrated the centenary of Rolls-Royce should get a look-in on my memorable concerts list!

As many Rolls-Royce-powered aircraft as the company could gather together came and demonstrated their engines while we played music. Anyone who knows Donnington Park knows it is alongside East Midlands Airport, and we had to liaise the evening performance and the flying display with holiday flights departing to the Mediterranean. This meant someone experienced in air traffic control radio communications had to liaise with the airport tower, display director, the holding display aircraft and me. At the end of the spoken introductions by the compère Ken Bruce, this chap whispered into my radio earpiece the right moment to start the music so the holding display aircraft could come in and perform. Every now and then, there would have to be a pause while we waited for the Airtours flight to Malaga to complete its climb-out, before being given the all-clear to play.

That voice in my ear was not some ordinary bloke who knew about communications between the ground and the air; he just happened to be Phill O'Dell, the chief test pilot for Rolls-Royce. His 'regular' office is the Rolls-Royce Spitfire! We have remained friends ever since and often meet up. Well, once you've had a man whispering in your ear…!

There were many RR-engined aircraft flying that day, but the one that remains fixed in everyone's head is the Harrier. It came and hovered above the tented stage while the full orchestra (something like eighty-six players) played Gustav Holst's *Mars*, the bringer of war from *The Planets* suite through amplified speakers. We were enormous. However, we might as well all have packed up and gone home! No one would have missed us. The noise from the aircraft was overwhelming and completely wonderful.

Phill O'Dell, known to everyone in the flying world as POD, did give the family and me the thrill of a lifetime. When the children were young, we went one year to the Biggin Hill Airshow where they were celebrating the Spitfire. So many marks of the aircraft were there, including Phill and the RR Spitfire. I rang him on his mobile and he invited us to go and see him. We found him in the packed arena of the airfield, and he took us to his parked aircraft on the Biggin Hill apron, promptly inviting each of us in turn to sit in the actual Rolls-Royce Spitfire that had flown with 16 Squadron at the end of the war. A huge privilege to be in one of the cockpits in which my father and uncle fought for their lives. Years later, Dominic and I flew to Biggin for tea in a PA28 and, as we landed, a Spitfire landed behind us. I took that as a tribute to my uncle and father, both of whom flew from Biggin in assorted aircraft.

Perhaps, for family reasons if nothing else, one concert stands out above all others. On 11 August 2018, at Blickling Hall close to Norwich in Norfolk, the National Symphony Orchestra and I performed an outdoor concert celebrating the hundredth anniversary of the formation of the Royal Air Force. The promoters had their doubts about the undertaking from the beginning, wondering whether we would achieve our ambitions and therefore audience numbers. To make sure they actually agreed to put it on, I offered to do it for a reduced fee enhanced by a percentage of profits. Sadly, their concern in the end was accurate! RAF aircraft were extremely busy with official RAF100 celebrations elsewhere and, ultimately, we were disappointingly light on display aircraft.

I managed to include Phill flying the RR Spitfire, the first time he would have flown and I conducted. Sadly, the Spit went U/S moments before take-off with tyre issues, and we have yet to achieve that particular duet. We were going to try again as the *Queen Mary 2* departed Southampton for our 2020 transatlantic crossing with the NSO on the top deck, but a certain virus put paid to that.

Other aircraft were taking part in the Blickling Hall evening, and you may say that was exciting enough, but also present were men and women from nearby RAF Marham who would perform the sunset ceremony for us. This is a ceremony that is performed at the end of the day, on bases around the world, and can range from an officer and a couple of junior ranks saluting as they lower the Union Flag, to a full-blown ceremony with band. We decided we would do the full-blown ceremony with band.

The original idea was to have the Central Band of the RAF playing, as there are a number of commands that have to be given and timed with music throughout the ceremony. As with the aircraft scenario, it was an extremely busy year for them as well and, in the end, they could not do it. What to do? Now, when I was in the cadets at Marlborough, the one thing you learned was never to volunteer for anything, but this was an opportunity I was not going to miss. I said I would do it with the NSO.

A lot of homework had to be done beforehand, most of which consisted of understanding the ceremony by watching the professionals do it on YouTube. Then I had to rearrange the music from a wind band arrangement to one suitable for playing by a symphony orchestra. I have a certain mastery of the music notation software Sibelius, so it did not take too long to sort and convert the *Last Post*, *Eagle Squadron*, *RAF March Past*, *Aircrew on Parade*, *St Clement* hymn tune and others into orchestral form. Then I had to learn the various commands and where they came: 'Present Arms', 'Shoulder Arms', 'Quick March' etc. The result of all that work became one of the most emotional and proudest concerts I have ever given. Surely not many civilian conductors have been responsible for the music at this wonderful military ceremony?

It was extraordinary, and everything from a musical point of view went well. The music, the poems read and, most of all, the participation of the men and women from RAF Marham made this the smoothest of events.

We reached the climax of the evening with the lowering of the flag, and as I stood there conducting the *RAF March Past*, I remembered sitting with my uncle in Westminster Abbey at the 1985 Battle of Britain Memorial Service. This time it was my turn to silently weep as forty fantastic servicemen and women marched, as had all my ancestors and my son was doing now, through the cheering and clapping audience, saluting the station commander of RAF Marham Group Captain Ian Townsend. For me, it filled a void that had been lying there all my life. Like so many times before and since, I wished they could all have been there to see it.

I miss them and hope they would have been proud.

Play-Out: Final Goodbye

As I sit writing this in the summer of 2022, the world is emerging from the turmoil of the Covid-19 pandemic, and who knows whether it will ever be the same again. However, it does give me a chance to take stock of my life.

I stated earlier that from the moment at my pre-prep school I first conducted an ensemble, I knew what I wanted to do as a career. And that is correct. However, at the back of my mind was also the allure of becoming a pilot. After all, my entire male family line had flown aircraft, perhaps I should. In the end, it was never a serious consideration. There was the little matter of the compulsory medical tests, and I had had enough of those. Then, I had conducted; I knew what that was like, and I liked it… a lot!

What is it like to conduct an orchestra? It is of course impossible to describe, and the closest I can get is likening it to an experience you never want to end. Most of us get that a few times in a lifetime. With conducting, it happens every single time. It appeals to so many senses: aural, visual, vestibular and proprioception. Aural of course is the main drug of choice as it can mean so many different things to so many different people, all from the same piece of music.

There is also the camaraderie, the sense you are doing something in which so many people are agreeing to willingly participate. I have often described conducting as the art of 'benevolent dictatorship'. These days, you can only achieve greatness with the consent of the people you are conducting. But there can only be one person guiding everyone along.

Let us say you are conducting Mahler's *Symphony No. 8*, the *Symphony of a Thousand*. There are anywhere from three hundred or more musicians, soloists and choirs taking part. In which case, there are anywhere from three hundred people who all think they know how the piece should go; a lot think they know better than you! There has to be one person with the overview, the personality to guide those performers to create something that is one single vision but also, by consent, persuading the performers that it is actually the vision of everyone on that stage. Us conductors cannot do it by bullying; we cannot do it by insisting; we cannot even do it by pleading. We can only do it by inspiring and bringing the performers with us. That, in a nutshell, is the art of conducting; that is the difficult part. My wife always says to anyone who rings up asking to speak to me and I am out, "Oh, he's off waving his arms around somewhere!" And she's right! This, in its simplest form, is what I do. Any book I write on the subject of conducting would be quite short: 'a conductor's own personal interpretation of a piece of music, performed with the understanding, consent and vision of all the performers on the stage'.

The arts industry took a severe beating during the pandemic, with musicians, lots of whom were freelance and not earning any income, retraining for other professions. We lost musicians from two generations: those already in the performing arena who had to do something else to earn an income and those who were about to enter the world of performing who couldn't even start!

I was lucky, as most of my career in terms of time is behind me and, financially, I was OK. I had saved and had no mortgage. I did what I could for others, donating to the Royal Society of Musicians two four-figure lump sums of money and putting my reduced hire library on the internet. These arrangements of well-loved classical pieces of music could help orchestras, if they were socially distancing when they restarted, to play great music again without the full complement of players.

I also became a volunteer for the Royal Air Forces Association. RAFA is a wonderful organisation that my paternal grandfather revived towards the end of the Second World War. As executive chairman, he created *Air Mail*, or *Airmail* as it is now called, its quarterly magazine, as a medium for promoting the organisation and as a means of keeping in touch with its members. Today, I follow in his footsteps and talk to ex-members of the RAF who, having devoted either a large or small part of their life to serving others, may now be struggling with loneliness or current circumstances. Further, I was hugely honoured when asked to become an ambassador for the organisation.

For me, being an ambassador is another link completing a circle that had a tiny bit missing. Since the RAF's inception, there has always been a member of my family serving, until my generation. With Peter Helmore's early death in the Bay of Biscay, it abruptly stopped. Now, in a very small way, I am linking the previous generation with the next, and I'm impossibly honoured. I shall do everything I can to ensure that I conduct myself (pun intended) so that my RAF forebearers would be very pleased.

Phantom of the Opera has come to an end for me. Though it has reopened, it has done so without me at the helm. As is only right, the future of the show is just that, the future and not the past. My last conducting performance of that great show was at Her Majesty's Theatre on 31 January 2020. I would like to think I will conduct it again, but it will have to be the right production with the right number of musicians in the orchestra! I will always have a huge affinity with that piece. What a genius Lord Lloyd Webber is.

I was one of the last freelance conductors to work before the worldwide shutdown. In February 2020, I played myself in the Netflix smash hit *The Crown*. The series is about the historical period of the reign of Queen Elizabeth II, and the moment which included me portrayed Princess Diana attending *Phantom of the Opera*. She was a huge fan of the show, watching many performances of her favourite musical. So most definitely, I can say I have played myself in *The Crown*, as I really did conduct when she attended.

We filmed *The Crown* in the Wimbledon Theatre, substituting for Her Majesty's, and had the full complement of musicians in the orchestra with some of the original *Phantom* musicians who would also have played while Diana was in the audience. What is more, the actress playing the role of Princess Diana was actually going to sing 'All I Ask', normally a duet within the show, as a solo.

We started at 7am, and I decided to do this properly and introduce her to the orchestra. This is what all conductors do with their soloists: "Please welcome so-and-so to the stage." On this occasion, the orchestra were situated downstage, and the actress was upstage. I called over to her, "Corinne." Nothing. A little louder, "Corinne." Still nothing. So now, as loud as was reasonable on a crowded film set, "Corinne." Zero, zilch, no reaction. It was at this moment the principal of the violas, a musician I know well called Mark Chivers, leant slightly forward and whispered very deliberately to me, "Anthony, her name is Emma." This fine actress's name is Emma Corrin, and as soon as I called out her correct name, she immediately came over for the introductions.

I think I got away with it though, as I left a long enough pause between calling the wrong and right names, as if calling Corinne to someone else. Goodness knows what I was going to call her if she had answered, and I had tried to introduce her!

My only excuse is that, at the time, we had an actress at Her Majesty's playing the understudy role of Christine called Corinne Cowling.

However, Emma Corrin had the last laugh. She gave an interview to the press afterwards, where she said she was very nervous singing live with an orchestra and was even worse after the first take. She went on to explain that the conductor came in and played the piece at such a completely different tempo from the way she had rehearsed it with her coach, it gave her a nosebleed! I guess after thirty-three years, I will get the tempo right one day!

After *The Crown*, I conducted a concert in St. David's Hall Cardiff with the London Concert Orchestra on 15 March 2020, followed by a Warner Hotel concert with the National Symphony Orchestra in Cricket St. Thomas on 18 March. How apt it should be those two orchestras!

When Covid-19 struck us all silent (such a cruel punishment for musicians and actors), lots of engagements were tentatively booked and then cancelled before we realised that was it, the end for the indeterminate future.

There is no substitute for performing live. The adrenalin rush that we all get as we walk onto the platform; the sustaining of fortissimo passages; and then, moments later, the quietist of pianissimos. The concentration required to perform at your best for two and a half hours is absolute. It is all very well sitting at home practising, but you have neighbours to think about, and you can always stop when you want and not when the music dictates. Your partner and/or children can interrupt; the phone can ring; or the shopping needs doing!

Wind instrumentalists, those who play flutes, oboes, trumpets, horns etc. called the enforced sojourn: lockdown chops. Like athletes and their bodies, musicians need to keep their lips, breathing, arms and fingers in tip-top condition for match-play readiness.

At the beginning of the pandemic, I made three videos with the LCO during lockdown, utilising the wonders of technology and creating something of which we can all be justifiably proud.

The first we did, on 10 April 2020, I think was the first to be made. As the first lockdown in the UK was on 23 March, it was very quick. I decided to do *Nessun Dorma* with new lyrics by Vaughan Meakins and dedicated to health workers around the world. I asked my good friend Wynne Evans, the famous tenor in the GoCompare adverts, to sing the solo. I knew how to synchronise everyone playing remotely, as we had done it with *The Two Ronnies* show back in the '80s, and ran it past the fabulous sound engineer Steve Carr, who confirmed it would work.

For the YouTube videos, I used the click-track principal, sending a computer software track to each musician, to which they listened in earbuds on a playback device, while playing live to another recording device such as a phone. Then it became a case of synchronising everybody together. That was simple: on the track I sent them, if the piece was in 4/4, I gave two bars counting out loud one, two, three, four in the time of the music. The musicians counted out loud the second bar, playing on the first beat of the third bar which was the first bar of the actual music. Steve then mixed the audio tracks, syncing everyone saying one, two, three, four, before cropping out those words and starting on the first beat of the third bar.

I asked my eldest son Dominic to mix the video using the same method. I reasoned, although he had never done anything like that before, being a pilot used to screens, dials, knobs and switches and with nothing to do as he was between delayed flying courses due to Covid-19, it would be right up his street. He thought a bit, asked for some video editing software and began a very steep learning curve as a vision mixer.

He also had previous of ingenuity! When the children were young, we used to keep a tuck box full of goodies such as sweets, Game Boys and the like under combination lock by the side of our bed, only to be opened as reward for good homework or playtime. Dominic obviously thought he should be rewarded more often than we did and somehow got hold of a small security camera and receiver, pointing the camera in the general direction of the combination lock so he could see the code we put in! The problem, of course, was the field of vision was quite high, and we did not discover the hidden camera until we realised the sweets needed restocking rather faster than they should have! We never did discover how long the camera had been hidden at the side of our bedroom, or what, apart from the combination number, he had seen!

The next YouTube video I posted on 5 May with the LCO was *Nimrod*, dedicated to all those who had died as a result of catching Covid-19. The first had put thirty musicians on the screen; *Nimrod* put forty-eight. The LCO gave a most moving performance of this quintessentially British piece of music, and I hope those who watched it and had been personally affected by the disease, got some solace and peace from the video.

Our third, posted on 24 June, was as a result of the world tearing itself apart. The divisions of Brexit and those who believed the pandemic was real, against others who thought it was a conspiracy made up to give power and control to some individuals and countries with a new world order. Some believed the government was doing a good job with Covid-19, and others did not. They all contributed to the anger felt by so many who had nothing better to do than vent their spleen on social media.

Why is it that people believe the perceived anonymity of social media gives them the right to say what they want to say and in any form they want to say it? I can't bear the animosity on social media and lack of politeness and intolerance of others' opinions, with the general attitude of 'I'm right and you're wrong'. There are so many armchair politicians and high-minded people who all believe they have a voice and are entitled to say what they think publicly, even if it hurts others. Since when did verbosity and vociferousness influence the majority? Since social media, that's when! I do not use Instagram or Facebook but occasionally Twitter.

With this new video, I wanted to heal rifts and try and bring people together so asked Katherine Jenkins whether she would like to do one with us. She quickly said yes and asked Marisha Wallace, the wonderful singer who had been in her 2019 Christmas show, to duet 'World in Union'. The video quoted the famous opening line of Shakespeare's play *Twelfth Night*, 'if music be the food of love, play on'. We had the LCO and a children's choir from Heath Mount School, a combined total of eighty-four people on the screen at the same time. Incredible to watch and listen to, but in terms of changing the world, I was probably aiming too high!

After doing those three videos, all of which can be viewed on my YouTube channel and, in my opinion, are absolutely brilliant, I stopped. They show the extraordinary ability of musicians and technicians (human beings), when challenged to do something different, to adapt to a new environment with consummate ease. It was incredibly unfair of me to continue asking musicians to perform for nothing. They are all superb professionals, and as such should be paid for doing their job. I know a lot of them enjoyed doing the videos, telling me that it continued the team spirit within the orchestra and kept the LCO alive. Many of them liked seeing their colleagues on screen, continuing to play with them, albeit remotely. However, it is not fair they should play for nothing, and as I was not earning an income, I could not pay them. I ceased doing them and missed them.

One of my proudest statements of those videos is that no artificial help was given to the soundtrack. What you hear is what was played. Yes, of course we added some reverb and EQ'd the sound a bit, but that is always done in a studio. Otherwise, what you hear is the undiluted sound with no editing from the phone microphones of the individual musicians in the glorious London Concert Orchestra.

Here I am looking back at the past; what of the present and future? The great restart began on 25 July 2021 when my orchestra, and appropriately Katherine Jenkins, met for an outdoor concert in Maldon, Essex. It was such an emotional occasion, every one of us performing with moist eyes. We maintained social distancing between us, and every string player had a stand to themselves, as opposed to the usual sharing. Masks of course were not worn; we were, after all, outside!

We are coming back, slowly but surely! Covid-19 will perhaps remain with us for a while, and we have to learn to live with it, yet have a normal life within any boundaries we want to set ourselves. Overseas tours are being talked about and engaged, and concerts at all the major UK halls with my orchestra have started. I am lecturing on board the Cunard ships again, and there is optimism in the air as the fightback against this terrible virus begins.

I hope to continue conducting until I drop, especially with my regular collaborators, which include Cunard and Katherine in particular. Then, there is my musical partnership with Raymond Gubbay Ltd and the LCO. I trust there are many more concerts with my friends in this organisation and orchestra, even the tough ones!

I am thinking of the regular New Year's Eve concert in Symphony Hall Birmingham, where we play through midnight, before hotfooting down to London and the midday rehearsal in the Barbican Hall and the traditional afternoon concert. Probably one of the last concerts of the old year and one of the first concerts of the new! Everyone needs stamina for these two concerts. With the exception of the pandemic, we've been continuously performing in Symphony Hall on 31 December since 1993, adding the next day in the Barbican in 1997.

It is now time to finish, and I am going to end with a hurried, life-changing conversation that happened at the beginning of my career. It comes out of a question I am often asked. Do I get nervous before a concert? Having played many big events, concerts and productions around the world, I can honestly say very, very seldom. The only time nerves come into play is if I think we're under-rehearsed, or the ability of the orchestra does not match what is required of them. This hardly ever happens, and I can remember only three occasions when there was nothing I could do but anxiously conduct and hope for the best.

The first was the Aldeburgh concert in August 1994 to which my old headmaster had attended. During the rehearsal, I forgot to rehearse a programmed piece of music with the orchestra until twenty minutes before the end. I had actually called an end to the rehearsal, when the leader of the orchestra asked me whether we were going to perform *Pineapple Poll*! My heart skipped several beats as I realised I had messed up the rehearsal time and had spent so long rehearsing the difficult *Four Sea Interludes* by Benjamin Britten, I had forgotten all about *Pineapple Poll*. This wonderful piece of ballet music, arranged by Sir Charles Mackerras of Gilbert & Sullivan tunes, lasts forty minutes, is rarely played and is tricky! I immediately cut the movements we were to perform down to twenty minutes and played it through, so at least the orchestra would have sight of this non-standard repertoire composition. Although the musicians in the orchestra were marvellous and played well, I was nervous that evening!

The second occasion was when I was rung up by the Philharmonia Orchestra in March 2000 and, at twenty-four hours' notice, asked to conduct them at the Malvern Festival. The person engaged to conduct was unable to adequately perform one of the pieces, and I was to discover why! Once again, I only had one rehearsal as the concert was the following evening. The programme on the surface looked very easy, and I knew all the repertoire, except for one piece: Ravel's *Tzigane*, a virtuoso piece for violin and orchestra. Marvellous music but, when I opened the score, really difficult to conduct! I was nervous then as well. I must say though, the greeting I got from the orchestra as I walked into the rehearsal room, as a different conductor to the one they were expecting, was gratifying: they cheered!

The final time was in June 2007 after I had conducted the Scottish Concert Orchestra in a programme at the Glasgow Royal Concert Hall and had left the hotel the following morning. I had arrived at the Central Railway Station to travel back to London, and had even got one foot onto the train, when there was a phone call from the general manager of the Royal Scottish National Orchestra (RSNO) enquiring as to my whereabouts. When I told him, he begged me to get off the train and come back to the hall. The conductor for that evening's concert was ill, and they wanted me to conduct it.

The programme was terrifying – it was Gilbert and Sullivan's operetta *The Pirates of Penzance*… in its entirety! I did not know it, had never conducted any music from it and arrived back at the hall an hour before the one and only rehearsal began! Pretty certainly, it was not the best performance of a G&S operetta that has ever been performed. We got through it though, and as the weak link amongst that fabulous orchestra, I was very nervous.

There is however, a moral to these occasions. You should know your repertoire intimately and never conduct a concert if you don't. Neither the RSNO nor the Philharmonia ever asked me to conduct them again!

My lack of nerves before a concert has its origin, and it dates back to 14 February 1988 and the beginning of my career, with a hurried conversation just before a concert at the Royal Festival Hall.

I was standing offstage about to conduct one of the world's great orchestras, the Philharmonia Orchestra, in a performance of Rimsky-Korsakov's dazzling orchestral showpiece *Scheherazade*. Leading the orchestra was their regular concert master and my old friend Christopher Warren-Green. The orchestra was onstage, fully rehearsed and tuned; the lights in the auditorium had dimmed down; and the audience was settled into an expectant hush. Chris, about to go onstage prior to me, saw me nervously pacing about, clearing my throat, fidgeting, peering round the door at the audience and asked me what the matter was. I explained that I was really nervous and was not sure I could go on. In the few seconds he had, he looked at me and said, "Is conducting what you want to do?"

"More than anything," I agreed.

"Well then," he said, "you have one of the world's great orchestras, the Rolls-Royce of orchestras, waiting for you. If this is what you want to do, either get out there and enjoy yourself or go home now and give it up!" With that, he turned round and walked onto the platform to his seat at the front of the orchestra.

I will admit, it was a jolt at the time but was the very best piece of advice that has ever been given to me. Pulling myself together, I followed him out and had the most wonderful time of my life.

I have been doing that ever since.